BLACK BELT®
B · O · O · K · S

THE ULTIMATE GUIDE TO
KNIFE COMBAT

THE ULTIMATE GUIDE TO
KNIFE COMBAT

Compiled by Jon Sattler

Edited by Raymond Horwitz, Jeannine Santiago,
Jon Sattler and Jon Thibault

Graphic Design by John Bodine

Front Cover Photo by Thomas Sanders

Cover Model: Tony A. Diaz

Back Cover Photos 1 and 3 by Rick Hustead

Back Cover Photos 2 and 4 courtesy of Emerson Knives

©2007 Black Belt Communications LLC
All Rights Reserved
Printed in the United States of America
Library of Congress Control Number: 2006927302
ISBN-10: 0-89750-158-6
ISBN-13: 978-0-89750-158-3

First Printing 2007

WARNING

BLACK BELT BOOKS
A Division of **OHARA** 🅿 **PUBLICATIONS, INC.**
World Leader in Martial Arts Publications

FOREWORD

At first blush, it would seem that reality-combat expert Jim Wagner and the Dyak headhunters of Borneo would have little in common. But one object, one tool, one weapon is a mainstay of civilization, bridging the chasms of history and culture with its utility and ubiquity. If the making of tools is the most humanizing trait, perhaps the knife is as old as humanity itself.

Perennially, the knife has been used as the metaphoric basis for countless adages and clichés; it has the ability to cut tension, describe wit and intelligence (or lack thereof: "He's not the sharpest tool in the shed.") and elevate mundane gossip to vicious, Caesarian backstabbing. Sharpened steel is as useful a literary tool as it is a corporeal one.

Mishaps are like knives, that either serve us or cut us, as we grasp them by the blade or the handle.
—*James Russell Lowell*

Literary flourishes aside, the sharpened edge is rivaled arguably only by the wheel as the most useful invention. What would medicine be without the scalpel? How would the Thanksgiving host serve turkey cutlets without a carving knife? Sculptors who free their artistic visions from the tough confines of clay, gnarled wood, and blocks of ice would have to resort to building sandcastles to satiate the muse. And, of course, the thousands of battles upon which modern civilization was built, the artwork those battles inspired, and the outcomes they produced would have been altogether different.

Black Belt Books is proud to present *The Ultimate Guide to Knife Combat*, which celebrates one facet of this versatile weapon: the brutal art of knife fighting and the lifesaving techniques of knife defense. A compilation of *Black Belt* articles written between 1982 and 2006, *Knife Combat* features the work of the foremost experts on the subject.

Knives have changed little over the millennia; the elegant simplicity of the short, sharp blade has only been improved upon through the materials used in its construction and various minute refinements in its shape. The karambit of the 11th century suggests the same deadly kineticism as the karambit of today, albeit the former lacks the features and modern design made possible by centuries of technological growth. But it could still cut you. And it would still hurt.

—*Jon Thibault*

CONTENTS

KNIVES
Keeping the Distance

by Joe Coelho • May 1982

There are many martial arts schools across this country, and for every school there is an instructor who has his or her own idea of what the martial arts should be. Some are interested in putting out top tournament fighters, while others are interested in having top *kata* performers. There are those who only teach street self-defense and others who only teach weapons, such as stick fighting. There is nothing wrong with teaching stick fighting as long as the instructors tell their students that they may not always be able to find a stick when someone attacks them. There is nothing wrong with putting out top tournament fighters as long as you explain to the students that most of their tournament techniques will not work if someone gets them in a head lock. Specific areas of the martial arts

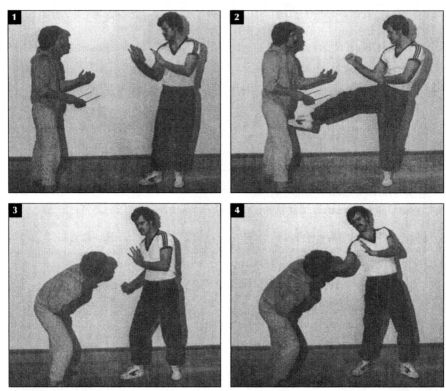

The defender holds his hands up to protect himself from a quick jab as the knife-wielding attacker approaches (1). Before the attacker gets close enough to use his weapon, the defender plants a front snap kick to his groin (2). The blow causes the attacker to drop his knife and double up in pain (3), paving the way for the defender's uppercut to his face (4).

The defender raises his hands in a protective position as the attacker advances (1). Not waiting for his assailant to get too close, the defender kicks his foe's hand and wrist (2). As the attacker's arm goes up and out of control, the defender pushes it aside and moves in with a finger jab to the eyes (3).

should be taught separately, thoroughly and realistically.

This is particularly important for self-defense training, especially when preparing to defend against a weapon, such as a knife. It is important to know how to defend against a knife for several reasons, the most important one being that it is available to everyone. If you check your local schools, you will find that there are very few students who carry guns, *escrima* sticks and *nunchaku*.

The quantity of knives in public schools is a real and present danger.

It is also important to understand the psychological advantage that you obtain by training with weapons. If nothing else, it increases self-confidence. If you know how to handle someone with a knife, then it should be much easier for you to remain calm against an unarmed opponent.

In the December 1981 issue of *Black Belt*, Dan Anderson—who has been training for the past 15 years and has been a nationally rated competitor for the last eight years—wrote about what training with sticks had done for him. "Since beginning my training in modern *arnis*, I have found my hand-eye coordination has increased, my ability to move in a relaxed flow has gotten to the point where I am not 'instinctively' backing away." The same thing can be developed if you train for knife attacks. You have better eye, hand and foot coordination so that you are able to deal with something as quick as a knife.

This is one of the reasons I recommend training realistically. If you practice with imaginary weapons, you will not develop the reflexes that it takes to deal with them on the street. Never say to a training partner, "Imagine you have a knife. OK. Now I'll practice taking it away." It is best to start out with a dull knife, such as a butter knife, for a more realistic effect.

Many instructors will not teach their students to defend against weapons until they are brown or black belts. What happens to a student who does not have a ranking belt and whose attacker doesn't care about rank? Should they perform inward blocks and chops as the knife is being jabbed into them? You simply can't have your students use the same techniques to stop a knife attack as they use to stop a straight punch.

Instructors teach students how to handle knife attacks by having someone jab at the student with a knife. The student is supposed to catch the wrist and find a pressure point, forcing his "attacker" to let go of the knife. I have seen this work over and over again in the studio, because they don't use knives and the "attackers" hold out their arms until the other guy finds a good pressure point or gets a good hold of the wrist for a takedown. Remember,

As the assailant commences with an overhead knife attack (1), the defender leans back as if afraid to get in position for a kick. The defender halts the progress with a side kick to his midsection (2). As the assailant steps back because of the force of the kick, the defender checks the knife with his right hand and follows up with a left-hand strike to the face (3).

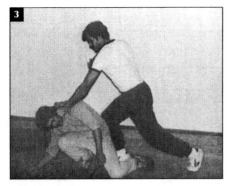

As the assailant commences his attack with his knee leaning forward (1), the defender plants a side kick on the forward knee and checks the knife with his lead hand (2), all the while keeping the knife far from his body. The defender finishes the attacker off, driving his knee to the ground and driving a reverse punch to his face (3).

almost every technique will work in the karate studio if the person who is being attacked knows exactly how he is going to be attacked.

The techniques demonstrated here show how to stop someone from getting close to you with a knife. Too many people get used to training for techniques, such as what to do if a knife is touching your midsection or throat. In other words, people get so caught up in trying to perform techniques for specific situations that they forget to keep as much distance between their throats and the knife as possible. There are many reasons to keep that weapon at a distance. If you strike at the knife with a kick and you fail, at least the weapon is still far enough away to perform a follow-up technique. However, if you wait until the knife is near your throat and your technique fails, you may find yourself in a very painful situation.

The kick may also knock the knife loose from the attacker's hand and possibly sprain or break the wrist, especially if you are wearing some good, hard street shoes. This brings up another point. If you reach in with your hands, you may get them cut, but if you use your legs, you have pants and shoes that the knife must first penetrate.

Keep in mind that if an attacker feels a good kick in that hand, he may realize that you know more than the average guy and stop attacking. Thus a little long-range action could spare you a few short-range cuts. Don't get carried away. If you are faced with a confrontation on the street, do not get into your horse or front stance—that will give away that you have martial arts training and he will be expecting a kick.

There are several things to keep in mind when training for a situation like this. One is to have your partner, as you get better, move the knife in unpredictable motions, such as circles, up-and-down motions and back and forth as you kick at his hand and weapon. It is very important to get used to kicking at the weapon without telegraphing so that the attacker does not pull it out of the way. Also, as you get interested in weapons training, remember to train for quick and realistic disarms and leave the more technical and flashy disarms for later.

GRADIENTS OF FEAR: TRAINING WITH THE KNIFE

How Do You Overcome Your Fear and Learn to Defend Against the Knife?

by J. Nagel • April 1983

"People think a lot of different things when they're faced with a knife," says Dan DiVito, an *arnis* expert and fourth-degree *taekwondo* black belt. "A lot of people are even more afraid of a knife than a gun. They think dead, cut, blood, scars, *ripping* of skin and tissue, eyes stuck out, internal organs punctured. There's tremendous fear and terror.

"*But,* there's a beauty in a knife. And what you have to do as a teacher, almost the hardest thing you have to do, is teach the person to get rid of all that fear and realize the positive energy about a knife. That doesn't mean you get cocky. It means you gain understanding."

DiVito has devoted himself to discovering new levels of understanding in the martial arts. He shares these ideas because he feels they are too commonly overlooked in self-defense training. Teachers commonly just show

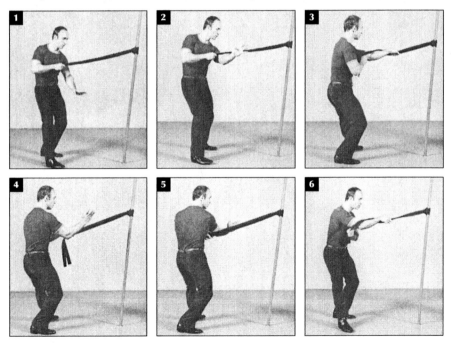

The most basic drill in DiVito's system. The left hand goes under (1) and around the belt (2), the body shifts—and the hand continues the counterclockwise motion, gripping (3) the belt and sliding downward. The opposite drill commences by moving over the belt (4&5), then around and gripping (6). Each motion should be practiced with both hands.

The same drill can be performed with a partner, adding in slight variations to increase practicality. DiVito's hand goes under (1), around (2) and grips his partner's wrist (3) as in the belt drill. The circular motion naturally deflects the force of a punch. The opposite motion (4-6) works equally well, and both can be combined with kicks.

students a few good techniques to use on the off chance that a murderous, knife-wielding assailant attacks them.

But what is often overlooked is the spiritual aspect of facing a knife. DiVito insists this is just as important, if not more so. It is the part of the training he begins with and never forgets.

"The first thing I do with a student who wants to learn defense against knives is teach him to face the knife itself," he says. "There are so many things you have to be able to handle. There's the opponent's motion, your own motion, the flow, the energy, the presence of the opponent, and then there's also just the knife itself. More elementary than any technique is the ability to have the knife in your environment and to face it with familiarity and confidence rather than fear."

For that reason, DiVito's knife-defense program features a unique "get acquainted" phase. He runs the new student through a series of physical drills and psychological exercises. This takes the student beyond the level of isolated techniques and to a whole new understanding of knife combat.

His first step is usually just to give the student a knife. Let him hold the knife, feel its weight, touch the point and edge, and move it around lightly in the air.

"You'd be surprised at the emotions people have going on about knives," DiVito says. "Some people feel they could never even hold a knife in their hand. Well, then, how could they possibly defend themselves against it?"

People are taught to face their fears in DiVito's class on what he calls a "gradient scale."

First, they become acquainted with the knife itself, and then they are introduced to a set of innocuous drills. To an untrained eye, this may seem like the furthest thing in the world from knife fighting.

The student begins alone, with a belt that is attached at one end to a post or doorknob. He performs various arm-circling and maneuvering drills at his own speed and without an opponent. The idea is not to teach techniques at this stage of the game, DiVito insists, but to get the new student to understand some basic *concepts* of movement, such as circling to the inside, circling to the outside, and in both small or wide circles. These are the basic motions of almost every parry, block or joint lock. Such individual drills allow a student to work from high speed to low speed, to innovate whenever he may feel ready, and most important, to grow comfortable with all the basic motions of self-defense.

Next, the same type of drill can be performed empty-handed with a partner. The student at this stage naturally begins to discover the concepts and techniques from the belt drill that can be applied to the human arm. "Empty-handed is a little more real than doing the drill with a belt," DiVito explains. "And we're trying to make it real. Make it real gradually, but make it real."

At some stage, the partners must work with knives. They can begin with rubber knives if they like because there's no danger and they get the general feel of the weapon. But DiVito also points out that "there's a whole finesse

In practice with a rubber knife, the whole situation becomes more realistic. The body shift (1&2) now proves important, as do the timing, distancing and skillful execution. The arm movements themselves are still nearly the same as in the first part of the belt drill, with one change: DiVito's right hand maintains control (3&4) and twists his opponent's knife hand away in a kind of wrist lock, preparing the kick (5).

The same basic motion as in the second half of the belt drill can be used to move in on an opponent. DiVito's hope is not to teach techniques per se, but to instill the concepts of evasion, circularity and counterattack. Here, he controls the attacker's knife hand (1&2) and moves in past the knife (3). Jamming the opponent's right arm with his own right shoulder, DiVito applies a choke (4&5).

to working with the knife, too, that you can only discover through actually doing it." When applying the blocks and parries or joint locks, the student must have an idea of where the point of a knife would be at each stage of a certain move, where the edge might be, and what an opponent could be expected to do with the knife while the disarm is attempted. "There's not much room for mistakes in handling a knife," DiVito says. "Either you win or you die."

DiVito's students eventually begin using wooden knives or real, taped blades during their drills. "That's just one more step in the process," says DiVito. "Working the drills with a stiff blade, instead of one that will bend harmlessly—you're not going to get cut or stuck, because the blade is taped. Yes, it's more dangerous than a rubber knife, but the student should be more prepared to deal with it by then, too. You have to feel that blade when you do the drill, because it's completely different working with a stiff blade than a flexible one. We try to get as close to reality as we can."

What DiVito is trying to do with these drills is subtle. Not only is he hoping to prepare a student physically for an encounter against a knife fighter, he also hopes to "establish a communication" between the student and the knife. Here, very unusual exercises come in.

"What I'll do sometimes," DiVito says, "is have the student *take* a cut. The blade is taped, of course, so nobody really gets hurt. But I'll have one student slash, then I'll say, 'OK, now take the cut, take the cut,' and the other student will actually move *into* the path of the knife. I'll have them

Finally, against a real knife, DiVito is confident, efficient, and brutal. His basic motion is that of the belt drill's first half, but performed with the right arm. From a balanced ready posture, he controls the attacker's knife hand and moves in (2). His right arm moves under and around in a clockwise motion, while his left hand still grips the opponent's wrist (3). As the circle is completed, DiVito's wrist lock drags his opponent down for a kick to the head (4).

do this with their eyes closed, too. Or I'll slow the motion down, slow it down, slow it down. What this does is allow the individual to take *control* of the knife. 'OK, you have the knife and I don't, but I have just as much control as you do.' You see, if they can intentionally *take* the cut, well then, psychologically, they can also decide, 'This time I'm going to *avoid* the cut,' and they can sidestep. There's a really powerful psychological barrier here that gets broken down."

This particular exercise is so powerful, says DiVito, that students often feel they can "see" the path of the knife blindfolded. There's such a strong emotion going on when you can't see and you know you're going to take that cut. You establish a whole new sensitivity to the weapon," he says.

Throughout this process, students are becoming acclimated, in a sense, to the knife. They are learning to move in certain ways against the knife, overcoming their own instinctual or irrational fears of the knife, and learning to understand it as a weapon. One area of crucial importance remains: the opponent.

"Some people think that a person's only going to move one way with the knife," says DiVito. "But they're wrong. A guy might not thrust with the knife; he may slice. Or he may chop at you. Maybe he's going to move in; maybe he's not. There are so many different ways to move with a knife!"

There are, in fact, as many ways to move as there are potential opponents. To deal with that problem, actual fighting scenarios are set up in DiVito's classes. "I'll put on different identities, that is, *be* different ways, and attack the students," he says. "I'll take a knife and fight them, as if I were afraid, or sloppy, or drunk, or overwhelming, or vicious because martial arts are not only arts of motion, they are arts of *being.* What happens is that you may get a guy who's big and vicious, or a guy who's little and sneaky—how do you handle a guy who's sneaky? Or, maybe there's a guy who looks totally unassuming, and all of a sudden he's a deadly killer. How do you handle that on the street? How do you even perceive that it's there? It's a confrontation of bodies, but it's also something else.

"So often," DiVito says, "what's going on spiritually is overlooked by the martial artist, or misunderstood. So what I want to do is develop drills and experiences that will handle that, meaning this: not just sitting down and thinking, but actually doing things that will make the guy more confident. And not just more confident, but drills that will take all this dispersed and scattered, terrorized energy and turn it into a more utilizable form. That way, the person faces a knife, and instead of being scattered all over and feeling weak and shaking, he is able to take that energy and use it to be centered, because he knows he can confront the situation. He can confront the knife."

SELF-DEFENSE AGAINST KNIFE ATTACKS
Let the Mugger Get the Point
by Jane Hallander • Photos by Jane Hollander • September 1984

Although basic self-defense techniques emphasize defense against unarmed opponents, the fact remains that there is a strong possibility of a weapon attack, such as an assailant armed with a knife.

What happens when a knife-wielding attacker lunges at you? Which of those basic self-defense techniques can you use without getting cut? What are some of the "dos" and "don'ts" of self-defense against a knife?

All martial arts contain self-defense techniques that are useful against a knife attack. The Korean martial art of *kuk sool won* is no exception. Kuk sool is a martial art comprising many facets of martial training—not just kicks and punches. Kuk sool won self-defense techniques also utilize pressure-point strikes, joint locks and throwing techniques.

Barry Harmon and his wife Choon-Ok Harmon, both fourth-degree black belts, manage and instruct a kuk sool won school in San Mateo,

In this defense against a straight knife attack, kuk sool won black-belt Choon-Ok Harmon readies herself as an assailant advances (1). She blocks the knife hand (2) to the outside and grabs his arm with her right hand. Grabbing the pressure point under his elbow (3), she pulls up on the arm while pushing down on his wrist. She takes the knife away (4) from her pained attacker, knees him in the chest and controls him by placing the knife at his throat (5).

Choon-Ok Harmon prepares to meet a straight attack (1), using a crossover cover (2) to grab her adversary's knife hand. She twists his wrist sharply (3), forcing him to release the knife, then turns the weapon (4) on her now fallen foe.

California. (Choon-Ok is the only woman in kuk sool won to have attained that rank.) One of the stages of training at their school involves techniques for defense against a knife attack.

One of the most important principles of kuk sool training is to "be prepared." This goal is attained by first learning the basic techniques and then realizing that those techniques don't work like magic. From the basics, kuk sool students learn to quickly change from one technique to another until one works rather than rely on only one or two techniques for all situations.

Of course, kuk sool students also learn that basic means beginning and that there are many variations to be derived from each basic technique. After absorbing the basic techniques, practitioners advance to the variations.

Students first learn about their opponent. In Barry Harmon's opinion, there are only two ways to hold a knife: inverted or straight. Knives held straight are used with either a forward thrusting motion or a sideways slashing action. When held in an inverted position, the knife can be used to stab straight down or to slash back toward its wielder.

Harmon stresses that no matter what position the knife is held, the defender should always be prepared to be nicked or cut slightly during defense. Getting cut is common because the defender's hands and arms will be coming into close proximity with the knife. "As long as it's not a serious cut, it's all right," he says. "Getting nicked is far better than being slashed or stabbed in a vital area."

For this reason, kuk sool students start their knife-defense training with rubber and wooden knives. When they've thoroughly absorbed the essentials of knife defense with the toy weapons, they advance into training with the real thing. From then on, all knife defense is done with sharp knives, under the theory that "there is no need to be on your toes if you're only used to a rubber knife." With sharp metal weapons, practitioners become acutely aware of the dangers involved in an actual knife attack.

There are several "do's" and "don'ts" the Harmons teach their students. Among the "do's" are:

1. When thrust at, the defender's body must evade the knife as quickly as possible. This is done by sucking in your waist and instantly pulling your body away from the oncoming attack. The Harmons consider this motion to be one of the most important concepts of knife defense. It's a common fallacy that a knife is short and may not penetrate the skin if the defender moves only slightly. Not all knives are short. Several inches can make the difference between life or death. Therefore, the ability to quickly

suck your body away from the attack becomes critical. In kuk sool, this sucking action is a swift movement that won't endanger the defender's balance or position.

2. If the defender has unlimited room, he should always retreat from any knife attack. If it's a sideways slashing attack, he should retreat until a definite forward lunge is made. It is best to counterattack when the knife-wielding assailant commits himself to a lunge. The defender shouldn't try to cover or block a slashing attack, which is not a committed motion and the weapon can be easily changed from hand to hand to evade the defender's counterstrike. When the assailant commits himself to a lunge, he is easily taken off-balance by a counterattack.

3. If the defender has any object at his disposal that can be used as a weapon, he should use it—a board, stick, piece of garment or dirt, which can be thrown into the assailant's eyes.

4. If the defender has what Barry Harmon calls "personal power" (intent and confident), he can often discourage the attack by looking straight into the assailant's eyes. If the defender doesn't have the advantage of experience, determination and practical confidence, he should look toward the base of his attacker's neck. This will give him a view of his opponent's entire body. If the defender looks only at the weapon, he easily can be tricked by an experienced knife-carrying assailant.

Along with the "do's" are certain important "don'ts" to defending against a knife attack:

1. The defender shouldn't try fancy techniques. He should always use simple, practical self-defense moves that don't require planning and thought.

2. He should not try to kick the knife out of his assailant's hand. The attacker's hand is faster than the defender's leg. The weapon can be kicked,

As an assailant moves in with an inverted slicing knife attack (1), kuk sool black-belt Barry Harmon ducks under the strike (2), then unbalances his opponent with a low spinning heel kick (3) to the back of his foot.

25

but only in the right situation, such as if one attacker holds the defender's arms in a bear hug and a second assailant strikes with a knife. Ordinarily, it's very dangerous to try to kick the knife away.

3. The defender shouldn't assume a martial arts stance before the attack. This not only broadcasts to the knife wielder that the intended victim may know a martial art but also impairs the defender's ability to move easily and quickly from side to side. Instead, he should stand square and prepare for anything. In this position, he can move easily to any defensive posture and can see every move his attacker makes.

4. The defender shouldn't punch or kick before he covers (neutralizes) the assailant's knife hand. Again, this is just practicality. If the defender punches or kicks before he neutralizes the knife, he can be easily cut.

Several practical knife-defense techniques are:

1. A cross cover/disarm against a straight attack. Cover the attacking hand with your hands crossed. Grab the knife hand and circle upward. The defender's thumbs will be across the back of his attacker's hand. This way the defender can press on a sensitive pressure point on the back of the assailant's hand while simultaneously holding the knife hand closed so that the knife can't be switched to the opposite hand. Bring straight downward pressure on the knife hand. This puts pressure on his wrist and will break it if the motion is performed quickly and suddenly. The assailant will release the knife.

2. Cover/disarm against a straight attack. The defender's left arm covers the knife-carrying wrist. His right hand reaches over and grabs the pressure point under the attacker's elbow and pulls upward. At the same time, his left hand pushes the attacker's wrist down. Now the assailant's arm is wrapped behind him in an armbar. The defender grabs the knife handle and pulls the knife out of the attacker's hand, kneeing him in the stomach. He can control his attacker by holding the knife at his throat.

3. Cover/disarm against an inverted knife attack. The defender's left hand covers the attacker's knife hand by pushing it up and away from him. At the same time, his right arm circles under and to the outside of the attacker's right elbow. With the defender's left hand at the attacker's wrist and his right controlling the assailant's elbow, he pulls straight down to lock the knife wielder's arm and dislocate his elbow. The defender can easily take the knife and use it to control the attacker.

4. Cover/arm lock against an inverted knife attack. The defender's right hand covers the attacker's weapon by pushing the knife to the outside. With the same action, the defender grabs his assailant's wrist with both hands so he is controlling the knife-bearing hand. The defender steps in front of his opponent, and with a circular motion, he brings his right elbow over the top of the attacker's arm to lock his foe's elbow under his arm. He applies pressure by dropping his body to the ground and takes the now disabled attacker down to a controlled position.

5. Cover/disarm against an inverted slicing attack. This is a double attack. First, the attacker slashes across in both directions. When that doesn't work, he stabs straight down. The defender ducks the initial slashing attack, and when the attacker lunges in to stab down, the defender steps behind him and covers the weapon with his right hand. At the same time, he grabs the wrist of the knife hand and pulls the attacker's arm back against the elbow joint. The defender's left arm comes up under his assailant's throat, bringing his elbow across the attacker's chest. He applies pressure

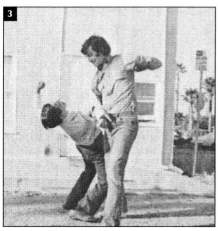

Faced with an inverted stabbing knife attack (1), Harmon blocks the strike with his left hand and, with his right, comes up under the assailant's elbow (2), locking it in his arm. Turning his foe via the arm lock, Harmon can now punch him in the face (3).

to the attacker's wrist, causing him to drop the knife, and to the windpipe, cutting off his opponent's air supply.

6. Kick counter/takedown against an inverted slice attack. The defender ducks the slice and steps to the rear of his attacker. He grabs the attacker's hair and, while pulling him backward and off-balance, kicks his foe in the

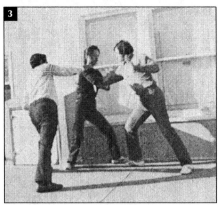

Backed into a corner and faced with two attackers (1), one wielding a knife, Choon-Ok Harmon "sucks" her body away from the knife strike (2) while the second attacker pushes her. She traps her foe's knife hand between her arm and body (3) and applies pressure to his arm while delivering a side kick to the unarmed attacker's midsection (4). She finishes the knife wielder with a hard knee to the stomach (5).

pressure point below the back of the knee to take him down.

7. Kick counter against an inverted slice attack. The defender ducks the slice and instantly uses a low spin kick to knock his attacker off-balance. This kick is not a sweep; it's a low kick, delivered to the leg with a nonstop, spinning body action. The kick, a specialty of kuk sool won, employs the heel as the kicking surface.

8. Cover/counterpunch against an inverted stab. The defender covers the weapon with his left hand by pushing the stabbing hand away from him. His right hand comes under the attacker's elbow, locking it between the defender's right and left hand. The attacker spins around in an attempt to relieve the sudden pain in his arm, and in the process of spinning, places his body in a position for the defender to punch him in the face.

9. Trap/counter against a cornered double attack. This is a special situation that requires a defensive technique that probably wouldn't work if the defender were in the open. In this instance, the defender is backed into a corner and is being attacked by two people, one with a knife. The empty-handed assailant pushes the defender into a corner, and the second attacker rushes in with a knife. The defender can't move or get away because he is in a corner. The defender bends away from the knife to position the weapon between his arm and the side of his body. The defender traps his opponent's hand with his arm so that the attacker's arm is pinned between his arm and body. The defender's right hand finds the pressure point on his attacker's upper arm and twists it to dislocate the elbow, simultaneously delivering a powerful side kick to the unarmed assailant. The defender then knees the now disarmed assailant and finishes the fight.

Knife attacks should not be taken lightly. They are life-endangering situations and must be treated as such. Only with the proper training should anyone try to defend against a knife attack. The best defense is always to run away. However, if there is no alternative except to fight back, kuk sool won offers a practical variety of self-defense techniques against a knife attack.

LONG KNIFE STYLES
The Silent Killers

by David E. Steele • October 1984

The year was 1967. The Special Forces captain led his small Montagnard force to scout a Viet Cong village. It was decided that one prisoner would be taken and the rest of the men in his "hooch" would be silently killed as a message to the lowland Communists to stay out of "yard" territory.

On the night of the raid, the attackers' faces were darkened and all equipment camouflaged. Regular weapons were carried, but the killing was to be done with a silenced M3A1 submachine gun and knives.

The approach to the village was made through heavy wind and rain. One of the "yards" acted as a guide for the captain, who would take out the perimeter guard. When the tribesman pointed out the Viet Cong standing in the trail, the captain drew his bone-handled *kukri*, a gift from an Australian officer. When he had judged the distance right, he struck a single blow, decapitating the sentry. The only sound was the body falling into the mud.

Once inside the compound, the raiders entered the hooch and found the sleeping Viet Cong. The tribesman with the silenced "grease gun" shot three of the Communists, but the two- and three-round bursts were not immediately lethal. The job was then finished with knives. The submachine gun was unexpectedly loud in such confined quarters, and as few shots as possible were preferred. Two other Viet Cong were dispatched silently with knives alone, one of them decapitated by the captain's kukri. All five died without making a sound. The one prisoner was gagged, leashed and led away. The mission was a complete success.

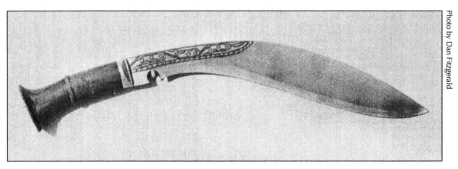

Photo by Dan Fitzgerald

This antique kukri has some decoration on the blade, which is rare because they were meant as field tools.

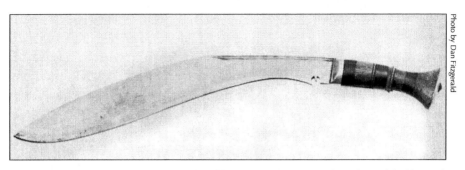

This buffalo-handle kukri has a 13-inch blade. Although unmarked, notice the traditional double notch at the base of the blade.

The kukri, usually associated with the Gurkha soldiers from Nepal, is one of the world's proven blades as both a weapon and a field tool. The Egyptians first developed the recurved, tip-heavy knife perhaps 3,000 years ago. They called it the *khopesh*, which the Greeks later renamed *kopis*. The Romans picked it up from them, though without the fanfare given to the *gladius hispaniensis* (Roman short sword), the standard blade in the legion. Through the Romans, the kopis design reached central Asia. The blade was expanded to sword length in the Nepalese *kora* and the Bengali *ram dao*. In shortened form, it became the field knife of Northern India and Nepal, which the Gurkhas renamed the kukri.

The typical kukri has a 9- to 13-inch blade, a short handle and a flared butt. The steel comes from Indian railroad rails or any other available source. It is tempered and sharpened by a local craftsman. There is a double notch at the base of the blade, and there are numerous stories surrounding the supposed purpose of this traditional decoration, none of which are verifiable. The handle is usually made of wood or buffalo horn.

Gurkhas have a great reputation as soldiers. They serve in the Nepalese army, as well as in the Indian and British armies, where they have served as mercenary units since 1815. In service, they wear the kukri as a field tool, last-ditch weapon and symbol of their calling. Before military service, they carried it at home in Nepal, using it daily for grass trimming, tree cutting, trail clearing and other chores common to poor mountain people. The kukri is their only tool for a multitude of functions. When they enter the army, they are already proficient in its use.

Gurkhas do not have a native martial art. They use the kukri as an extension of their arm. They can behead an enemy soldier with the same body movement as cutting off a tree limb. Because modern close-quarters combat does not involve much sophisticated "parry and riposte," Gurkhas do not need a sophisticated system. Based on their speed, naturalness of movement and willingness to engage in hand-to-hand combat with the enemy, they are more likely to kill their enemy than vice versa. At this time, the British army does not provide any close-quarters battle training for Gurkhas, although off-duty *taekwondo* (Korean karate) clubs are available on some posts.

There are numerous World War II accounts of Gurkhas using the kukri in battle. This was no doubt because of the British army's lack of small arms and ammunition, compared to the Germans or the Japanese. Thus, hand-to-hand combat was relatively common when ammunition ran low or during night combat and ambushes.

Photo courtesy of Graciela Casillas

Boxer and martial artist Graciela Casillas demonstrates the double-sword kali technique. Kali is the best-known fighting art of the Philippines.

Imperial War Museum photo

During World War II, Gurkhas (above) used both kukri and fixed bayonets. Kukri, with their weighted tips, made for powerful strokes.

The recurved blade of the kukri puts its weight toward the tip, making for an extremely powerful blow. It is not designed for thrusting. The most common stroke is decapitation, although a hand or foot could be taken off just as easily.

Perhaps the most famous story of a kukri-wielding Gurkha came out of the 1943 Tunisian Campaign. An Indian army Gurkha on night patrol stumbled across a German trench. As he put it, "I recognized him (the German soldier) by his helmet. He was fumbling with his weapon, so I cut off his head with my kukri. Another appeared from a slit trench, and I cut him down. I was able to do the same with two others, but one made a great deal of noise, which raised the alarm. I had cut at the fifth, but I am afraid I only wounded him. Yet perhaps the wound was severe, for I struck him between the neck and the shoulders."

The technique used by the Gurkhas is similar to the techniques used by the Dyak headhunters of Borneo. Dyak tribesmen practice the decapitating stroke with the traditional *mandau,* a machetelike jungle knife sometimes

The mandau sword/jungle knife (below) was used by the Dyak headhunters of Borneo (left). The handle was sometimes decorated by human or goat hair.

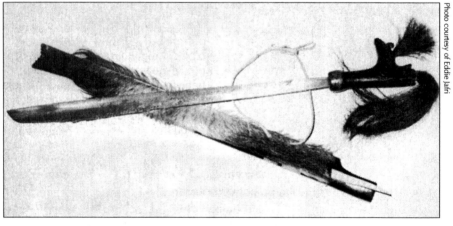

decorated with human or goat hair. The technique is not a complete fighting system with blocks, angling or fancy footwork. It is geared to the task of beheading. While it is not a sophisticated style like Indonesian *pentjak silat,* it is good enough for a jungle ambush.

The main advantage of a long blade over a short one is its ability to parry an opponent's weapon. Even a 4-inch blade can kill easily when thrust to the neck or abdomen, but it cannot block an enemy's blade, and its slashes are not likely to kill or dismember. A blade more than 9 inches long is better suited to close combat because it can be used for a full range of martial arts techniques.

Few people today fight with swords, but quite a few, especially in Asia and Latin America, fight with sword-length field knives. The Philippine *kris* and *bolo,* the Indonesian *golok,* the Malaysian *parang* and the Mexican machete have figured in numerous martial arts as well as Saturday-night mayhem in jungle villages.

Asian long-blade styles have been around for several thousand years, but some of them are adaptable to modern weapons while others are museum pieces. For example, Chinese saber and straight-sword styles are still taught to advanced *tai chi chuan* and *wushu* students, but they are not likely to see service in modern combat or street fighting. The saber was, however, used throughout World War II by cavalry and Communist soldiers who had not yet captured a rifle from the Chinese nationalists. Mao Tse-tung himself mentions the "great sword" in his classic book on guerrilla warfare as the first weapon of the partisan.

One Chinese weapon that does seem to have application in modern usage is the butterfly knife. This is a short sword with a D-guard, customarily used in pairs. Shaolin monks who could not carry conspicuous weaponry hid them in their boots.

Chinese butterfly knives are used with short, chopping strokes. In most of the weapon's defensive techniques, one knife blocks the enemy's staff or sword technique while the other attacks with a short, direct chop or thrust. The D-guard protects the user's hand. A large *quillon* extends from the guard to disarm the enemy after the blade deflects his weapon (block, catch, twist). Butterfly-knife techniques have also been used to good effect with kitchen choppers (cleaverlike kitchen knives) by youths in Hong Kong street gangs.

Most Japanese long-blade systems were developed around the *katana*, a single-edged, two-handed sword used for dismounted combat in Japan's more recent samurai past. The earliest battles in Japan's history were fought with straight, double-edged, Chinese-style swords. Later the *tachi*, used by cavalry, became prominent. The tachi was like a large katana slung edge-down from the armor while riding horseback. The katana was more maneuverable for close combat afoot, because later battles stressed infantry tactics. It was worn edge-up through the sash, suitable for instant

Photos by Dan Fitzgerald

downward strokes from the *saya* (scabbard). Worn in combination with the *wakizashi* (short sword), the katana became the most obvious symbol of the samurai class, who ruled Japan for several hundred years.

Although Japanese noncommissioned officers and officers carried katana-like swords (*gunto*) in World War II and used them in close combat, that will unlikely occur again. Infantry equipment for modern armies is judged in terms of "weight penalty," and a samurai sword is as bulky as a modern assault rifle. Also, a shorter, one-handed edged weapon such as the bolo or kukri is not only a lighter, more efficient field tool, but it also allows hand-to-hand combat in the extremely tight confines of a trench, foxhole, tent or ditch.

Traditional sword techniques are still taught in Japan in numerous schools of *iaijutsu* (sword-drawing art), *iaido* (meditative sword system based on iaijutsu), *kenjutsu* (sword art) and *kendo* (fencing with a bamboo sword). These systems have many physical, mental and spiritual advantages, but they are not very practical for modern combat because they depend on the presence of a very specialized weapon, which is the source of their appeal to many Japanese. They find a discipline that is totally removed from the modern world and that promotes the aggressive Japanese spirit *(Yamato damashii)* irresistibly attractive.

The samurai, of course, being more practical than some of their modern

Hawkins Cheung demonstrates (1) the butterfly-knife technique versus the staff. Notice the footwork (2) as the left knife blocks the enemy's staff while the right knife (3) attacks simultaneously with a short, direct chop or thrust. Butterfly knives originally were carried in boots by Shaolin monks who were not allowed to carry conspicuous weaponry.

counterparts (actual fighting has a way of promoting pragmatism in weaponry and technique), also had short-sword and knife styles. These styles were usually taught under the title *tantojutsu* (half-sword art) and were generally combined with empty-hand *jujutsu* (the art of suppleness). Tantojutsu is rarely taught today, usually as a "finishing touch" for jujutsu or kenjutsu black belts, and then only in certain styles.

The Filipinos are more practical, especially because fighting with edged weapons is still common on the islands. The arts of *kali, escrima* and *arnis de mano* can be employed with virtually any field knife or fighting blade. These blade types are too numerous to mention, especially in the Moro areas, and some may have several local names. However, most fit into the kris (double-edged straight sword, sometimes with a wavy blade) or bolo (machetelike chopping blade) categories. The Moro *kampilan* is an example of the latter, and it is quite similar to the mandau, because the Majapahit Empire that was based in Java once connected the Philippines and Indonesia.

The Indonesians, who are spread out over 13,677 islands—Java, Sumatra, Borneo and Bali being the best known—are a seafaring people, who are traditionally fishermen and pirates. There are more blade types in Indonesia than in any other place in the world. The "national weapon" is the kris, which is smaller than the Philippine variety, with a straight or wavy

Photo by Dan Fitzgerald

Photo by Robert Battica

Photo by Dan Fitzgerald

Pentjak silat instructor Eddie Jafri (dark pants) demonstrates the curved rentjong versus the kris (1-2), and the Indonesian short knife (3) against a long-blade attack.

thrusting blade. The best-known styles are the Javanese and Balinese kris. Most Indonesians are Muslim and therefore do not make "graven images" (realistic pictures of people). But the Balinese are Hindu-Buddhist, a remnant of the original religions in the area before the Islamic proselytism. The Balinese, therefore, carve beautiful human forms into kris handles, while the Javanese tend to use a more stylized "birds-head" grip.

In the 16th century, the Dutch began their conquest of Indonesia, exploiting its wealth of natural resources. They were finally thrown out by the Japanese in World War II and kept out by Indonesian patriots. These jungle fighters used their blades and pentjak silat to fight both the Dutch and the Japanese.

Long-blade styles are common everywhere in Asia, not just in the Philippines or Indonesia. The Burmese practice *bando*, sometimes incorporating the Gurkha kukri. (Gurkha officers were once stationed in Burma with the British forces.) The Koreans practice *hwa rang do* and certain other styles. As long as there is war and a traditional warlike spirit, the long blade will be taught in Asia. Firearms are still rare outside the regular military, and self-defense and guerrilla fighting in the rural areas are still conducted with the jungle knife.

A HAPPY UNION
Hapkido and the Knife

by John Earl Maberry • Photos by John J. Hayland III • November 1984

When you think of the Korean martial art *hapkido* and its use of weapons, you rarely think of the knife—the cane maybe, or the staff, but not the knife. This is because, for the most part, training with the short combat knife is seen only in soft-style hapkido.

Hapkido is broken, rather roughly, into three styles: hard, intermediate and soft. Most hapkido instructors teach the hard style, which is popular around the world and has a greater visual dynamism. Intermediate-style hapkido resembles a cross between *taekwondo* and *aikido* and is just now becoming popular. Soft-style hapkido still labors under the blanket of relative obscurity. The hard style primarily teaches how to defend against knife attacks, and the intermediate form does not use the knife at all. Only the soft style utilizes a systemized series of knife-fighting techniques and principles.

Soft-style hapkido knife science is a unique blend of Asian and Occidental knife-fighting concepts. It incorporates the older Korean empty-hand knife-fighting counters, the close-range knife strikes of the Japanese arts, some Chinese interceptions and double-knife techniques, and the combat-efficient knife movements taught to domestic American armed forces. The latter influence is owed heavily to two martial artists who trained

The early hapkido knife-fighting posture used a hidden knife grip and a high forward guard to allow for parries and grabs.

together in Korea for more than 15 years: Joshua Johnson and Byong Park, both high-ranking *hapkidoka* and members of their countries' armed forces.

Johnson—president of the Soft Style Korean Hapkido Federation of North America—was a U.S. Marine Corps master sergeant specializing in preparing small-unit groups for secret missions. Park was a lieutenant in the Republic of Korea army before retiring to private business a few years ago. The pair met as classmates in a Korean martial arts school in 1960. They trained together in Korea and later served together during two tours in Vietnam.

While training together, Johnson showed Park some of the Marine-style knife-fighting techniques, which differ from Asian knife fighting in terms of approach to the opponent, point of entry of the cut or stab, and the type of knife used. They worked together on these principles for more than a year, and when it came time for Park to test for his third-degree black belt,

This updated version of the hapkido knife posture uses a more forward knife grip to allow for faster striking and a lower guard to protect more of the body.

41

he used a Marine-style "K-Bar" for his knife-defense techniques. Naturally, this caused the test examiners—a panel of five expert hapkido instructors—to ask him about the type of knife he was wielding and why he was performing techniques unfamiliar to them. Park and Johnson explained that the knife-fighting techniques they developed had proved superior to the concepts originally taught to them in hapkido.

To prove their point, Johnson asked that he be allowed to demonstrate the techniques personally to the panel members. He selected five of the largest black belts in attendance to use as attackers. Johnson was armed with a dull metal blade coated with talcum powder. Powder marks on the *gi* would indicate cuts or stabs. The attackers had similarly prepared knives as well as sticks.

The first few attacks were one-on-one, with Johnson executing simple countermoves to sudden aggression. He demonstrated a clever hidden-

The traditional military-style rear knife attack is used almost exclusively by hapkido students in the U.S. armed forces.

Two hapkidoka prepare to spar using dull metal knives coated with powder. The powder marks on the gi will indicate cuts.

blade posture that kept the knife down and out of view and used his lead hand to perform hooking blocks. He also performed fast draw-and-cut techniques (the Japanese influence) and some quick Chinese hand traps and counter-cuts. Then he focused on quick incapacitation techniques taught by the military to hamstring an attacker or otherwise limit his practical mobility.

Johnson also fought against multiple attackers, using his opponents' own bodies as shields against the others. When he was done, Johnson had managed to simulate severe damage to each of the attackers while receiving only two superficial "cuts."

Despite the eclectic nature of the demonstration, the panel was impressed. So impressed, in fact, they assigned Johnson the task of transforming his knife-fighting concepts into a teachable system. Ultimately, he did so. Johnson's system, although updated often since 1964, breaks down knife fighting into the following categories:

1. Knife grips: standard and personal
2. Knife-fighting postures: aggressive and defensive
3. Knife applications: slashing, slicing, cutting and stabbing
4. Blocking and parrying: offensive and defensive
5. Knife attacks

6. Unarmed knife defenses

7. Armed knife defenses

8. Sparring

9. Situational problems

10. Ceremony

The first section, knife grips, deals with how to best hold a knife. Holding the knife so the blade points downward from the edge of the hand is called a spike grip and is not recommended for practical use. Holding the knife so that the thumb and knuckles brace the hilt is called the hook grip because, in certain Chinese-influenced techniques, the upper edge of the knife and the knife wielder's wrist can trap and hold an attacker's arm. There are other grips, such as the forearm-braced grip and throw grip, but the hook grip is most often used and is more practical.

The hapkido practitioner prefers to keep his knife out of the opponent's reach by leading with the empty hand. This allows the lead hand to trap while the knife darts in and out to inflict whatever damage is required. Johnson favors the hidden-knife posture. This stance allows the fighter to use his lead hand to block, parry or hook and gives the feet freedom to shift stances, evade, kick or advance. The knife itself is kept low and back, held

A quick downward slash to the leg succeeds in both stopping the kick and incapacitating the limb.

lightly against the hip. The thumb is pressed under the hilt for direction when cutting. Because very few stabs are used, the hapkido knife fighter prefers a grip that will allow fast, short-range cuts and slashes.

An alternative grip and posture bring the knife higher so it can be implemented faster. The guard is dropped slightly to allow the elbow to protect the ribs, stomach and back. Unlike the previous stance, this is a more aggressive posture and is more often used in knife-against-knife confrontations.

Hapkido knife strikes are based on depth rather than just target. Small, circular motions are used to injure, with penetration broken down into slashing, slicing and cutting. Slashes cause surface injuries and are designed to draw blood and generate pain without doing serious, irreparable harm. In hapkido, the attacker is almost always offered a chance to back down, even after initial blows are exchanged. Slashing attacks allow the foe to back out of a knife fight while still in one piece.

Slicing strikes take the fight a step further and are designed to cause heavy bleeding, major tissue damage and partial or total incapacitation—but again, not fatally. There is a strong sense of life backing up hapkido's ethical code. Life is taken only when no other avenue remains. Slices can therefore be as dangerous to the defender as they are to the attacker, but they are a calculated risk the martial artist should be willing to take.

When a hapkidoka is forced to cut, he cuts to the bone, severing muscles, tendons and organs. This attack is used only in extreme cases.

Hapkido instructors also teach a few extreme knife penetrations, such as minor or major stabbing. A minor stab inflicts pinpoint wounds and is used in much the same way as a slash to cause injury without death. Major stabs are always fatal and are designed for warfare. These are some of the military techniques incorporated into hapkido. The Marine-style throat wrap and stab (seen countless times in war movies) taught in hapkido is a technique reserved for military personnel and advanced students.

Blocking with a knife is an overlooked concept in most martial arts. Hapkido, however, sees value in knife blocks. The style has a lot of what are referred to as "single-movement defenses." These techniques use the knife to block the attacker's arm or hand, not just his weapon, thereby accomplishing both defense and the infliction of a debilitating injury.

Suppose an attacker tries a cut with his knife. Utilizing hapkido's single-movement defense, the defender cuts deeply across the attacker's knuckles. In most cases, this would cause the attacker to drop his knife. Variations could include a blocking cut to the attacker's inner wrist, forearms, etc. A blocking cut to any muscle or tendon used to support the knife hand will work in one's favor.

The hapkidoka can also use the knife to block a kick. A simple slice to a leg not only would hurt the attacker, but could also do enough damage to the supporting muscles to severely restrict mobility. An immobile assailant cannot press his attack, and the defender can retreat without further injury to either party.

Even though Johnson wrote extensively on using the knife to attack, very little offensive theory is taught in most soft-style hapkido schools. Because the point of self-defense is just that—defense—there are few instances that warrant a direct attack, especially an armed direct attack. These techniques are reserved for military and advanced students who wish to know the entire scope of hapkido training.

On the other hand, knife defenses—both armed and unarmed—are taught to all soft-style hapkido students. These defenses mirror the kind of techniques you will see in any good martial arts school. The attacks are practical and the kind one is likely to encounter in a real knife attack. Most of the unarmed defenses against knife wielders utilize trapping blocks and immediately immobilizing the knife arm. This is most often followed by a joint-breaking technique, kick, hand strike, takedown or disarm and possible counter-use of the knife. Very few throws are used in hapkido against knife attackers because of the uncertainty of the weapon's location during the throw.

Suppose the knife wielder has a grip on the defender's lapel and is using the knife for intimidation, perhaps as a stimulus for cooperation in a robbery. Implementing a simple red-belt-level knife defense, the hapkidoka can use both of his hands to snare the attacker's wrists. The right hand holds the grabbing wrist in place, while the left gains a controlling grip on the knife hand. The fingers should be wrapped around the edge of the hand and the thumb on the backside for leverage. With a deft twist of the wrist, the defender snaps the attacker's wrist inward, dragging the man's own knife across his inner arm and behind his elbow. (Depth of the cut is determined by the intensity of the threat.) Continuing the downward motion, the defender performs a basic pressure wrist lock so he can break the attacker's knife wrist or use it to control him in another way.

Although basically a simple maneuver, this technique illustrates the hapkido concept of controlled aggression. The defender could easily inflict permanent or minor damage, depending on his desire. He doesn't have to injure the attacker seriously if he doesn't want to. His moral judgment dictates his actions.

Armed hapkido knife defense generally uses the knife to stop the attack

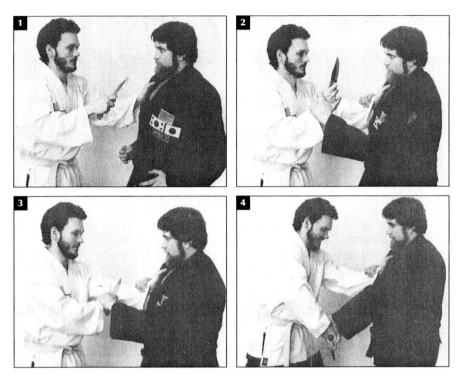

In this sequence, the attacker uses a lapel grab (1) and his knife to intimidate the defender. The defender grabs both of the attacker's wrists (2), holding one hand in place while controlling the other. This allows him to snap his knife hand down, causing him to cut himself (3). The trapped knife hand is twisted down (4), where it can either be broken or locked.

in a nonlethal way. Sometimes this means causing serious damage to muscles or tendons. Other than military students, hapkidoka are rarely taught to take a human life. This sets hapkido knife fighting apart from most forms of knife fighting. In hapkido, the knife is a tool one can use to restore peace, not take lives. But like any weapon, including the hands and feet, it can be a lethal tool, as well.

There is some knife sparring in hapkido schools using variations on the *ippon kumite* rules, the first "serious" strike ending the match. Hapkidoka do not use live, sharpened knives when sparring, as do some schools. Aside from the obvious legal problems this kind of training can generate, everyone makes mistakes. And when working with knives, mistakes can be fatal. Safe measures are therefore taken.

In hapkido knife sparring, each fighter generally uses a wooden or dull metal knife coated with colored powder (a different color for each fighter so accidental self-inflicted cuts will show). Point values are determined for the various body zones, and the judge awards points by observation.

"Situational problems" are one of the most educational and enjoyable aspects of hapkido knife training. These scenarios simulate potential combat situations, such as street confrontations, house break-ins, sudden fights and armed robbery. The defender walks through the scenario expecting no trouble. The attacker(s) enters the scene but may or may not attack. The teacher secretly tells the attacker whether he should engage. While students should be prepared for an attack, they shouldn't jump every person who comes close. In these situations, the defender and attacker must try their best to inflict mock injury on the other. Again, dull, powdered weapons are used because they're good tools for learning.

Although the short, American-style knife will probably never gain the almost universal respect weapons such as the *katana* (Japanese sword) and the *jo* (short stick) have earned, it is still a worthy and formidable weapon. It has been the strong right arm of many servicemen and will probably continue to be so, no matter how advanced other forms of weaponry become.

THE FOLDING KNIFE
A Pocketful of Trouble

by David E. Steele • April 1985

G iven a choice, most people would want a big knife to fight with. It can be used for parrying and to keep a safe distance from the opponent. It can also be used to make deadly slashes and decapitating strokes.

In most civilized countries, however, carrying a big knife would be unusual, unnecessary (for utility purposes) and conspicuous. The most common defense knife in such countries is the pocket folder.

The folding knife is the easiest blade to carry in modern clothing, especially with

Photo by Dan Fitzgerald

The custom 4- and 5-inch balisong folding knives above possess flattened clip points.

beltless slacks. There is no problem strapping it on in the morning—just drop it in the pocket and walk. With a locking blade, the folder can serve as a sheath-style boot knife or a push dagger.

Different states and localities have different laws regarding how or whether such knives can be carried legally. Generally speaking, however, a knife carried in the pocket will not turn up except in a search, and a legal search must be preceded by probable cause for detention or an arrest. Therefore, a citizen who avoids bars and other potential trouble spots will probably never have any police official discover his knife unless he uses it. And if he has to use it, the offense of having carried it (which is generally irrelevant to the question of whether it was employed reasonably for self-defense) will probably be the least of his problems.

Because the knife is generally considered deadly force both de facto (in reality) and de jure (by right), it is appropriate for use only in life-threatening situations. At least that is the way courts tend to look at the matter. However, a closed knife, especially a well-designed weapon like the *balisong*, can be used as a *yawara* stick for attacks that could be construed as serious but less than life threatening. Cuts to the extremities can often end an empty-hand attack, but explaining to a court that your intent was merely to stop your opponent may not be convincing. The court may consider the minimal damage you inflicted to have been serendipity (a happy accident) rather than a demonstration of your skill and control as a martial artist.

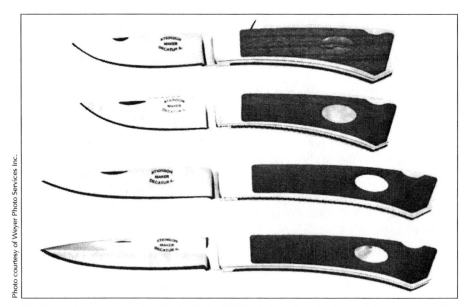

The blades above are examples of rocker-locked folding knives. Note the diamond-shaped cross section of the blade at the bottom, a feature designed for penetration.

Some jurisdictions make a distinction between "cutting" and "stabbing" as far as charges and penalties are concerned. The theory is that a stabbing is much more likely to be fatal. In fact, a knife cut anywhere but on the neck is not likely to be fatal. Many jurisdictions, however, make no such distinction; once the knife is used in any way, the charge is likely to be a major violent felony (assault with a deadly weapon, attempted murder, mayhem or another appropriate charge). Merely brandishing the knife combined with a threat is usually enough to be considered assault with a deadly weapon, which is another good reason to keep the knife out of sight until circumstances justify its use.

Today, police officers carry knives (boot knives or folding hunters) as last-ditch defensive weapons. The most common blade they carry is the buck-style, rocker-locked hunting knife. Uniformed patrol officers routinely carry these on their belts for cutting screens, seat belts, etc. Because the officer has a revolver, Mace and a baton as part of his regular gear, the knife is not likely to be used as a weapon unless he is off duty or working undercover.

In New York City, for example, a blue steel .38 revolver is as indicative of a police officer as his badge because it is standard issue to all local departments to eliminate confusion in shootouts. This presents problems for undercover officers, who might have to stash both their gun and badge before approaching someone for a "buy." Because a knife is standard operating equipment for a New York junkie (the weapon is easy to get and cheap—not taking up extra cash that could go toward buying dope), undercover officers also sometimes carry them. For instance, Anthony Schiano—nicknamed "Solo" for his habit of operating alone—was well-known for carrying unusual weapons while working the narcotics detail undercover. His favorite weapons were the lock-blade folding knife and a wire with large nails for handles. The latter could work as a garrote, a flail or improvised handcuffs depending on the circumstances.

In the case of an undercover operation, it may be advantageous to use a typical, comparatively cheap street knife, something that will not attract unnecessary attention and that can be ditched, if necessary. For police officers operating off duty, however, especially if the knife is the

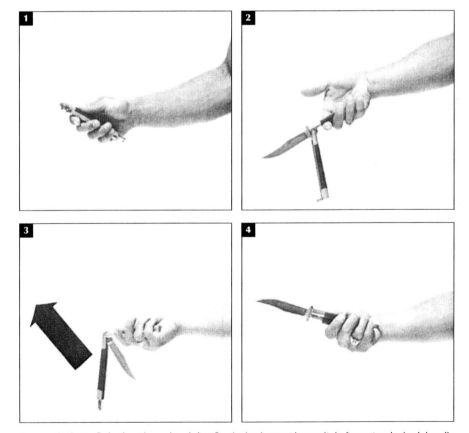

To open the butterfly knife with one hand, first flip the latch (1) with your little finger. Let the latch handle drop free (2). Turn the now latchless handle and flip it up (3) to the open position (4), edge up.

only weapon the officer is carrying—some officers prefer the blade to a gun, especially if they are exercising in outfits that would make concealing a gun difficult or impossible—a carefully designed and manufactured folding fighter is recommended.

The folding fighter may be double-edged, but its most important characteristic is a sharp, stabbing point—the main difference between it and a conventional folding hunter. The stiletto blade and the flattened clip point are two of the best shapes. The "Wee-Hawk" blade—designed by custom knife maker Jody Samson and used on some 4- and 5-inch Bali-Song knives from Pacific Cutlery—is an example of the flattened clip point. This style allows good penetration but has more blade strength than the stiletto.

Bali-Song is the trade name for the highly refined Pacific Cutlery version of the traditional Philippine *balisong* butterfly knife. This weapon, which appeared in the Batangas province in the 1940s, was named for the "butterfly" scissor action of its split-handle design. Another name for it was "click click," which is the sound it made as it opened or closed.

The balisong utilized traditional Philippine martial art techniques designed around the *daga* (dagger). The ancient sheath dagger, incorporated into the Philippine arts of *kali, escrima* and *arnis,* was supplemented by the balisong, a knife more appropriate to the urban lifestyle and modern clothing of the 20th-century Philippines.

The balisong was an excellent design limited by the quality of materials and workmanship available in the Philippines. Jungle and barrio workshops could not produce high-quality knives because they were limited to whatever materials were at hand—plastic from toothbrushes for the handle, old car springs for blade steel, etc.

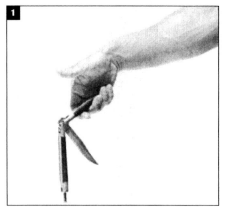 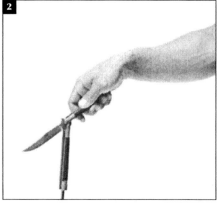

To close the butterfly knife, let the latch handle drop back down (1). Turn the latchless handle 180 degrees (2) and flip it up (3) to the closed position (4).

Les de Asis of Pacific Cutlery in Los Angeles took the balisong into the modern era with first-rate materials and craftsmanship. Noted martial artists like Dan Inosanto, Leo Gaje, Jeff Imada and Graciela Casillas prefer these knives for demonstrations. They have been used in the martial arts films *The Big Brawl* and *Sharky's Machine* because of their visual appeal.

There are many flashy ways to open and close the balisong. In reality, the fighter only needs to know how to open it to a "natural" blade-forward position and a way to open it to the blade-downward "dagger" position. Once a blade can be opened quickly with both hands, these two methods are quite sufficient. As Inosanto says, "The art comes in after the knife is open."

Street tactics do not need to be excessively complicated, either. For example, one common Philippine technique is to spit in the opponent's eyes (preferably with tobacco or betel nut juice), kick him in the shin (to cause pain and distraction), draw the balisong and use it closed as a yawara stick, then, if necessary, open it behind the hip (so the enemy cannot kick it away) and slash and stab from several different angles.

Most books on knife fighting show knife against knife techniques. This is a dangerous business at best, because on the street it is always best to have a weapon that gives you an advantage over your opponent's weapon. For example, gun against knife, stick against knife (the stick has a reach advantage, although it has to be used properly), and knife against empty hand illustrate obvious tactical (if not always legal) advantages.

Of course, the greatest advantages are common sense, tactical awareness, and an understanding of current laws and court cases. For example, one security guard at an aircraft manufacturing plant was demonstrating knife techniques on another guard with a 2-inch pocket blade. Both men

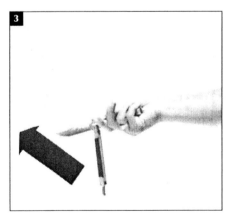

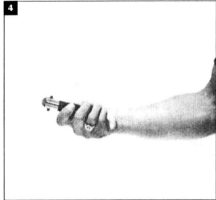

were former police officers. The other guard turned out to have a knife phobia, something no one knew. He became angry, and though he had not been hurt in any way, he reported the demonstration to the plant's bosses, who had been trying to find a way to get rid of the demonstrator for his pro-union, anti-management activities. They tried to charge him with assault with a deadly weapon but could not because he did not have the required evil intent. They tried to charge him with violation of a company rule, but there were no rules about knives, and no person or property had been damaged. They finally suspended him just on general principle, and because the incident involved a knife, it was hard for him to find a federal or state agency to press his discrimination case. He finally got assistance, but it took a year before the company was forced to remove the trumped-up incident from his file. The moral of the story is to practice or demonstrate knife techniques only on other martial artists with the right attitude, and don't display a knife unless you intend to use it.

If a police officer asks for the knife you are wearing, even if you are convinced you are carrying it legally, your best bet is to give it to him or let him take it from you, whichever he prefers, because he has a great deal of latitude in acting to protect himself. He may just be removing it temporarily while he talks to you and will give it back after you have answered his questions satisfactorily.

In one case, a Veterans Administration hospital police officer was called to a disturbance at the emergency room. The officer found a 30-year-old, 6-foot, 180-pound man kneeling outside the ambulance entrance cursing the emergency-room staff for not treating him first. The investigation showed that he was probably under the influence of strong pain medication and close to being a prescription addict. The officer noticed that the man was carrying a Gerber FS-II rock-blade folder on his belt, which is illegal on VA property because it has a blade more than 3 inches long. Given the man's agitated state of mind, the officer did not feel he would give up the knife voluntarily, so with his left hand, the officer reached to unsnap the sheath from the man's belt. Suddenly, the man flipped over on his back, drew the knife and threw it past the officer's leg through an open car door to the front seat of the man's auto. It was evident he had not intended to throw the knife at the officer but wanted to keep it from being confiscated by tossing it in his car. When the officer reached in the car to pick up the half-open knife, the suspect tried to slam the door, which ended up hitting the officer in the hip. This was the last straw for the officer, who subdued and handcuffed the man, charging him with disorderly conduct and possession of an illegal knife. A less-benevolent officer could have added felony assault charges to the list.

The courts consider the knife as deadly force in the same way as a gun. However, unlike the gun, a knife makes a poor weapon to threaten with. Many individuals will see the knife only as provocation, forcing you to use it. So your best bet is to keep it out of sight until needed.

In another case, a police officer whose department did not allow officers to carry guns off duty was shopping at a local firearms store. Because he was wearing "police pants" (with distinctive sap and flashlight pockets), he became the object of an assault by a 250-pound mental patient. The man gave the officer a violent shove, which sent him flying into a rifle rack, knocking six long guns on the floor. The officer, because of his martial arts training, was not injured when he fell. When the psycho walked over cursing, the officer grabbed his shirt and told him he was under arrest. The suspect grabbed the officer's left hand and, using both of his hands, tried to break the officer's thumb.

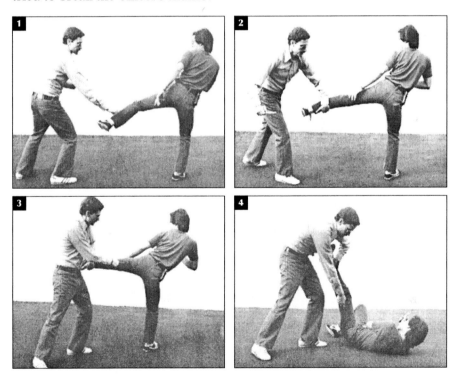

The folding knife can be your best defense against a kicking attack. As your assailant kicks, maintain your distance and cut (1) to his shin. Grab (2) the attacker's kicking leg with your free hand, and follow up with a stabbing thrust (3) to the thigh. Maintaining control of your opponent's leg, dump him to the ground (4) and, if necessary, inflict a second knife thrust to the thigh. Remember to use only as much force as is needed to end the conflict.

In spite of appearances, the officer actually had the advantage because his enemy had tied up both of his hands on the officer's one. This allowed the lawman to draw the balisong he always carried off duty, keeping it out of the suspect's sight. Store employees, however, sprayed the suspect with Mace, spraying the officer in the process. Even so, the officer was not incapacitated and would have maimed the suspect except for fear of the legal consequences of using "deadly" force when the suspect had "only" sprained the officer's thumb and not yet attacked in a way that would convince a jury lethal force was necessary. Fortunately, the suspect backed off and was subsequently apprehended by the local police.

In this case, the officer protected himself against both the suspect and the courts, keeping his knife in reserve until the circumstances required it. He still occasionally wears his uniform pants off duty, but he is more careful now where he shops. Police-hating psychos are common enough on duty without having to deal with them off duty.

SURVIVAL KNIVES
When It's Just You Against the Wilderness
by Mark Jackson • February 1987

There recently was a well-meaning soul who volunteered for a survival test armed with nothing but what he could carry in the hollow handle of his "Rambo" knife. He fully intended to make it through the duration of the two-week test, but he had to call it quits before the course ended. "I knew I was in trouble the first couple of days," he said. "I lost my knife when I threw it at a squirrel. It took me two days to find it, and I went hungry all that time since I couldn't build any traps or start a fire."

Anyone facing a similar emergency should have as many survival aids as he or she can comfortably carry. And above all else, one should be certain to have a sturdy knife.

The Rambo knife combines the features of the fixed-bladed knife and the spring-locked knife. The former follows the classic design reaching back to the cave men, who ground flat stone to an edge.

The knife parallels the development of the sword. Each culture has tended to produce a smaller version of the bladed weapon that its soldiers carried into combat. For the Japanese, it was the *tanto*, the Chinese had the *chi-shou* and the English had the dagger (or Scottish dirk).

In 1825, the U.S. frontiersman Jim Bowie designed the knife that bears his name. It was 10 to 15 inches long with a blade width of 1-3/4 inches. It was single-edged and curved at the tip. The razor-sharp edge allowed Bowie to skin a deer, while the specially designed tip let him penetrate an opponent's body more easily than with a conventionally forged weapon.

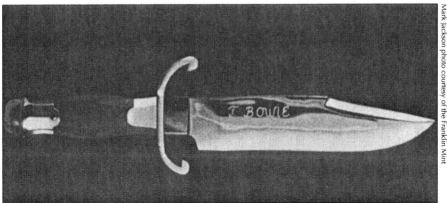

Mark Jackson photo courtesy of the Franklin Mint

The bowie knife, named after frontiersman Jim Bowie, is the forerunner of most modern-day survival knives. Above is the Franklin Mint's replica of this famous early American knife.

The blade's width, and the fact that it was sharpened on one edge, were significant in that these factors did not detract from the tensile strength of the steel. The knife was also balanced for throwing, enabling the user to dispatch a foe while remaining out of arm's reach.

This utility approach to the manufacture of a knife was a concept that other knife makers would pursue for the next 160 years. Twenty-five years after Bowie saw the prototype for his knife, the British firm of Joseph Rodgers & Sons Ltd. produced the Norfolk Sportsman's Knife for the Great Exhibition of 1851. This pocketknife had 75 blades and was the result of two years' planning and manufacturing.

The first improvement on this design was the addition of a spring in the handle to reinforce the position of the blade. The pocketknife was first customized for dual usage with the addition of a second blade at the opposite end of a larger one, which was made to sharpen the tips of quill pens (hence the term "pen knife"). Most of the 75 blades in the Norfolk Sportsman's Knife were forged with the 1851 Exhibition (a forerunner of the modern-day World's Fair) in mind. They bore filigree of floral designs, landscapes and portraits that show that Joseph Rodgers & Sons wanted to be a focal point of conversation wherever their knife was displayed. Among the ornamentation, they also included scissors, tweezers, a corkscrew, a fork, a leather punch and several picks and hooks.

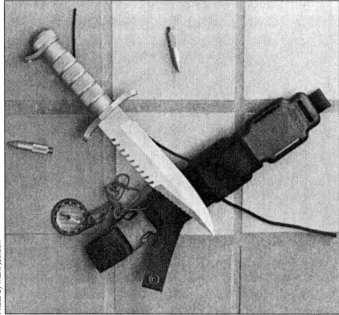

Photo by Mark Jackson

The Buckmaster, manufactured by the Buck company, is said to serve as a grappling hook while also addressing other survival needs, including providing a compass that fits into the sheath.

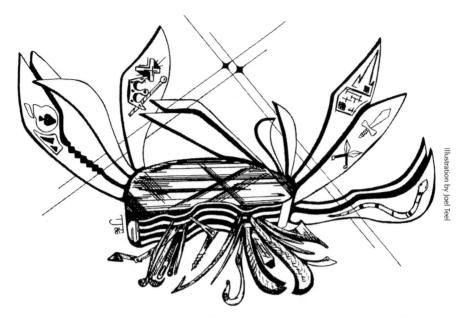

Illustration by Joel Teel

Joseph Rodgers & Sons Ltd. produced the Norfolk Sportsman's Knife for the 1851 exhibition. This pocketknife had 75 blades, including scissors, tweezers, a corkscrew and a fork.

Knife forgers have continued Bowie's concept of devising blades for specific applications. For at least two decades, fishermen and divers have used fixed-bladed knives with sawteeth filed in one edge for scaling fish. The filet knife has a flexible blade so the cook can easily separate the meat from a fish's skeleton. For at least three decades, engineers enjoyed a spring-locking knife with a folding foot-long ruler, calipers for measuring the thickness of small objects, and screwdrivers for repairing or assembling equipment. In 1897, the Swiss Army assigned the Victorinox the task of manufacturing a pocketknife for military application. Still in production, these models fulfill the promise of utilitarian application that was evident in the Norfolk Sportsman's Knife in 1851. Roughly an inch wide and 3-1/2 inches long when closed, these knives give the user a magnifying glass, wood saw, fish scaler, leather pouch, reamer, wire stripper, hook disgorger and metal file at his disposal. The U.S. Army has its own version of this spring-lock knife called the Camillus. Both versions are usually available in knife stores for side-by-side comparison by consumers.

Whether spring-locked or fixed-blade, the manufacturing process for all knives is essentially the same. Steel of the appropriate dimensions is hammered or forged into shape with a portion called the "tang" extending in a thinner section to the rear of the blade. The knife maker then "tempers" the

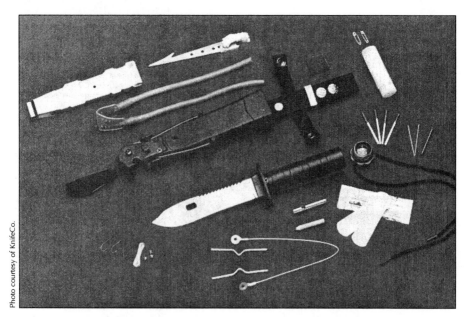

KnifeCo's Survivor blade is multifaceted, offering the user everything from a slingshot, matches and Band-Aids to a compass, spear, fish hooks and line, needles and thread, and a whistle.

blade so it will have the degree of hardness he desires. In this step, he heats the blade to an ultrahigh temperature (1,400 degrees Fahrenheit for most steels; 1,740 F for stainless steel) and then dips it suddenly in cold water. He reheats the slightly brittle blade to toughen it so it can retain an edge. The knife maker observes the color of the steel to judge the temperature of the blade (the hotter the steel, the tougher the blade). If the steel has a red-brown color, it has a stronger amount of temper than steel with a straw color. When he sees that the blade has the desired temperature, the smith cools the steel to complete the process that determines the hardness of the blade.

The knife forger keeps the tang soft so he can fit the metal inside the handle for the knife. Until 1981, knife handles were made of wood, ivory, plastic, gold, silver and tortoise shell. The handle was a solid cylinder and, outside of serving as a substitute hammer, had no function but to provide a grip for the blade. Then, in the summer of 1981, Sylvester Stallone asked Jimmy Lile, known professionally as the "Arkansas Knifesmith," to design a "different" survival knife for his film *First Blood.* Lile took the assignment on the understanding that he would not be creating "another attractive movie prop" but "one basic tool to do a variety of jobs." The result was the now world-famous tool for combat and survival—the Rambo knife.

Lile imagined himself in an isolated survival situation and deliberately limited his resources to only one tool with which he would have to get by. After careful deliberation, he adapted the basic design for the bowie knife to perform the following functions:

1. Cut firewood and shelter materials, and slice up his food with a long cutting edge.

2. Hold a compass so he could have a true bearing for escape.

3. Hold necessities (e.g., matches, medicines, needles and thread) in a hollow handle. This would be waterproof when capped and could be fitted onto a pole to make a spear or gig.

4. Contain screwdrivers for working on any gear.

5. Carry a nylon line for fishing and snares.

6. Provide a flat surface for pounding.

7. Have sawteeth carved in the side of the blade opposite from the sharpened edge, enabling one to cut poles for shelter and spears for fishing and defense, and also carve through the canopy of a downed aircraft.

8. Be a dependable offensive or defensive weapon.

Lile selected 440C high-carbon steel for the blade so it could cut open the canopy of an airplane and withstand the stress of survival and combat. The cross guard had a Phillips screwdriver on the top and a standard cross-bit

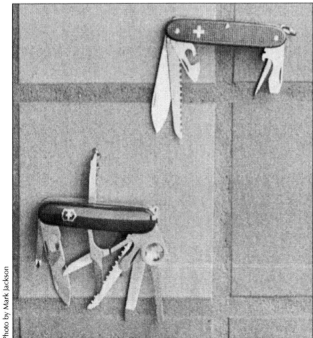

Photo by Mark Jackson

The famed Swiss Army knife comes in several models. Among the utilitarian devices these knives contain are a magnifying glass, saw, fish scaler, leather punch and wire stripper.

screwdriver on the bottom end. There were also two holes for attaching the knife to a pole. A butt cap contained a small nonmagnetic compass with a replaceable "O" ring that kept the hollowed handle watertight. The compass was sealed with clear plastic to give the knife a flat surface. Lile wrapped nylon around the handle and placed a folder inside the hollowed tube for cutting lengths of nylon as he needed them. The knife was about 14 inches long (the blade about 9 inches, the handle about 4-7/8 inches).

Five years after Lile forged the knife for Stallone, survival knives of similar design began appearing on the market in abundance. Lile maintains that his survival knives "are the most popular and imitated knives in the world but still unequaled." However, just as Lile worked from the basic design of the bowie knife, so have other knife forgers expanded on his concept of a multifunctional blade designed for survival.

The most controversial survival knife may be the Buckmaster, whose manufacturers claim it will serve as a grappling hook while also addressing the needs served by Lile's knife. On both sides of the hand guard, the Buck company has attached two 2-inch anchors that are supposed to provide the grip should the user need to climb up or rappel down an obstacle. One ties a rope through a hole at the rear of the handle to apply the Buckmaster in this fashion. The survivalist might consider removing the anchors and slipping his rope through the two holes in the hand guard. Because the knife measures 12-1/2 inches from the handle to its blade tip, one might use

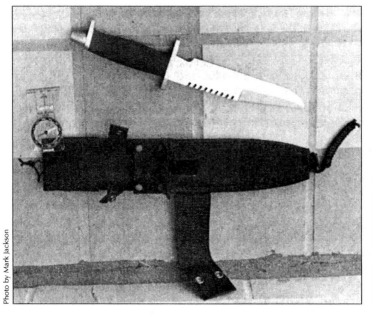

Photo by Mark Jackson

Gerber calls its survival knife the BMF (Basic Multi-Functional). It has a solid rather than hollow handle and enough saw-teeth on one edge to allow for three inches of sawing "stroke."

the entire Buckmaster to suspend his weight in an emergency in which he does not have access to a grappling hook (and when he can find sufficient support for the knife).

Instead of inserting a compass within the butt cap of the hollow handle, Buck has designed a case in the sheath for carrying a Silva Type 12 compass. This use of the sheath to hold additional supplies has also been developed by other firms trying to provide as compact a design as possible for carrying survival tools. The Gerber company has designed a sheath with removable clips for holding any materials the user wants to carry. Like the Buck company, Gerber has made a pocket on the sheath for a small compass, which one carries separate from the knife.

Gerber calls its survival knife the BMF (Basic Multi-Functional). It has a full tang instead of a hollow handle, and the blade has straight edges that taper to the "clip point" (curved tip). Like the Buckmaster, it has enough sawteeth on the top edge to allow its user three inches of "stroke" for sawing action. It is 3/4 of an inch longer than the Buckmaster and is also constructed of 440-grade steel.

KnifeCo has a customized sheath for its survival knife, The Survivor. The sheath has compartments for a signal mirror. Clips fit in the top to form bands for a slingshot (the rubber tubing that fastens to the clips can also function as a tourniquet). One aims the slingshot by bracing it against the hip and centering the midpoint between the prongs on the intended target. Because one can use this weapon only against very small game at a range of less than 30 yards, he might consider using the slingshot simply to improve his aim for larger weapons or if he has no other means of procuring food. The sheath also contains a small fishing harpoon that the user would probably find more effective by attaching it to a pole.

KnifeCo blades are forged with 420C stainless steel. This metal differs from the 440C high-carbon steel in that it does not have the tensile strength for cutting the dense plastic of a jet's canopy.

Before embarking on any sojourn that will lead to a wilderness locale, one should hedge one's bets as tightly as possible. Survival conditions require as many supplies as one has available for the duration of the emergency. No one can guarantee that a system of training or a collection of materials will assure survival in all conditions. But possessing a good survival knife such as those discussed in this article can go a long way toward bringing you back alive to civilization.

THE ART OF KNIFE THROWING
A Cut Above Other Forms of Self-Defense

by Brad Bayler • Photos courtesy of Young C. Choi • May 1987

The martial arts have been in existence since the beginning of recorded history. They have been effective because they were developed from actual combat. The techniques were lessons directly from the real-life experiences of many men. Any martial art that was not effective could not survive the test of time. After all, who would pass down fighting techniques if they did not work? And who would be foolish enough to train in these techniques if they did not work?

The fighting techniques of the Korean people have been tested over the years, with deadly results. Looking at the history of Korea, it becomes immediately apparent why the inhabitants developed fighting arts.

Koreans have never invaded another country; they are a peace-loving people. But their neighbors have invaded them time and time again. The martial arts to Koreans meant survival. And these arts were used in a way that protected their country and way of life.

The martial arts as they were originally practiced and as they are used today are very different. They have evolved into a scientific way of fighting. Because of this evolution, some aspects of the martial arts are fading out of existence.

In this day and age of firearms, the practice of the sword, and other classical weapons, is becoming obsolete as a form of self-defense. Even rarer than sword training is the practice of throwing daggers or knives. While one may never use these weapons in a real-life situation, their fighting principles

 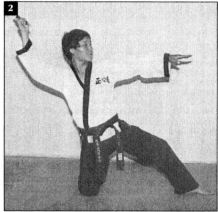

To throw from a kneeling position, point (1) your left foot at the target with your rear leg at a 90-degree angle to the target. Shift (2) your weight back.

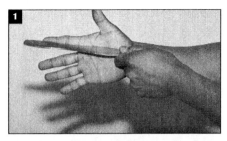
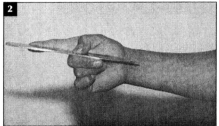
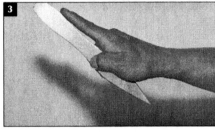

Proper knife grip: Place (1) the edge of the knife along your index finger. Hold (2) the knife lightly between your thumb and curled middle finger. Roll (3) the wrist downward to jettison the knife.

can be of use to any martial artist.

One practitioner of knife throwing is Young C. Choi, who teaches the art of *chung sim do* in Lancaster, California. Chung sim do translates to "the study of the mind and body."

In ancient times, rocks were thrown as weapons and used as vehicles for the development of the mind. The individual throwing the rock would concentrate on a particular target. While he concentrated, the target grew in his mind and appeared very large, thus making it easier to hit. This is really the same principle as aiming a rifle at a target or shooting an arrow in archery. By concentrating and focusing on the target, everything else is

Then move it forward (3). Your knee and head should be in a straight line as the knife is thrown (4).

excluded. This sort of exercise is called *hang sang sim*, which means "to have a stable and calm mind." The development of hang sang sim comes from breathing and meditation practice.

There are several fairly simple methods for developing hang sang sim. One method is to take a piece of paper and draw a circle on it, then draw a dot in the center of the circle. Hang the paper on a wall, sit down at any distance you want and focus on the dot in the center of the circle. When, in your mind, you can make the dot fill the circle, you are developing good focus and concentration. Even though the dot is actually small, in your mind it will appear to be large.

Along with the development of the mind comes the development of the body. Proper technique and body mechanics must be practiced until the moves become second nature. In order to concentrate on fighting your opponent, it is important to focus and concentrate solely on him and nothing else. If you do not concentrate on the opponent and watch how you are throwing your techniques, you will be defeated.

This is like driving a car. The mechanics of the car are learned first before you drive on the freeway. When you drive, the mind concentrates on the road, other cars and obstacles. You do not think about what your feet or hands are doing; they react to what the mind wants to accomplish. If you were driving down the road and thought, Let me observe my foot, and now my hand, it should be no surprise when you crash into something.

It is important to understand the mechanics of a thrown knife in order to be successful when employing the weapon.

Throwing Positions

There are four basic methods of throwing a knife. The most common method is from a standing position. The second position is throwing the

Basic throwing form: Focus (1) on the center of the target while keeping your back leg straight. Your left hand points (2) to the target while you bring your right hand up and bend (3) your wrist at a 45-degree angle.

knife while on the run. The third position, a kneeling posture, is done on one knee. In the fourth basic knife-throwing posture, the practitioner rolls from the ground to a kneeling position.

Distances

Obviously, the closer you are to a target, the easier it is to hit it properly.

In chung sim do, practitioners concentrate on three throwing ranges: short (10 to 20 feet), medium (20 to 30 feet) and long (30 to 40 feet). Ranges longer than 40 feet tend to be largely ineffective because of a variety of factors: wind, knife vibration, etc.

Principles of Knife Throwing

There are two major principles to consider when throwing a knife. The first is the principle of revolution. When throwing the knife, it must make only a half revolution from your hand to the target. At close range (10 to 15 feet), this is easy to do. But at greater distances (20 to 40 feet), the knife must rotate on its horizontal axis to keep it at a half revolution.

The second principle is that of rotation. To make the knife rotate, you must apply slight pressure with your index finger on the tip of the blade as the knife leaves your hand. The weight, shape and length of the knife will have an effect on both the revolution and rotation.

Obviously, one cannot explain in words all the factors involved in knife throwing; the accompanying photographs will help clear up many of the readers' questions.

It should be remembered that the knife is not simply an in-hand weapon; it can also be employed as a throwing tool—and just as effectively. If one simply learns the basic principles of knife throwing, it will open up a whole new area of training and self-defense for the martial artist.

Shift (4) your weight and elbow forward and, without moving (5) your wrist, slide (6) the knife out of your hand.

THE BOWIE KNIFE
The Biggest and the Baddest Blade of All!
by David E. Steele • June 1987

Since the dawn of civilization, knives, first made of bronze, were used in warfare. Bronze gave way to iron, then steel. For the last few thousand years, steel has been the metal of choice for knife making.

One of the advantages of steel is that it can be hammered or ground into almost any shape. Different nationalities favored different knife styles, generally adding their own special qualities and effectiveness. In Europe, for example, the heavy single-edge chopping knife (hand ax) held sway from the Dark Ages to the mid-13th century. From the 13th century to the present, the dagger has been the favorite European combat knife. In Japan, the most popular fighting knife of the ruling samurai class was the single-edge "half-sword" (*tanto*). In Indonesia, the premier knife was the wavy-bladed thrusting *kris*. In Nepal, the tip-heavy, recurved *kukri* is favored over all other blades, a design that goes back 3,000 years to the Egyptians.

Some of these countries developed complex martial arts around empty-hand techniques and various weapons, including the knife. In the Philippines, for example, the arts of *kali* (from *kalis* meaning "blade"), *escrima* and *arnis* were adapted to available weapons, including the stick (usually made of rattan, a vine that can be shaped and fire-hardened), and various edged weapons of Malay, Spanish or American origin. The Philippine arts are eclectic and adaptable to available technology and weaponry. In the 14th century, the southern Philippines were part of the Majapahit Empire ruled from Java, Indonesia. The kris was an integral

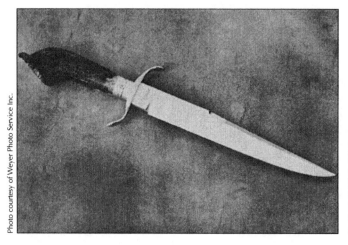

Photo courtesy of Weyer Photo Service Inc.

This classic fighting bowie knife with a stag handle was made by C. Gray Taylor. The long false edge, associated with Henry Schively of Philadelphia, is characteristic of the so-called Mexican bowie.

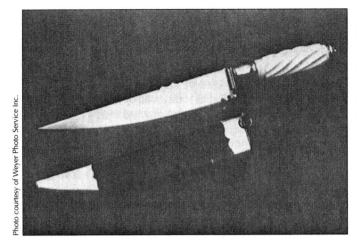

James Schmidt made this version of the "Mediterranean dagger," the immediate predecessor of the bowie knife. This dagger was commonly used by French and Spanish settlers in America.

Photo courtesy of Weyer Photo Service Inc.

part of Indonesian weaponry, and it found its way to the Philippines, where it was made larger and stronger, capable of acting as a jungle knife as well as a thrusting weapon.

Some islands in the Philippines remained Muslim, while most became a colony of Catholic Spain. Although the Spaniards forbade the natives to own or practice with weapons, the Filipinos undoubtedly continued to do both, adopting some of the Spanish weapons and their names for them (e.g., *espada y daga*—sword and dagger). Rapier and dagger dueling was probably the most distinctive form of combat practiced by the conquistadores and passed on to the Philippines.

In 1898, when the islands passed from Spain to the United States, the Philippine rebels realized that they would have to acquire modern firearms. When no guns were available, they used bush knives, the most famous of which was the Moro *kampilan*, a design almost identical to the Dyak *mandau* of Indonesia. American officers found their .38-caliber revolvers inadequate to stop the knife-wielding Moros, so they requested a reissue of the .45-caliber revolvers of the Indian wars and the development of a .45-caliber automatic (resulting in the eventual issue of the Colt M-1911 automatic).

While the Filipinos preferred their bush knives before the American occupation and the development of cities, they started to adapt their arts to American-style weapons, particularly ones that could be concealed in modern clothing. The *balisong* (butterfly) knife was developed in Batangas province from an American folding knife design (patented in 1872). From about 1940 on, this was the premier Philippine knife, and the most popular blade style was the American bowie. The Philippine arts emphasize the bowie blade the most, but this weapon can easily fit into Korean, Japanese

69

Photo by Richard Heinzen

This bowie knife was crafted by Roger Russell of New Mexico. The bowie retained its popularity through the Civil War. Its use as a defensive sidearm declined shortly thereafter.

or other arts. Because armor is no longer routinely worn, the armor-piercing blades developed for Japanese *yoroi kumi-uchi* (grappling in armor) are no longer necessary, and *tantojutsu* (the Japanese knife art) can be carried out with a bowie as easily as the traditional half-sword.

Basically, the modern bowie is another name for a knife with a clip-point blade. However, the evolution of this knife is at least partly the history of

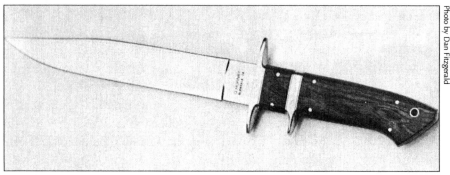

Photo by Dan Fitzgerald

The Hornby subhilt fighter, a modern version of the bowie knife, makes an excellent military-style combat knife. It's useful when a soldier runs out of ammunition or cannot use firearms.

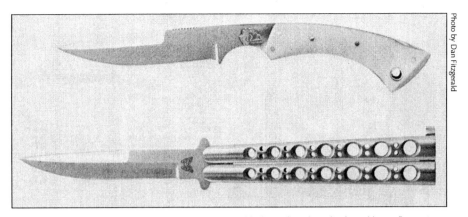

Photo by Dan Fitzgerald

This "Wee Hawk" clip-point knife comes with a bowie blade made in boot knife and butterfly versions. Butterfly knives are often associated with the Philippine balisong.

early America, and the special value it holds for Americans can only be understood with a little background information.

During the American colonial period, most knives were imported from England. Even after America gained its independence, Sheffield cutlers dominated the U.S. market until after the Civil War.

For many years, Americans who could not afford British knives made their own or had them forged at a local blacksmith shop. The crude knives carried by Kentucky riflemen to cut the patches for their rifle balls were of this type. The handles were usually made of wood or deer antler, and sometimes a homely saying might be carved into them for decoration.

The first major American knife factory was begun by John Russell in 1834. His plant was located at the "Green River Works" in Greenfield, Massachusetts. Russell copied British knife-making techniques and managed to make a success of his business in spite of the trademark infringement practiced against him by Sheffield cutlers. Russell is famous for only one knife design, an upswept "skinner." The shorter 6- to 8-inch blade was used by mountain men for taking beaver pelts, while the longer 10-inch blade was a favorite with hunters for butchering buffalo.

The Russell knife was simple, with riveted wood handles, no different from modern meatpacking knives. Its historical reputation comes from the mountain men, buffalo hunters, exploration parties and Indians who used them. Mountain men were prone to settle disputes over beaver "plews" by driving their skinning knives into their enemies "up to Green River" (the trademark at the base of the blade).

Most of what we think of as the United States was not under English

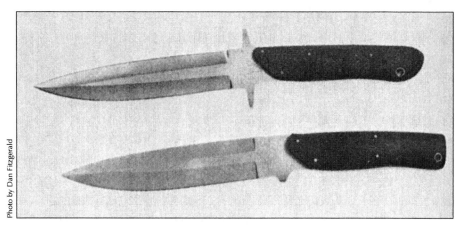

Gil Hibben's craftsmanship is displayed in these two full-size bowie knives. This classic design is still as effective as it was when Jim Bowie disemboweled Maj. Norris Wright in 1827.

rule in 1776. The Spanish and French owned much of the continent, and their influence was shown in cutlery, among other things. The *hauswehr* (peasant knife) of medieval Europe had developed into the "Mediterranean dagger," a favored sidearm of Spanish sailors and French noblemen. This knife was as effective for cutting off a slice of beef as for dispatching a foe. Basically, it was a single-edged knife with a tapering point and no separate *quillon* (cross guard). The width of the blade toward the handle kept the fingers from sliding forward onto the edge. In design, it was virtually identical to the French chef's knives and the Argentinean gaucho's knives that descended from it. The Mediterranean dagger served as the model for the prototype of the most famous knife in American history—the bowie.

The Bowies grew up in Louisiana, a territory owned by France until Napoleon sold it to the United States to acquire money for his armies. The Bowie family was involved in land clearing and speculation, a heavy backwoods job. Rezin Bowie, an avid hunter, had constructed a large hunting knife, one that would not break on bone or wood. This knife was a Mediterranean dagger except for its more pronounced sweeping curve toward the tip and an inconspicuous quillon at the hilt. The blade was about 9-1/4 inches long. From his prototype, Bowie later had special versions made by a surgical instrument maker named Searles in Baton Rouge Louisiana, which is why this knife style is sometimes called the Searles bowie by collectors.

Around 1825, Rezin's brother Jim Bowie became involved in a quarrel with Maj. Norris Wright. This feud eventually resulted in blows and an exchange of pistol shots. Perhaps because of the ineffectiveness of this exchange, Jim wanted something more reliable than a handgun. At that time, pocket pistols were single shot and usually small caliber, with a marked tendency to misfire. So Rezin lent his brother his hunting knife, and soon after, Jim Bowie and Wright met up again. Bowie was serving as a second in a duel at the Vidalia Sandbar, and Wright was a second for the opposing side. The principals exchanged fire without effect, but then a general melee broke out among the parties. Wright shot Bowie in the arm and hip, then tried to finish him with a sword cane, but Bowie managed to grab Wright and disembowel him with his knife. Bowie was already well-known in New Orleans society, and this fight was widely reported and exaggerated in the newspapers. By the time his wounds healed months later, Bowie was nationally famous.

The Vidalia Sandbar was Bowie's only documented knife fight, but it was enough to make every settler heading for the frontier want a knife just like Bowie's; although, for lack of a photograph, they weren't sure what kind of knife that was. Eventually, every big knife was called a bowie.

Bowie was not a fencer. He used the knife as an extension of his impres-

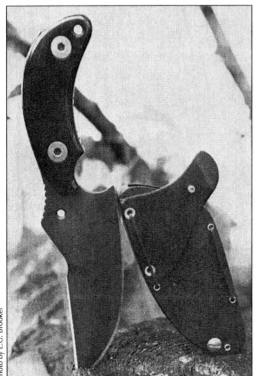

Photo by E.G. Brooker

Watch out for this new Jerry Price fighting knife, with darkened blade and synthetic sheath. Note the stylized bowie blade, which is also widely used in folding and survival knives.

73

sive physical strength. He was prepared to accept whatever his opponent could throw at him, until the man was close enough to grapple with. The knife he wanted was not a quick dart-and-thrust weapon but a tool heavy enough for deep slashes and capable of lopping off limbs and cleaving skulls. The Bowie family eventually ordered other knives, some from a knife and surgical instrument maker named Henry Schively in Philadelphia. It was apparently Schively who came up with the idea of adding a double guard and clip point with a sharpened false edge (ideas that we now associate with a "classic bowie"). Which knife Bowie had with him when he was killed at the Alamo in 1836 is unknown, but the only design historians are certain he used was the Searles bowie at the sandbar. Nevertheless, it will always be the classic bowie that most people will associate with his name.

Bowie knives retained their immense popularity through the Civil War. The decline of the bowie as a defensive sidearm most likely came in 1813, when a metallic cartridge was introduced for the heavy Colt revolver. The brass-cased cartridge eliminated the ignition problems of the percussion revolver. A man armed with a knife could no longer expect to get close to his opponent before he was cut down by .44- or .45-caliber slugs.

The military, however, was still concerned with edged weapons because soldiers could run out of ammunition or run into circumstances that prohibited the use of firearms. This became common in World War I, where fighting in the trenches could make a bayonet-equipped rifle unwieldy. Also, night patrols and sentry neutralization required quiet weapons. The

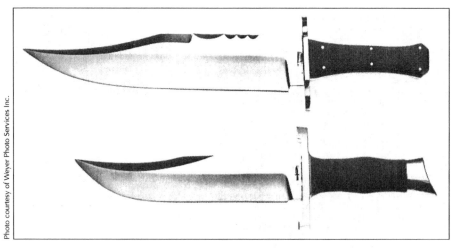

Photo courtesy of Weyer Photo Services Inc.

Here are two versions of the fer-de-lance double-ground bowie designed by David E. Steele. The standard model is pictured above; the one below has been modified for tantojutsu practice.

trench dagger, sometimes equipped with a knuckle-duster handle, became a favored weapon.

In World War II, particularly in the Pacific theater, soldiers wanted a "combat utility" knife more versatile than the single-purpose dagger. The answer was a modified bowie knife. The double guard and clip point were still there, but the blade was shortened to less than 8 inches. The most famous of these knives was the Ka-Bar used by the Navy and Marine Corps, though most collectors would say the Randall Model 1 was the best knife of this type produced during World War II.

After its success in World War II, the revived bowie retained its popularity through the Korean and Vietnam wars. Sawbacks and hollow handles were sometimes added to create a "survival knife," but the basic bowie shape was retained. To lighten the blade, a double-grind shape was developed by R.W. Loveless. This made the blade double-edged and as light as a dagger, but the bowie shape made the knife stronger and it cut better than a dagger.

The bowie blade is also widely used in folding knives. In conventional, rocker-locked knives, the back edge (swage) is not sharpened. On fully enclosed models like the balisong, a sharpened false edge can be used without risk to the wearer. This design is especially popular for commercial balisongs made in the United States. These knives are now widely used in martial arts demonstrations and movies.

THE POCKETKNIFE
Versatile Blade Offers Portable Protection

by Doug Witt • Photos Courtesy of Doug Witt • November 1987

The pocketknife has two apparent advantages. It's a tool first and a weapon second, making it very difficult for the government to mandate controls on it. Second, it doesn't make noise like a gunshot, and there is no bullet to trace. These factors give the American citizen a break from otherwise restrictive self-defense measures.

Imagine, if you will, that it's late at night and an assailant jumps out of the bushes on a side street, attempting to crush your skull with a lead pipe. Fortunately, you avoid the pipe, then slash with your pocketknife to his throat. You now have two choices: Leave the area immediately, or call the police, in which case you will have to explain why you were on the street so late at night, what you were doing in that area and why you carry a pocketknife. The "victim" assailant, if he is alive, will likely sue you for using a knife. This is better than having your skull crushed like an eggshell, however.

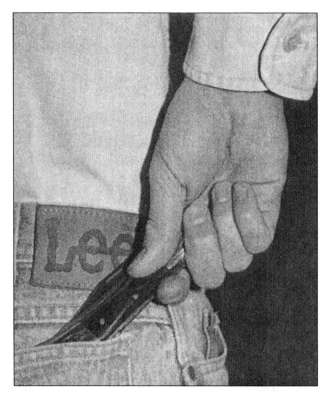

The back pants pocket is perhaps the No. 1 carrying spot for a pocketknife. From here, it can be easily drawn and implemented, provided that no other objects are in the pocket.

One-handed openings of any knife are made easier by attaching a clamp-on "flicket" device, which has a shelf for the thumbnail, allowing the blade to be opened quickly.

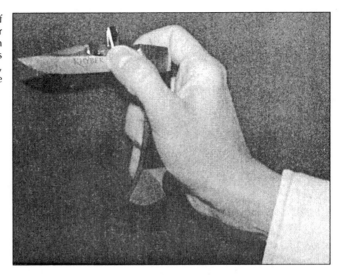

There may be times when you must be ruthless and fight with lethal fury to save your life or a loved one. Close-in pocketknife defense requires skill and sometimes the ferocity of a mad animal. If you can't muster this survival instinct, you may wind up dead. It's your choice.

Choosing a Pocketknife

Until the late 1970s, one's choice of a pocketknife was limited primarily to factory-production knives. Since then, however, an expanding group of knife makers has appeared who will customize a blade in any manner you choose. Buy the best knife you can; it can last you a lifetime.

Your self-defense knife should be as large a model as you feel comfortable carrying. Actually, with the blade inside the handle, and gripping it in your fist, both ends of the handle should stick out a half-inch or so. The blade should also be as straight as possible, not a large, curved "skinner" blade. The blade design should allow thrusts either between ribs or into the throat, eyes, ears or temple. A double-edged blade allows sweeping slashes in both left- and right-hand movements.

A short person should carry the longest blade possible for a longer reach and for deep thrusts into vital kidney, lung or groin areas. Short, 3-inch blades act like a razor for slashes to the wrist, face, neck and legs yet still allow penetration. Belt-buckle knives are used for punching thrusts—not much penetration but still a bloody wound.

Drawing the pocketknife quickly and getting the blade out are essential. Opening the blade quickly is solved in a number of ways. By using lubrication on the pivot point of the blade, you can quickly open the knife with your thumb and index finger. If this doesn't work, you can purchase a "flicket" at a cutlery store. This device clamps to the blade and has a shelf for the thumbnail to flick open the knife. Some pocketknives are designed for one-handed opening. The Gerber Paul knife has a button on the hinge which, when squeezed, releases the blade.

Gentlemen should carry the knife in a coat pocket or back pants pocket, and nothing else should be carried in that pocket. Speed is cut drastically if you have to feel around in a pocketful of items. Depending on the knife size, ladies can carry one in their bra or coat pocket. Avoid carrying a pocketknife in a purse.

Concealment

The purpose of concealing a knife is not to avoid legal problems or make sure the police don't see you are carrying it. Rather, concealment insures that your assailant believes you are defenseless, giving you the advantage of surprise. You must have time—no matter how short—to bring your knife into action. Therefore, tell no one—wife, husband, brother, sister, relative or friend—that you carry a knife for protection. Maintain the element of surprise. Remember that many attackers are known by the victim. Check your local laws on carrying knives and balance that knowledge with your need to carry a pocketknife.

A pocketknife can also be an effective weapon for home defense and is a fine alternative to using a gun. Above the entrance to your home, glue a container to hold your pocketknife. When answering any questionable door knock, grab your knife first. Incidentally, your weakest point of defense is between your house and car. Try to carry your knife open, in a concealed fashion, until you are in the car.

Grip

Holding a pocketknife would seem simple enough, but guess again. With the wrong grip, your slashing techniques are limited. The right grip makes you an artist with the blade. Best of all, your seeming expertise with a knife will often scare the hell out of an assailant. If you can avoid a life-and-death fight by merely looking like a knife fighter rather than a helpless victim, so much the better.

The "foil" grip is perhaps the best method of holding the knife. Just like taking a golf club or fishing pole in hand, the thumb rests on one side of the handle. You will find that holding the handle in this manner gives you a lot of wrist action for short slashes in close-in knife fighting. Without a guard like most sheath knives have, you can bang up your thumb as you bury the blade in the assailant's body, hitting bones, buckles, buttons or other hard objects. But slashes across the throat, face and arms don't cause thumb damage. If the handle end of the knife sticks out of your fist, you can use it to drive into the skull, cheekbone, nose, etc.

Don't ever throw your knife. You are instantly unarmed and at the mercy of your assailant. And he might use your own knife against you.

Stance

There is no one accepted stance for knife fighting. The assailant's attack will be so fast that the most you can hope for is to be balanced. You should move back for added distance while drawing your pocketknife. A close-in fight will consist mostly of pivoting in a semicircle as you slash the assailant. If your assailant has a knife, your stance should be a balanced, upright position, not hunched over. You want him to come to you. Your free hand

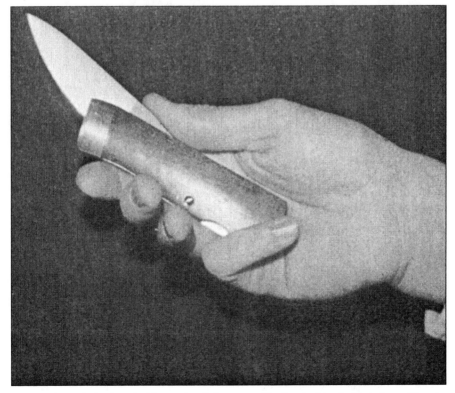

Benchmark's pocketknife is ideal for one-handed openings. The thumb slides the blade forward into the locked position while the weapon is somewhat concealed in the hand.

and arm will help you remain balanced. If you can reach in your pocket or purse for coins, or pick up sand or rocks from the ground, throw them in his face, followed by a knife thrust to the neck.

Knife Cuts

Unlike a speeding bullet, which results in the sudden expulsion of bodily fluids, causing muscular collapse, a knife slash produces no hydrostatic shock. The pain and perception of damage to the body are slow, unless the slash was such that a large amount of blood was lost in a few seconds. The assailant would then drop to the ground. As the victim, you want to produce a psychological shock to the assailant with slashes to the arms, face and legs. An attacker who sees his own blood may faint, recoil or lose confidence. You must instill in your own mind that if you see your blood first, it will be a signal to get even more vicious.

If possible, avoid this type of attack. But if you have no choice in the matter, come prepared with a pocketknife rather than a razor, unlike the man on the left.

Knife Practice

There is a psychological barrier to overcome in cutting someone into a bloody mess, even in self-defense. In an attack, you must respond automatically and do what you have practiced. Practice by filling an old pair of overalls with straw and hanging them up in a garage or basement, out of sight of other people. Next, cover the blade of your knife with tape to dull the edge. Determine where the knife will be carried. Then, very slowly, take the knife from your pocket in such a manner that you are also opening the blade at the same time (if it's a one-handed opener). Speed will come with practice. Practice the proper grip with lots of wrist action. Make some slashes, slowly, at the overalls, followed by some thrusts. Visualize targets such as the throat, stomach and legs.

Practice at home until you feel comfortable with the knife grip and slashing and thrusting movements. The purpose here is to build speed, skill and confidence in handling the pocketknife. During an attack, you don't want to think about it; you want it to happen automatically.

DAGGERS OF THE DARK AGES
The Knives of Medieval Europe and Japan
by David E. Steele • Photos by Dan Fitzgerald • December 1987

The term "dagger" can refer to any stabbing weapon. Historically, the word has been applied to single-edged, clipped-point, double-edged, triangular, quadrangular and cruciform blade designs. Today, it is not unusual to hear the term "folding dagger." Also, a lock-blade folding knife, when carried in the pocket, was construed as a dagger in recent California case law.

Currently, the most fashionable daggers are double-edged, a design that dates back to the Bronze Age, and the Japanese dagger, which dates back to the rise of the samurai (warrior) class. Collectors and custom knife makers are most familiar with the single-edged Japanese dagger, but double-edged models are also common.

With the exception of the *pugio*, a short, broad dagger worn on the left side by Roman soldiers, the dagger was out of favor in Europe between 4 B.C. and A.D. 12. During this period, the Celtic LaTène culture superseded the Hallstatt culture in Europe. Conditions in most parts of the continent were primitive. A versatile, single-edged chopping tool was the favored weapon. The most famous fighting knife during this period was the scramasax (hand ax) used by the Vikings, Germans, Franks and Anglo-Saxons. During the Dark Ages, Europeans required an all-purpose tool with weight and strength behind the tip, and an edge for a strong, chopping stroke that could build huts or decapitate enemies.

The dagger started to reappear in the 12th century, often in the form of a short sword. Sometimes these daggers were called *misericorde*, because they were used by dismounted knights to dispatch an enemy or cause him to beg for mercy. Some of these daggers had a narrow, diamond cross-section blade to allow for piercing through mail, joints in armor or the eye slits of a helmet.

Contrary to movie depictions, daggers were rarely thrown. Bashford Dean reports one instance in 1386 in which English troops threw their daggers at the French, finishing them with their swords. This is essentially how Japanese samurai used the *shuriken* (throwing spike), *kozuka* (utility knife) or *umabari* (horse needle). The dagger would be thrown to distract the enemy long enough to close with the sword.

The era of the dagger began in the 13th century. As styles developed, methods of carrying the weapon changed, too, although they were generally geared to an "ice-pick-style" draw. The dagger was usually worn vertically in front, a position favored for speed. The dagger could also be worn vertically or at an angle on the right. Occasionally, the dagger was worn together with a pouch; this style was carried over to the Scottish dirk worn with the sporran.

Throughout the later Middle Ages, the fighting dagger was designed with a large guard to prevent the hand from running onto the blade. This was

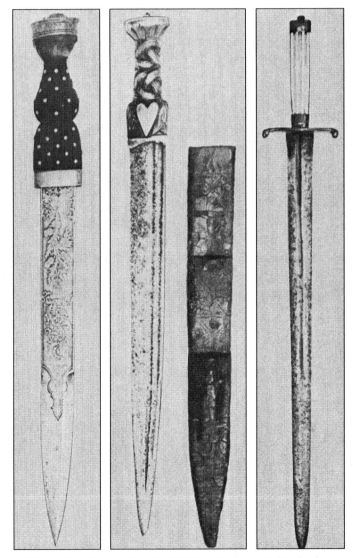

At left and middle: two Scottish dirks. At right: an English naval dirk. The decorative "thistle" handle is evident on the 19th-century Highland model (middle).

important because the dagger was used ice-pick style to allow maximum power in punching through a mailed shirt or padded armor. The large guard would obviate the need for sophisticated hand positioning like that used by samurai in wielding the *yoroi-doshi* (armor-piercing dagger). The most common European daggers of this time, the *rondel* and *baselard*, also had large flat pommels, making withdrawal simple and secure while providing good surface for the left hand to reinforce blows.

In Europe, strength was emphasized over skill. The distance between opponents was point-blank grappling. Most knew only the right-handed ice-pick stab combined with a left-handed grab for the enemy's knife wrist. By the 16th century, however, there were more sophisticated methods, most of which have been left unreported. The martial arts in Europe were not associated with religious ritual, like they were in Japan, so techniques were not passed down through the centuries by rote. Still, artists' drawings from the period show that the following techniques were known: jamming with the body, armbars, underhand thrusts, sidestepping away from thrusts, grabbing the enemy's dagger out of its scabbard, stepping on the enemy's foot and, when disarmed, grabbing the enemy's knife arm for a break or throw.

Daggers were also used for hunting during the Middle Ages, although a sword was more often used for killing the animal. Later, a special set of hunting knives called a *trousse* was developed for disjointing the game. Perhaps the most common daggers used for hunting were the peasant knife (*hauswehr*), the Irish skene (a dagger of substantial size, not like the

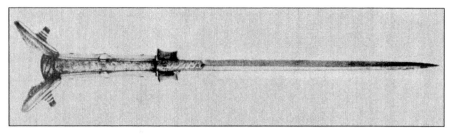

Above and below: Italian eared daggers, circa 1500. Note the blade decorations and carved handles. Both were obviously designed as status symbols for the gentry class rather than fighting tools.

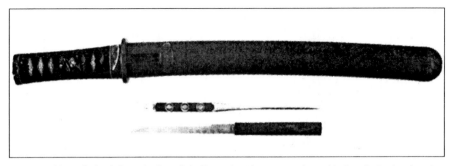

A mounted hamidashi (fighting knife with half guard) with a wrapped ray-skin handle (top), a kogai or skewer (middle) and (bottom) a kozuka (utility knife, sometimes used for throwing).

later Scottish *skene dhu* worn in the stocking when wearing kilts), and the *ballock* dagger. There is also a famous drawing by Stradanus of an armored knight using a *quillon* dagger against a bear.

There were seven major dagger designs developed in the Middle Ages: the rondel, the baselard, the quillon dagger, the ballock or kidney dagger, the eared dagger, the *cinquedea* and the peasant knife. These are terms used by modern scholars and do not necessarily reflect what the blades were called in their own day.

By the 16th century, European daggers had become more ornamental and, most significantly, the quillon dagger had developed into a parrying weapon used in combination with the rapier. The most elaborate form of the parrying dagger was the *main gauche* (French for "my left"), which was used in Spain until the 18th century. This rapier-and-dagger style of dueling gave rise to the "blade forward" use of the dagger, an innovation that is now thought of as the mark of the knife fighter in Western countries. Actually, this method was only effective because armor had become lighter with the introduction of firearms (there was no use in wearing heavy armor when it could be penetrated by musket balls). Another interesting 17th-century dagger descended from medieval designs was the Italian stiletto, which had no cutting edge but was triangular or quadrangular in cross section. This thrusting weapon saw continued use in various bayonet designs and was popular in World War I as the M-1917 trench dagger.

The first and possibly the most interesting medieval design was the rondel, named for its circular-style guard and pommel. It saw use among the knightly classes of Western and Central Europe between 1325 and 1550. The large disc guard was excellent for preventing the inexperienced user from running his hand onto the blade when a powerful ice-pick stab was used. For fighting in armor, this design was unsurpassed.

Like the Japanese yoroi-doshi, single- and double-edged versions of the rondel were produced with reinforced points. Occasionally, triangular-bladed versions are found, presaging the later Italian stiletto. Eventually, however, the rondel design became decadent, with thinner blades, reduced guards and leather scabbards.

The second major design, the baselard, named for the city of Basel in Switzerland where it originated, was probably the most widely used dagger in the 14th and 15th centuries. Eventually, it developed into the Swiss or Holbein dagger, which was later adapted into the Nazi dress daggers of World War II.

By the 15th century, knights had ceased carrying the baselard, but civilians and foot soldiers continued to do so. The baselard had a large guard and pommel, but it was straighter than the rondel, so that the grip was shaped like a capital letter "I." It came single- or double-edged with a flattened diamond cross section. It was usually worn on the right side or in front, suspended from a sword belt or girdle. Very long baselards might be worn on the left like a sword, slung either from the belt or from a baldric across the right shoulder.

The quillon dagger appeared in the 13th century. The earliest design resembled a shortened sword with a long cross guard. It was generally a knightly weapon worn on the right side. It is sometimes found with a large hollow pommel.

By the 15th century, these blades had started to develop into left-handed daggers for rapier-and-dagger dueling. This style is still used in the Philippines, a former Spanish colony, where it is known as *espada y daga*. There, the rapier has been replaced by a stick or bolo, and the dagger is sometimes replaced by the *balisong* (butterfly knife).

On later quillon daggers, the guards were usually made of iron and faced forward. They were strong enough to catch a sword and shaped to hold it. There was also a ring to protect the thumb. The blades were straight and double-edged, sometimes with sword-breaking notches. The most elaborate form, the main gauche, used long, straight quillions with a cup-style hand guard.

The quillon dagger was usually carried on the right toward the front or at the back with the hilt to the left for fast use with the left hand. Even so, it was also carried on the right or at the back with the hilt to the right, evidently for use without the sword.

The ballock dagger, known as the kidney dagger to the prudish Victorians, had a handle and guard conspicuously made to resemble the male sex organs.

It is sometimes found with a reinforced point. It was popular in the 14th and 15th centuries, and by the 17th century, it had developed into the dirk in Scotland. The ballock dagger was worn at the front or on the right.

The Scottish dirk was at its most practical when it resembled the earlier ballock dagger. The handle on later specimens, the so-called "thistle" shape, was impractical for serious stabbing, and the stones set in the pommel show its development into Highland dress decoration. Early dirks were substantial single-edged daggers with grips narrowing toward the pommel, shaped well for the ice-pick stab. In combat, the dirk, which had an average length of 18 inches, was held in the left hand with the blade extending below the shield while the right hand wielded the broadsword. The sword, shield and dirk could strike disabling blows to the enemy.

The eared dagger, used from the 14th through the 16th centuries, is named for the two discs at the pommel. It was an elaborate, upper-class dagger worn more for decoration than utility.

The cinquedea was an elaborate Italian dagger with a wide blade that was used in the 16th and 17th centuries. It was said to have a blade five fingers (*cinque diti*) in breadth, from which it derives its name. It was often decorated and not very practical.

The peasant knife (*hauswehr*) was a home defense weapon of the poorer classes in Central Europe. Some were double-edged, but others were simply large butcher knives with guards. These eventually developed into the Mediterranean dagger, the bowie knife and the French chef's knife.

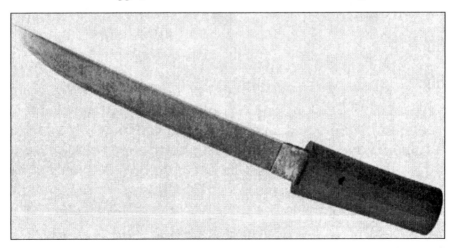

The tanto was one of the most common knives in Japan during the Tokugawa period, although it was still considered a secondary weapon by many samurai warriors.

The peasant knife, most commonly a single-edged dagger, settled many a score among gypsies, serfs and others of the "lower orders." The peasant could not afford to have a knife for every purpose. For example, when a Polish peasant was pressed into military service by the local king, his only weapons were his knife and whatever bludgeon he could improvise from a convenient tree limb.

The development of European daggers can best be seen in contrast to another feudal culture, the Japanese, from the ninth century to the 19th. Before the 17th century, the knife most used by the samurai class was the yoroi-doshi, a single or double-edged armor-piercing dagger with a reinforced point. It was used by dismounted knights to stab into weak parts of armor, in conjunction with empty-hand grappling techniques, a style called *yoroi-kumi-uchi*. The yoroi-doshi was generally single-edged and shaped like a short version of the sword (*tachi*), with all the usual mounts, including a *tsuba* (circular guard) and a lacquered wood sheath. It generally resembles a *tanto* (literally "half-sword," a fighting knife), but with a stronger blade.

Knife-fighting expert Jeff Imada demonstrates the weapon's versatility: as a thrusting device (1), as a cutting tool (2)

One school that still teaches yoroi-kumi-uchi (grappling in armor) is the Yagyu Shingan Ryu in Japan. The technique involves unbalancing the opponent and then plunging the yoroi-doshi into a weak spot in the armor. As with any sophisticated *tantojutsu* (Japanese knife fighting) style, the trick is to control the body of the opponent during the strike. This is especially difficult to do in armor because loose-fitting samurai armor does not provide a secure handhold, not to mention its penetration resistance. This school generally uses a simple ice-pick grip on the dagger, which is secure enough because of the substantial tsuba on the yoroi-doshi.

The Takenouchi Ryu in Japan also uses the ice-pick grip when striking with the *kodachi* (short sword) or other single-handed edged weapons. Their style is called *kogusoku* grappling, and again the trick is to control the enemy's body, often with an empty-hand technique, before the dagger finishes him. The samurai developed techniques based on practical experience, and experience showed that a man cut or stabbed could still be extremely dangerous. Therefore, it is important to control the enemy's movements throughout your attack.

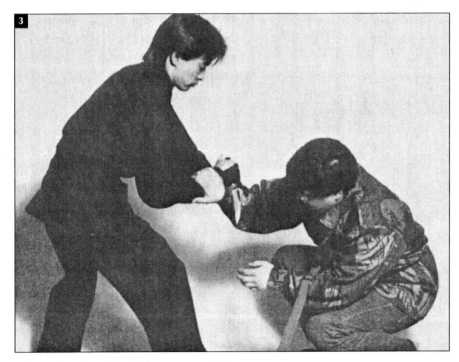

and in conjunction with a takedown maneuver (3).

The ninja also practiced their own styles of tantojutsu, just one more in a long list of weapon arts these operatives were expected to learn. The best-known *ninjutsu* style taught in the United States is *togakure-ryu*, which has its origins in the Iga province of Japan. The evasion and grappling techniques taught in this style are quite sophisticated, utilizing two standard grips that do not depend on the size of the guard to keep the fingers off the blade. The first is an underhand grip, which places the butt of the knife on the meaty part of the hand beneath the fifth finger. The other is an ice-pick grip, with the butt secured by the thumb or index finger.

Other sophisticated hand positions are taught in some rare styles of tantojutsu. Most Japanese daggers have short handles by Western standards, and some have very small guards or none at all. Various methods were taught so that there was always a thumb, finger or palm pressing against the pommel, so as to put the bone structure and body weight behind the thrust—especially important when striking an opponent in armor or one protected by heavy clothing.

After Japan's warring period (A.D. 1603, the beginning of the Tokugawa Shogunate), the samurai no longer wore full armor on a daily basis. The most common knives were the tanto (with full guard), *hamidashi* (half guard) and *aikuchi* (no guard), anyone of which might be chosen to supplement the long and short swords (*katana and wakizashi*) carried at all times by the samurai. In the Tokugawa era, the aikuchi became the favorite knife for both male and female samurai and even replaced the wakizashi for committing *seppuku* (ritual suicide).

By the late Tokugawa period, when full armor was rarely worn, some schools of tantojutsu began to emphasize the blade-forward, cut-and-disable style of knife fighting over the older approach, which usually finished with an ice-pick stab through armor.

There is no comparison in sophistication of knife techniques between Europe and Japan. By the turn of the 17th century, tantojutsu was as highly developed as any martial art in Japan and was usually taught as a secondary art in *jujutsu* and *kenjutsu* schools. This does not mean all samurai, much less peasant conscripts, were highly trained in this art. The bow and the sword were the primary weapons in medieval Japanese warfare, as they were in Europe. Of the 18 weapons usually taught to samurai, these were the most important, and secondary weapons like the dagger were given little thought in some schools.

The Japanese also developed a wide variety of specialized utility, stabbing and throwing blades to supplement the main dagger, which was carried at all times. The most common of these knives were the *kogai* (skewer, occasionally used to put wounded soldiers out of their misery by piercing the ankle vein), *kozuka* (utility knife, sometimes used for throwing), *shuriken* (spikes, often used by ninja to distract or disable pursuers), *shaken* (throwing star, another distraction weapon, sometimes tipped with poison to kill) and *umabari* (a stiletto carried in place of the kogai by samurai in the Koga province and occasionally used for throwing).

Medieval European styles of dagger fighting are virtually unknown in the West. The most common style used today was adapted from saber fencing, which descended from rapier-and-dagger dueling. The knife is held blade-forward with the thumb along the back of the handle. This style has some advantages and should not be underestimated, but for close-range grappling, it is not as practical as the medieval styles and certainly lags far behind tantojutsu.

While the European styles of the Middle Ages have died out, the dedicated student of knife technique can still find a few legitimate tantojutsu schools in America, Europe or Japan, although he may have to search hard and serve a long apprenticeship in empty-hand technique.

BOOT-KNIFE FIGHTING
The Street Style of the '80s
by David E. Steele • April 1988

Any concealable, fixed-blade knife can be termed a "boot knife." It may be carried on the belt, in the waistband, under the sleeve, in a pocket as well as in a boot. The usual blade length, given the limitations of modern clothing, is 3 to 6 inches.

Martial artists of many styles, usually those termed "combat arts," carry and practice with boot knives. Among the better-known knife arts are Japanese *tantojutsu*, Philippine *arnis*, and Indonesian *pentjak silat*, all of which usually teach the short knife as an adjunct to empty-hand fighting.

A blade less than 9 inches long provides little, if any, safe distance from the opponent. It has little power to parry the opponent's blade. This is why the aforementioned styles emphasize evasive tactics and empty-hand grappling techniques when teaching the short knife. Face-to-face knife dueling should be avoided; its likely result is serious injury to the "winner." Instead, the knife should be concealed until the opponent commits himself and his initial attack has been evaded.

In tantojutsu, whether of the ninja or samurai variety, the student usually spends years in empty-hand training before going on to the knife. The objective is to keep the student from becoming "married" to his knife, to

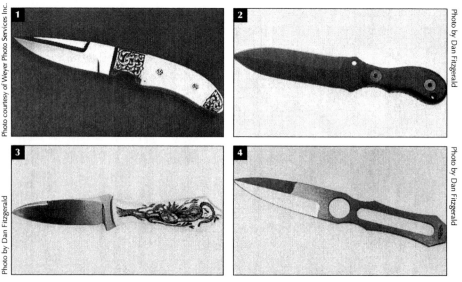

Boot knives for the discrete fighter: Jim Hammond's "Stingaree" (1), Jerry Price's triangular blades (2), Chuck Stapel's scrimshaw handle model (3) and Pass' skeletonized model (4).

Photo courtesy of David E. Steele

Former kickboxing champion Graciela Casillas never goes on a survival hike without her Al Mar dagger strapped to her leg. The engraving reads: "The daughter of a lion is also a lion."

remind him that he has three other weapons available (two feet and one hand) and that body mechanics are far more important than having the most sophisticated fighting knife available.

"Sidestepping" is probably the most important move in Eastern knife fighting. It is critical to avoid the enemy's initial thrust. Once this occurs, the opponent is vulnerable to any number of counters, usually beginning with an attack on his weapon arm.

In one samurai tantojutsu style, the body is taken out of the line without actually moving the feet by executing what is called a "knee, ankle, hip" pivot. This is an extremely efficient move but requires precise timing. In arnis styles like *pekiti-tirsia*, the feet are turned and heels raised in addition to turning the body. This is similar to pentjak silat, which sometimes requires students to do a thousand of these turns in each practice session. In fact, traditional pentjak silat instructors will occasionally tie one student's sash in a large loop containing his opponent. One student in the sash loop will thrust with his dagger while the other performs this evasive turn.

After the turn, the counterattack is usually delivered first to the weapon

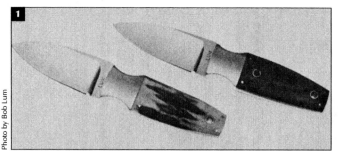

State-of-the-art boot knives: single-edged dirks by Bob Lum with stag and cocobolo handles (1), an ivory-handled model by Jimmy Lile (2) and another pair of Bob Lum designs (3).

Photo by Bob Lum

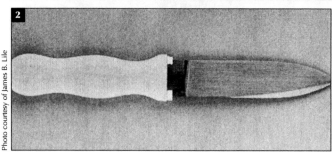

Photo courtesy of James B. Lile

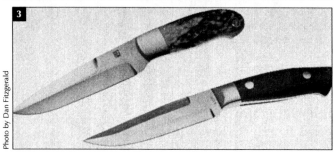

Photo by Dan Fitzgerald

arm. This not only takes away the enemy's best weapon, it also gives him a serious wound to think about. This initial counter is usually a cut, though it may be a stab or even an empty-hand check, lock or throw. The knife may be held blade-forward or in a reverse grip. One of the most effective methods is a tantojutsu grip in which the blade lies along the forearm. Even a double-edged blade will not cut into the forearm when utilizing this grip because knives cut by "drawing." In this position, the forearm adds weight behind the blade when blocking and cutting the enemy's wrist.

The reverse grip also allows various hooking techniques to catch and control a wrist or ankle. In this way, the reverse grip is more versatile than the blade-forward grip, although it does give up some reach.

After the initial counterattack to the weapon arm, the usual follow-up is a killing thrust. Cuts from a short knife are not likely to be fatal unless they are directed to the throat, a comparatively small target. Vital organ damage and uncontrollable bleeding are best accomplished with a thrust.

A knife thrust into an unprotected body is surprisingly easy. However, it can be complicated by factors such as heavy clothing or body armor (convicts often put books or magazines into their clothing to protect against a stabbing attack), bones, dangling equipment or a badly designed blade that is too blunt, flexible or fragile at the tip. This is why knife-fighting styles designed for cold climates or fighting in armor, like tantojutsu or *yoroi kumi-uchi*, emphasize putting the body weight behind the thrust.

The smaller the blade, the easier it is to conceal. However, it takes at least a 4-inch blade to reach all the vital targets in the thoracic cavity. Some martial artists carry three knives (one for each hand and one to throw), and the primary knife should have a blade of more than 4 inches in length.

High-quality folding knives like the custom *balisong* (Philippine butterfly knife) have some concealment advantages over the boot knife, but most folders are weaker at the blade-and-handle juncture than a sheath knife. They are also harder to clean and slower to draw.

Boot knives can be concealed in a number of ways. The sheath can be cemented, sewn, clipped or Velcroed into a boot. It can be looped or clipped onto a belt. It can be hooked onto a shirt or jacket lining. Sometimes it can be taped to an ankle, thigh or forearm, or it can be tied or taped to the outside of a boot or military suspenders. It can be clipped onto the cargo pocket of military fatigues or onto a pack. It can be clipped inside the waistband at the front or back or simply carried in a large coat pocket. The methods of concealment are only limited by the user's ingenuity. The most-concealed positions are usually the least accessible and vice versa. One of the fastest methods is to hide the knife behind the forearm or in an object (like a book or sack) carried in the hand.

Those martial artists who carry a boot knife often opt for the front inside waistband carry, concealed by a loose shirt—just like police officers carry their off-duty guns. Knife-using cultures, like those in traditional Japan and modern Indonesia, favor the front carry because of its speed and usually use a hardwood sheath for safety. However, in case of a surprise attack, the fast draw is secondary. When attacked suddenly, the martial artist must first take his body out of the attacking line ("easier to move the target than the arrow") and then may have to reply empty-handed before drawing the knife. Even so, developing a fast draw can be an advantage, eliminating the need for a drawn-out defensive fight. This was the reason for the Japanese fast-draw sword art of *iaijutsu*, the principles of which were applied to the *tanto* (half-sword or knife).

A working knowledge of anatomy is also helpful to the knife fighter. He should know where the kidneys, lungs, heart and major arteries are located, as well as the possible effects of blows to each area. The martial artist should be prepared for various reactions depending on the part of the opponent's body that is injured. For example, the reaction to most "felt" cuts (the opponent may not feel certain cuts or thrusts until later because of adrenaline) is to pull away. Knowing this, the martial artist can place his blade so that the enemy's reaction will impale him further. For instance, in one tantojutsu cut, the blade is started at the perineum, where the enemy's startled reaction will cause his crotch to be cut through as he pulls away. Likewise, thrusting directly to the front of the throat can cause the enemy to successfully pull away, but hooking the blade into his lower jawbone will keep the knife from twisting out, and his struggles will only tear up more of his throat.

Carrying the boot knife in a boot is not a very good idea if the knife is one's only weapon. If so, the knife should be carried at the waist or above in case the martial artist is knocked down in a sudden attack. Drawing the knife from a boot is also a long, conspicuous action. An enemy can not only counterattack but can also make it difficult for the martial artist to surreptitiously move the knife into a better position to counter an expected attack. The only way to fast-draw a knife from a boot is if one is sitting down, as in a car. Otherwise, the martial artist must choose whether to raise the foot or go to a kneeling position.

The boot knife is usually either single- or double-edged. In some cases, it may have no edge at all, used purely as a thrusting dagger. Traditional Japanese examples of the single-edged blade are the tanto, *hamidashi*, *aikuchi* and *yoroi-doshi* (an armor piercer). Japanese double-edged blades are less common but can be found, like the *himogatana* or *kwaiken*. Thrusting blades include the *umabari*.

Indonesian knives are too numerous to describe. The *kris* is the best-known example of a two-edged thrusting dagger. The *rentjong* may be single-edged or unsharpened. The rentjong, incidentally, is usually carried these days in the waistband under a loose shirt.

In the days when most martial arts were developed, boots were uncommon. Bare feet or sandals were far more common in the Orient. An exception was the Shaolin monks of China, who often carried large butterfly knives in their boots. Because of their religious calling, the monks used these large choppers to disable rather than kill their attackers. Of course, in those days disabling wounds were often fatal because of infection. Inci-

Photos by Dan Fitzgerald

Boot knife defense against a kick attack: Check and hold (1) the opponent's kicking leg with your free hand, then dump him onto the ground and deliver (2) a knife thrust to the thigh.

dentally, knives of this size would be difficult to carry, much less conceal, in modern boots.

The best blade material for modern boot knives is high-carbon, stainless steel, such as 104CM or 440C. The guards should be nickel-silver or stainless steel to minimize corrosion and only long enough to keep the fingers from running onto the blade (larger guards would not ward off an enemy's blade and could interfere with a fast draw from under clothing). The handle should be synthetic rubber, impregnated hardwood, Micarta or one of the other modern plastics—something that is secure, warm to the touch and virtually indestructible. The sheath should be top-grade leather or, preferably, one of the modern plastics like Kydex. Plastic sheaths are less flexible and make more noise than leather, but they are virtually impervious to rain, snow or sweat. Most concealment locations will adversely affect sheaths, handles, guards and blades if they are not immune to moisture damage.

Virtually all traditional knife-fighting techniques can be used today, but modern clothing and weapons must be taken into account. The modern fighter probably isn't wearing a kimono and carrying an aikuchi. Instead, he will probably be wearing designer jeans and toting a boot knife.

THE NUNCHAKU VS. THE KNIFE
Which Is the Better Weapon for Self-Defense?

by Larry A. Ytuarte • Photos by Louise C. Ytuarte • March 1989

You're reading a book or an article on *nunchaku* self-defense techniques in which a person is confronted by a knife-wielding assailant. The defender slips his nunchaku around the waist of his attacker, gives a twist and sends the brute flipping onto his back. Or the defender parries a knife thrust, adroitly steps inside and gets the attacker in a nunchaku choke hold. Or the defender knocks the knife from the person's hand with the nunchaku, lunges forward and down, wraps the nunchaku around the assailant's ankles and sweeps him off his feet. How do you feel when you read something like that? Do you buy it? Do you honestly think it would work?

Imagine yourself in the role of the defender in a real-life situation. You're walking down a street—alone. Suddenly, someone approaches. This someone is holding a knife. By his words and actions, you have no doubt that he intends to use the knife on you. It's a narrow, dead-end street. Consequently, your best defense—escape—is not possible. But you do have your nunchaku with you. You grab hold of the sticks and face your attacker. In that precious fraction of a second, you have to decide what you are going to do.

Ask yourself this: Do you really want to get close enough to attempt slipping the nunchaku around his wrist? (There's a hand at the end of that wrist, and there's a knife in that hand.) Do you really want to try to parry a knife thrust? (Remember, this is for real.) Are you really sure that, under such circumstances, you could be accurate enough to knock a knife out of someone's hand? (Hands are pretty small and very mobile targets.)

If your answers to the preceding questions are "No," well then, what *do* you do?

Something *practical*. Something *realistic*. Something that has a very good chance of working.

You may only get one chance.

The Technique

Whatever self-defense technique is used, it should meet the following criteria:

- It is fast.
- It is unexpected.
- It does not require unrealistic accuracy or power.

• It leaves you in a good position to strike again or withdraw in the event your attacker is not neutralized.

With these criteria in mind, the following two variations of a practical nunchaku technique against a knife attack are proposed. Both variations share the same general outline: 1) a feint (to draw the attacker's attention away from the direction of the actual strike), 2) the strike itself, and 3) good final position (ending in a stance that is neither awkward nor defenseless). One variation uses a forehand swing of the nunchaku to the attacker's head, the other a backhand swing. Let's analyze the steps in each variation.

The Forehand Variation

In this nunchaku defense, the defender squares off against the knife-wielding attacker and leads with his left side. The nunchaku is held in a ready position over the right shoulder. The defender leaves a fairly large distance between himself and the attacker (always a good idea when up against someone with a knife). The defender then throws a low (about knee-high) front kick with the rear leg (his right leg). This serves three purposes: It draws the attacker's attention down and away from the nunchaku, putting the assailant, at least for a moment, on the defensive; it closes the gap between the two combatants, while the attacker is on the defensive, putting

In the backhand nunchaku defense, the two opponents face off (1) and the nunchuck stylist feints (2) a low kick, then unleashes (3) a high backhanded nunchaku strike to the head, re-chambering (4) the weapon for a possible follow-up strike.

him in range of a nunchaku strike; and it pivots the defender, turning him in the same direction as the upcoming strikes, thereby adding power to the swing of the nunchaku.

The feint-kick is not meant to connect with the attacker's leg; it is meant to divert attention downward. (Glancing down at the attacker's knee just before throwing the kick can help draw his attention downward.) The kick should look forceful enough to put the attacker on the defensive, but it is not necessary to make contact. This allows the defender to maintain a safer distance because the striking range of nunchaku is considerably greater than that of a kick or a knife.

The real strike is a full-swinging nunchaku forehand to the attacker's head. The strike should begin when the feint-kick has reached full extension. Don't lose the momentary advantage over your attacker by taking time to plant your foot after the kick and *then* begin your strike. It will be too late. Strike while you are retracting your kicking foot. The pivoting motion of your swing and your own forward momentum will bring you to the final position. After the nunchaku strike, the defender is balanced and mobile, ready to skip back from the attacker, if needed. The nunchaku is in excellent position for an immediate follow-up backhand strike if the attacker has not been neutralized.

The Backhand Variation

In the backhand nunchaku defense, the defender leads with his right side. For reasons that will be explained, the nunchaku sticks are held 90 degrees apart, and the right hand grips the stick in a palm-up position. Again, the defender keeps a good distance between himself and the attacker. The defender then executes a low side kick—again a feint—to draw the attacker's guard down. This kick can be preceded by a skip to help close the gap, if needed.

The nunchaku strike is delivered in a backhand type of motion to the right side of the attacker's head. It is hard to generate as much power with the backhand swing as can be generated in the forehand strike described earlier, but holding the sticks 90 degrees apart helps. This gives the striking stick a greater arc to swing through, increasing its speed and therefore producing a more forceful blow than would be the case if the sticks were held in a straight line with respect to each other.

After the strike, the defender is balanced and mobile, his footing remaining virtually unchanged during the technique. The nunchaku has been caught in an across-the-back position with the left hand, making it very easy

THE ULTIMATE GUIDE TO KNIFE COMBAT

to execute a powerful follow-up forehand strike. It is for this reason—to be able to swing the nunchaku all the way around and across the back—that the stick is held palm-up in the right hand. Holding it palm-down would greatly restrict the arc of the swing.

Which Variation Is Better?

Neither of the variations is the better of the two. Like all self-defense techniques, both have their good points and their bad points. For most people, the forehand variation will deliver the stronger blow. This is a serious consideration. However, the backhand variation has the advantage in that, during the course of the technique, the defender only presents his side to the attacker, while in the forehand version, the defender pivots and, if only for a fraction of a second, gives the attacker a potential frontal target. Your best bet is to practice both and see which of the two you feel more comfortable with.

Handedness

In the preceding nunchaku techniques, the defender was right-handed. If you, as the defender, are left-handed, simply reverse your stance. In other words, in the forehand variation, you would square off leading with your right side and the nunchaku over your left shoulder. You would throw the low front kick with your left leg (the rear leg), pivot and swing the nunchaku with your left hand.

In the backhand variation, you would square off leading with your left side, and the low side kick would be thrown with the left foot. You would swing the nunchaku with your left hand, bring it around your left shoulder, down across your back, and catch it in your right hand. The attacker in the preceding scenarios was also right-handed. What if you are confronted by a left-handed attacker? Does it matter?

Not very much, for the reason that this is a long-range technique aimed at your attacker's head. Whether he holds the knife in his left or right hand will have little bearing on how successful your strike is, especially if your feint-kick is convincing and draws his guard down from the head-level strike.

However, for the sake of completeness, it could be argued that the best strike would be one in which the nunchaku swings toward the side of the attacker on which he holds the knife. In other words, against a right-handed attacker, a right-handed defender might want to use the backhand variation, while a left-handed defender might want to use the forehand version. (The stances are reversed against a left-handed attacker.) The reason for this is that, under these conditions, the attacker's free hand and arm are rendered almost useless. If he attempts to block the nunchaku strike, it will most likely be with the arm and hand holding the knife. Forcing him to block with this arm has two advantages: It momentarily renders the knife useless, and if the strike is blocked, the blow to the arm may leave the assailant unable or unwilling to continue the attack.

Practice

Learning self-defense techniques is very much like learning to juggle. You can read an article on how to juggle 10 times, but you won't be able to juggle until you put the article down, pick up three objects and start doing it. Juggling involves thought, intuition and quick reflexes. It requires practice.

The same sort of thing can be said about self-defense. Reading about a technique is not enough. Timing, distance, accuracy and power will not come from reading about a technique. These are developed through practice.

If you have a friend who shares your interest, practice together. Take turns in the roles of defender and attacker. Use a rubber knife and hollow plastic or foam-rubber nunchaku. Wear headgear and eye protection. (If you

In the forehand nunchaku defense, the two opponents square off (1) and the nunchuck stylist feints (2) a low kick, drawing the knife stylist's attention down before striking (3) to the head with the nunchaku. The nunchaku practitioner then prepares (4) for a possible backhanded follow-up.

don't have these things, *do not* practice with someone.) Drill the technique until your timing is right. Vary your distances from each other when you square off. Have the assailant vary the aggressiveness of his attack. Get comfortable with both variations. When you feel comfortable, include the follow-up strikes.

Practice by yourself with real nunchaku against a target. If you don't have a training bag, a stack of five or six cardboard cartons makes an excellent target. Arrange things so that the topmost carton is about head size and at about head height. Aim only for the topmost carton, drilling the technique to increase your power and accuracy.

* * *

In a self-defense situation, it is the fastest and least expected technique that has the highest chance of success. Drill for speed. Make the feint-kick convincing. Reach a point at which the technique becomes more of a reflex action than a conscious, premeditated act. Practice.

THE DO'S AND DON'TS OF KNIFE DEFENSE
Be Prepared or Be a Victim

by Jane Hallander • Photos by Jane Hallander • September 1989

What weapon raises the most fear on the street? The first thing that usually comes to mind is a gun. But does a gun really carry the most deadly potential?

Perhaps not. The knife may possess the deadliest potential. According to law-enforcement statistics, you are more likely to face a knife-wielding attacker on the street than one armed with a gun.

Moreover, assailants who bear a firearm know the exact capabilities of their weapon. They have already measured the risks involved in pointing a gun at an innocent person. However, knife-wielding assailants often do not realize their weapon's potential and are more apt to seriously cut the defender without intending to do so. Add that to the fact that even a small knife cut to a major artery can kill another person, and the knife becomes a very dangerous weapon to defend against.

Most martial arts systems exclude firearms from their self-defense training. Gun-toting assailants are generally best handled with a lot of serious talking rather than disarming attempts. Knives, on the other hand, are taken into consideration in most martial arts. Unfortunately, not all martial arts systems take a realistic look at knife defense.

Jim Mather, a San Jose, California-based karate instructor, has a reputation for teaching solid, traditional, practical self-defense. Besides training several world and national karate champions, Mather has found himself pitted against opponents who were sometimes high on drugs like PCP or were just plain mean.

Mather maintains that someone skilled with a knife will usually not let the defender know it until the defender is cut. For that reason, Mather starts his students' knife-defense instruction by teaching them which types of opponents will likely have knives. He wants his students to avoid those individuals at all costs.

"The problem is that a well-made, sharp knife cuts as soon as it touches, and good knife fighters always have good weapons," Mather asserts. "They will never come after someone with a wide-open, straight or overhead thrust. Instead, they make no major commitments but perform maneuvers that are difficult to block and counter, such as small slashes, slices or pokes. I tell my students to stay away from this type of individual if they can."

Mather imparts some valuable do's and don'ts to help his students decide

Karate instructor Jim Mather (left) demonstrates a knife defense: He steps away (1) from the slashing direction of the knife, then grabs (2) the knife-bearing hand. Mather then moves in close, elbowing (3) his assailant in the head to weaken him, before disarming (4) the opponent.

what kind of defense to use, should they become involved in a knife fight. For instance, if the knife is visible, the position of the blade before the assailant strikes will often tell what kind of blow is coming. If the knife tip is pointed upward, the strike will probably be similar to that of a hammer. A downward-pointing blade tip indicates an ice-pick-like strike. Any kind of ripping action starts with the blade pointed slightly up, while pokes, slashes and slices are initiated with the knife tip up and the cutting edge of the blade pointing down.

If the knife tip is down but the cutting edge is up, a diagonal slash will probably follow. Some assailants will even use the butt end of their knife as a blunt object to hit with. Others are experts at rapidly switching hands, making it difficult to judge where the attack is coming from. Mather believes that the average knife fighter starts with the tip of the blade up and the cutting edge down, making short slashes and pokes.

The head, face or eyes are among the favorite targets of knife-bearing assailants. These are painful but not usually fatal targets. However, the neck and throat are potentially fatal areas and should be protected. The

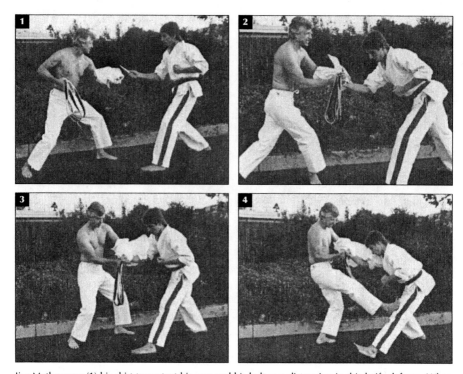

Jim Mather uses (1) his shirt to protect his arm and his belt as a distraction in this knife defense. When his assailant strikes, Mather grabs and traps (2) the knife hand, placing it (3) in a wrist lock before kicking (4) the attacker's knee.

same cautions apply to the chest, heart and lungs because cuts to these areas do not have to be deep to kill.

However, an accomplished street fighter will often attack the defender's arms, causing him to lose the ability to counterattack. Defenders should do their best to protect the inside areas of their arms and legs because major arteries and veins line the insides of these appendages.

Although this all sounds very discouraging, should a confrontation with a knife-wielding attacker take place, there are viable defenses available. The first and most important defense is to avoid the fight or run away. If the assailant cannot reach his intended victim, he can't cut him. When evasion is not possible, a block or deflection of the first cutting action is essential. Mather does not recommend trying to catch a knife-wielding hand; it involves too much risk.

If possible, the defender should throw an object at the assailant or otherwise distract him, creating an opportunity to either run away or counterattack. If an opening is created, there are several counterattacks that will stop the knife wielder. Knife fighters, like everyone else, have to be able to see to attack. A counterstrike to the eyes, temporarily blinding the attacker, will often end the confrontation. The assailant must also be able to breathe to fight. Taking his breath away by striking the throat or solar plexus can quickly stop the attack. If access to the eyes or throat is not possible, attacking the assailant's arms or legs can slow or stop him, allowing the defender to escape.

Attacking the knife hand itself is risky and should only be attempted as a last resort. Anyone who tries to kick the knife hand had better expect to get cut in the process. The best types of kicks are fakes toward the knife hand that force the assailant to deviate from his set pattern.

The countering techniques one employs depend on the type of knife attack. For instance, the direction of the assailant's slashing arc determines whether the defender should move to the inside or outside. A general defense pattern might be:

1. First, evade the knife's line of travel. If the knife travels in a straight line, the defender should move to the left or right. The defender should be close enough to counterattack but not close enough to be cut by the knife.

Using (1) his shirt to protect his arm and his belt as a weapon, Mather strikes (2) his knife-wielding attacker in the eyes with the belt, distracting him (3) and opening his defenses for a front kick (4) to the groin.

2. The next step is to control the attacker's hand. Grabbing the hand is safest when the blade is pointed away from the defender's body.

3. The knife should be taken away from the attacker. This can be done either by manipulating a wrist or elbow joint, causing the assailant to drop the weapon, or by striking the knife-bearing arm. Hitting and stunning the attacker will often force him to drop the weapon.

4. The final step is to insure that the assailant does not continue the fight. After disarming the attacker, attempt to disable him as quickly as possible with solid karate blows.

Mather encourages students not to overcommit to a situation, such as a grabbing technique that makes them lose control of the attacker's knife. They need to always be in a position in which they can easily move out of the knife's striking range. Mather calls such mobility "the option to leave."

One should never defend against a knife attack barehanded, if at all possible. Sticks, dirt, belts, coats or shoes, etc., can be employed for self-defense. A coat wrapped around the defender's leading hand offers some protection and can be used as a distracting target. Belts wrapped loosely around the hand can either be effective distraction devices or painful whips when used to counterstrike.

Mather's students incorporate knife defenses into their regular training regimen. They develop the timing necessary for good defense and counter-attack through regular sparring practice. Only by training with a partner can the student learn to react instantly to the unexpected. Rubber knives are used in sparring situations, lending realism to the drills.

One hopes, of course, to never have to use his knowledge of knife defense. But should the situation arise, comprehensive training in both the mental and physical aspects of knife defense can save lives.

KNIVES VS. GUNS
How the Police Deal With Knife Attacks

By David E. Steele • December 1989

Until recently, police officer survival classes had minimized the danger of edged weapons. In 1987, the last year of detailed figures on the subject, 73 police officers were murdered nationwide. Handguns were used in 48 of these murders, rifles in nine, shotguns in nine, knives in three, automobiles in two, and two officers were wounded by gunfire and burned to death in their cars. Statistics like these do not point to a large knife threat, but among civilians, knives are second only to handguns in fatal attacks. Now, however, as a result of intelligence gathering on prison inmates, who kill each other and corrections officers on a regular basis with improvised knives and spears, there is reason to believe that a "knife subculture" is developing. Convicts practice knife fighting in the "yard" with toothbrushes or pencils. They use this knowledge when they get back on the street.

Photo by Dan Fitzgerald

Most police officers believe that at contact distance, it is safer to first fight empty-handed against a knife-wielding assailant before attempting to draw a gun.

109

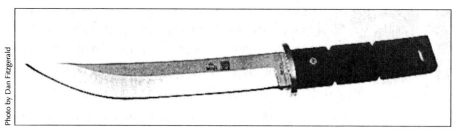

Tanto-style knives, such as the one above, are noted for their cutting ability as well as being able to penetrate body armor.

Satanic cults, particularly those practicing what is called "chaos magic," put emphasis on mutilations with steel objects. *Palo Mayombe*—a religion brought to the Caribbean by Bantu-speaking slaves from the Congo—was the ritual system associated with the recent machete killings in Matamoros, Mexico. In that case, human sacrifices were offered to Satan to protect the participants' drug-running operation. Ritual daggers are almost always among the paraphernalia used by satanists. Certain minority groups, especially those from agrarian societies in which edged tools are everyday implements, also form part of the "knife culture."

This is not to imply that there is anything inherently evil about knives or people who carry them. Knife collectors, hunters, fishermen, meatpackers, military personnel, martial artists, housewives and others enjoy using and becoming proficient with knives. Some of these people may even carry knives for defense. "Knife subculture" simply refers to those who carry knives to intimidate or injure innocent human beings. Some peace officers underestimate the danger presented by the knife subculture or individuals who have a knife available when distraught (such as drug users, emotionally disturbed people, suicidal people, etc.). A popular cartoon on a current police calendar shows a dozen 9 mm holes in a knife-wielding assailant. The caption reads: "The best reaction is overreaction." Unfortunately, the reality of such a situation could be quite different, especially at contact distance, where the knife wielder may have an advantage. Police training tends to go "in straight lines"—officers are taught to stand straight, march straight, shoot straight. Martial arts styles, however, especially ones that associate with knives, tend to go toward circular movements, with abrupt changes in speed and direction.

The trained martial artist does not focus on "center of mass" like in conventional pistol training. He is taught to close, then strike many times to vulnerable spots as they become available. At close quarters, using an ice pick, an Indonesian stylist could strike 10 times a second to his opponent's eyes or other preferred target with a bladed weapon. If such an opponent were that close, it would be utterly futile for an officer to go for his gun. The only real knife defense at very close range is with empty hands, trapping the enemy's hand or spinning him away long enough to draw a handgun.

Like most Americans, police officers like to "buy their way" to success. The current fashion in police circles is the high-capacity 9 mm automatic. However, except for SWAT, narcotics enforcement and high-risk patrol in large cities, it is difficult to justify high-tech automatics when simpler, cheaper and more reliable revolvers will do.

Certainly the 9 mm automatic is no more intimidating to an expert knife wielder than a revolver, because once he gets close, you will be lucky to get off even one or two shots. In order to draw and fire two rounds before contact, the knife artist must be advancing from no less than 20 feet. At close distance, it is more realistic to expect to get cut, then use empty-hand defense until the gun can be employed. Of course, if a revolver or baton is already in hand at the time of the attack, the odds of avoiding injury improve dramatically. For that reason, police officers often conceal a flashlight or small stick under the forearm when interviewing suspects.

Philippine stylists Leo Gaje and Dan Inosanto have both shown on video how easily a knife-wielding attacker—even when starting from what seems to be a safe distance—can overpower an officer. The flowing movements of the trained martial artist dominate the "straight thinking" police tactics every time. Fortunately, authorities in the line of duty rarely encounter

Photo courtesy of Heckler & Koch

The current fashion in police circles are high-capacity 9 mm automatics such as the Heckler & Koch P9. While superior for military service, the jury is still out on its superiority over the revolver for police work.

knife artists this skilled.

Another question is that of stopping power. At the turn of the century, Moro guerrillas in the southern Philippines chopped up quite a few U.S. Army officers, seemingly impervious to the .38-caliber revolvers most officers carried. However, contrary to legend, the .45-caliber Colt revolver brought out of mothballs and the .45-caliber Colt automatic developed for Philippine service did not do much better. In fact, even the Krag rifle didn't always stop the *juramentados* on their suicidal missions for Allah. A combination of adrenaline, fanaticism, native "painkillers" and leather bindings on their limbs that slowed bleeding made the Moros difficult to kill. The Moros were also highly skilled in *kali,* the foremost martial art of the Philippines. Contrast this with the average American officer who could not "place his shots" under pressure. Shot placement (preferably in

Photo courtesy of Eddie Jafri

The flowing movements of trained knife fighters, such as kris-wielding Indonesian stylist Eddie Jafri, have been shown to dominate "straight thinking" police tactics.

the head, heart or spine) is still critical in pistol effectiveness, even with modern hollow-point ammunition.

As far as the "perfect" gun for dealing with a knife factor, the old expression applies: "The second-best gun for the job is the one you have with you at the time you need it." Once again, shot placement and tactics are more important than magazine capacity because distances are close and the gun hand can be deflected. At contact distance, it is best to think like a knife fighter: Use the gun in one hand, deflect the knife with either hand and pick your target carefully as if for a thrust—upper chest, neck or head.

The point to remember is that a gun is not a magic wand, and the basic principles of maneuvering (blocking, evasion, feint, counterattack) still apply. With sufficient training and adequate forethought, the officer might have a stick or flashlight in one hand and a gun in the other—the stick can be used to deflect, stun or disable in combination with the gun (like using a sword and dagger in Renaissance-style dueling). The number of rounds in the magazine is relatively unimportant; the first couple of solid hits are the most important. Fighting at contact distance can mean that the gun will be jammed by bits of flying flesh and clothing or the opponent's movements. Fast, violent movements can cause some unexpected problems.

In cavalry days, officers on horseback who preferred revolvers to sabers did so because a bullet could not be parried, not because of increased range. Often cavalrymen, in order to minimize the inaccuracy of shooting from a moving horse, would ride up on their enemy and put the muzzle against his chest before firing. Obviously, it is better to take advantage of the pistol's superior range by confronting a knife-wielding assailant at a distance. Even in this scenario, it is safer to be behind cover or approach the attacker from the back or side. However, a good knife practitioner will not let you see the knife until you are already cut. It can be hidden in the palm or concealed in dozens of places on the body. Traditional Philippine martial artists always carried at least three knives—one to throw and one for each hand.

Violence is a form of communication, and like any other language, some people have a larger vocabulary than others. The vocabulary is structured into grammar and then into style. The self-defense and weapons techniques taught at police academies or at martial arts seminars are just the ABCs. Real fluency comes with years of empty-hand, knife, stick and firearms practice, as well as an understanding of human nature when placed under extreme pressure.

ARMED DEFENSES AGAINST A KNIFE ATTACK
Counterattacking With Your Own Weapon Increases Your Chances of Survival

By David E. Steele • March 1992

It is no secret that the handgun is the preferred weapon for murder in the United States. According to FBI statistics, a pistol is used in 50 percent of all U.S. homicides. Ranking second—and accounting for 19 percent of America's homicides—is the knife.

A knife is like a handgun in that it is highly concealable and it kills by penetration, causing hemorrhaging and damage to vital organs. A knife has the added advantages of being lighter, cheaper, more readily available and quieter than a handgun, leaving no ballistic residue for later forensic analysis by law-enforcement agencies. Damage to the victim is also more easily controlled with a knife than with a gun. A knife victim can be injured, maimed or killed, depending on the intent and skill of the attacker, whereas a firearm carries with it a constant risk of paralysis and death.

In the United States, the armed individual most likely to confront a knife fighter is a uniformed police officer. A police officer usually carries a revolver and a nightstick, along with other defensive gear. The most dangerous type of knife fighter is the one who conceals his weapon until the last instant. However, it is more common for a knife fighter to attack with a simple thrust or slashing motion. A police officer can counter such attacks by maintaining his distance from the assailant, then using the baton's greater reach to disable his hand or arm.

Each officer must decide whether he can disable the attacker with his baton or whether he should go directly to his revolver. Some believe the revolver should be drawn first because it is the most intimidating weapon on the officer's belt. However, there are often serious repercussions when employing firearms, and immediate action, rather than the threat of action, may be the best move.

In Los Angeles, sheriff's deputies were called to a residence by parents being threatened with a knife by their teenage son. One of the deputies approached the boy, talking soothingly to him while concealing his PR-24 baton behind his back. When the deputy got close enough, he performed an upward spinning technique with his baton, breaking the boy's forearm and sending the switchblade caroming off a wall.

If an officer is trained in any of the Philippine martial arts, he could undoubtedly use a nightstick more effectively against a knife than a PR-

Photo courtesy of Taser Systems

Photo by Dan Fitzgerald

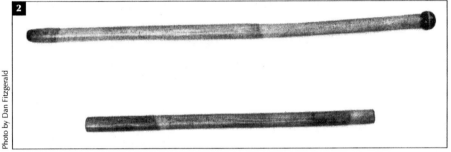

Photo by Dan Fitzgerald

There are a variety of weapons both a police officer and an average citizen can choose from to defend himself on the street, including a stun gun (1), cane or stick (2), or a registered handgun such as a .357-Magnum revolver (3).

24 baton. The straight stick does not hit as fast or as hard as the PR-24. An experienced knife fighter familiar with PR-24 baton techniques would have a substantial advantage if the deputy's first spinning strike missed because the deputy would invariably follow up with a reverse spin at the same angle. A straight stick or a knife, conversely, can move instantly from one angle of attack to any other within 360 degrees. However, if an officer is not trained in these arts, he can do little more than bat at his enemy's hand, using the baton's two-foot reach advantage, then following up with a strike to the temple or side of the neck (targets generally avoided during an unarmed attack). It is also possible to simply thrust with the baton in the off hand or throw the baton at the opponent's face, thus allowing the officer time to draw his revolver.

If an officer decides to use his revolver, he should not consider it a magic wand. If a knife fighter is on drugs or has gone berserk, he may not go down even with six well-placed .38-caliber slugs. If this occurs, the officer should not attempt to reload in the face of a continuous charge. Instead, he should backpedal, sidestep, or otherwise evade the attack until he can get some obstacle between himself and his opponent. Then he may decide to use his baton until the attacker goes down from a loss of blood. As soon as the attack is broken off, the officer can take the time to reload.

If an officer is stabbed before he has time to shoot or take evasive action, he should remember that knife wounds produce no hydrostatic shock like bullet wounds often do. Unless the knife has pierced the heart, spine or brain, it is quite possible to continue fighting. The most dangerous knife wounds are deep, penetrating thrusts. Big, ugly slashes may take hundreds of stitches to close, but unless they cut the throat or are not properly treated in time, they are not likely to be fatal. In other words, the officer must keep fighting as long as he is physically able and must not succumb to the psychological shock of large, gaping wounds.

What about Mace? Won't that stop a knife fighter? The answer is that Mace and other tear-gas sprays do not work consistently on subjects

Photo by Dan Fitzgerald

Improvisational training is an excellent way to develop solid self-defense skills. In the example above, defender Hawkins Cheung (right) has removed his shoes and placed them on his hands in an effort to defend against a knife attack.

who are psychotic or under the influence of alcohol or drugs. Moreover, manufacturers do not recommend tear-gas sprays for use against armed opponents. A knife fighter, for example, does not need the full use of his eyes or nose to close the distance and stab you repeatedly.

Not everyone carrying a concealed knife poses a threat to an officer's safety. Many individuals who carry knives today do so not for felonious purposes or to assault police officers but to protect themselves from criminals. When disarming suspects who have not shown an intent to use their knives, an officer should exhibit more than a little common sense. His objective should be to keep the situation as calm as possible. It is not a good idea to have the suspect lay the knife on the ground because some knife fighters can use this as a ploy to scoop the weapon up for a groin attack. It is also not a good idea to order the suspect to drop the knife on the ground because he may have some attachment for the weapon and might become hostile if it was damaged. The best tactic, perhaps, is to have the suspect slowly lay the weapon on a table or car, then turn away.

If the knife is concealed or if it is drawn for the purpose of attack, the preferred tactics are quite different. The important thing to remember in searching for a concealed knife is to not let the searching hand get trapped in the suspect's pocket and to not search from an imbalanced position. Either of these mistakes could allow the suspect to throw or trap the officer while drawing a weapon with the other hand.

While patting down a subject, an officer should be aware of the number of places a knife can be concealed. It could be hidden in a paper sack or in the card pocket of a library book. It may be part of a comb or a belt buckle. Several knives are marketed in the outward shape of a fountain pen. Razor blades and needles may round out the knife fighter's concealed arsenal. Some Chinese martial artists are adept at concealing needles in their mouths and then blowing them into an opponent's eyes.

Some officers are afraid of suspects who throw a knife. They may respond mechanically, using their service revolver at a distance at which they would not engage even a proficient knife fighter. Officers do this because shooting policy and training films have made them aware of the extra distance at which a thrown knife may be deadly. The fact is, however, that accurate knife throwing is a skill possessed by very few, and usually by professionals rather than knife fighters.

Some people are so filled with frustration that they will throw anything at hand when an officer tries to apprehend them. This may include knives, but the chances are that such a weapon will do no more damage than a thrown rock or piece of pipe. In most of these situations, the officer's best tactics are to duck, seek cover, draw his weapon, and allow the suspect an opportunity to surrender.

When faced with a knife-wielding attacker, it is obviously preferred to have a weapon of your own to counter with. Most handguns have definite advantages over a knife in terms of intimidation and stopping power. Employing a handgun at contact distance does not require the skill and determination of using an edged weapon. Those who have not trained with a knife should rely on a firearm as their weapon of choice to counter a knife attack.

If firearms are not available, other weapons can give you the advantage over a knife-wielding assailant. Among your choices are stun guns and sticks. Blunt instruments, such as a baton, may be used in conjunction with Mace, the tear gas acting as a blinding powder, allowing the defender to get in close more safely. If you are suddenly confronted by a knife-wielding assailant, various environmental weapons such as shoes (worn on the hands), rolled-up newspapers, briefcases, etc., can be used to fend off the initial attack.

Remember to remain calm and focused. You *can* defend yourself in a knife attack, whether you are armed or not. If you possess a weapon, as well, you increase your chances of survival dramatically.

THE KNIFE-FIGHTING TACTICS OF THE U.S. MARINE CORPS
Grips, Stances and Targets
by Robert Safreed • Photos courtesy of Robert Safreed • September 1992

It's midnight in the jungle, and a United States Marine Corps infantryman crouches in the grass. His M-16 assault rifle, emptied of bullets, lies somewhere in the thick underbrush, near the bodies of the soldier's slain enemies. He is alone, and he is far from home, behind enemy lines. Yet he is unafraid. He still has his knife, and in close combat, that is all he needs.

* * *

According to Jim Advincula, a longtime U.S. Marine Corps knife and close-combat instructor, basic knife-fighting techniques are far more effective in close-combat situations than fancy or advanced techniques. For the average grunt, simple is deadly.

Advincula's Oceanside, California, martial arts school is located near a military base, and the *isshin-ryu* karate and *escrima* instructor is frequently

Jim Advincula (left) demonstrates the "triangle" stance, with his knife to the front and shield hand covering his chest. This is the preferred knife-fighting stance. Standing with the free hand forward (center) rather than the knife hand or using a reverse grip (right) is not recommended.

called on to teach U.S. servicemen the finer points (excuse the pun) of knife fighting. Following are some of the major principles Advincula covers with his trainees.

Grip

The first thing Advincula shows his knife-fighting students is how to grip the weapon. The terrain and environment are rarely ideal for close combat. Rain, mud or snow will make the handle of a knife slippery and difficult to manage, and wearing gloves only makes it more difficult to wield the weapon efficiently. Therefore, it is necessary to select a simple, strong grip that can be used in any situation. Close-combat instructors generally teach four methods of gripping a knife:

• *Reverse grip.* Some instructors advocate the use of the "reverse" grip, with the knife held along the wrist. However, Advincula claims this method limits your techniques and only allows for slashing maneuvers, which are

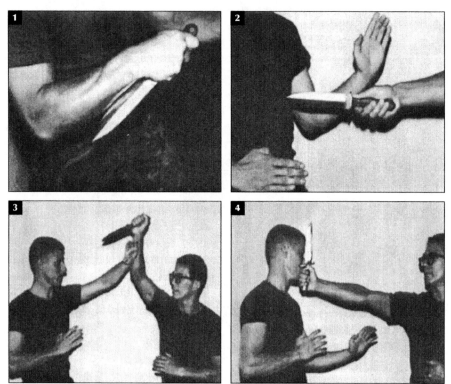

There are four basic methods of gripping a knife: the reverse grip (1), tile fencer's grip (2), ice-pick grip (3), and hammer grip (4). The hammer grip is the preferred method because you are less likely to lose your grasp of the weapon and you can use the knife in combination with a punch.

usually ineffective in a close-combat situation because the blade doesn't penetrate the target or generate much power.

• *Fencer's grip.* Most instructors teach the "fencer's" grip, in which the knife handle is gripped firmly between the thumb and forefinger, with the other fingers wrapped loosely around the handle. While this grip may be suitable for small knives like a stiletto, it isn't suitable for blades with large grips. If your hand is hit during combat while employing the fencer's grip, you can lose your grasp on the weapon.

• *Ice-pick grip.* The "ice-pick" grip enables deep penetration against soft body armor, heavy clothing or other protective outfits. To achieve this grip, simply hold the knife handle in your fist, with the blade pointing down. There are drawbacks to this grip, however. When raising the knife for a downward strike, you not only telegraph your intentions and expose your chest area but also make it easy for your opponent to see the weapon. Moreover, the ice-pick grip does not provide parrying or thrusting capability, and it is easier for the opponent to block a knife strike delivered in this manner.

• *Hammer grip.* The hammer grip is preferred over all others. A knife held in this fashion is less likely to be knocked from your grasp, and it can also be used in conjunction with a punch or to deliver butt-end knife strikes. A hammer grip is achieved by grasping the knife at the handle and forming a tight fist. Keep the wrist flexible, as if using a hammer or hatchet. This enables you to lock the wrist tightly when needed.

The hammer grip provides great penetration and power, allowing the blade to easily cut through heavy clothing. There is also less likelihood of injury to the user's thumb, unlike with the fencer's grip. The hammer grip can be used for chopping, slashing and especially thrusting techniques.

Stance

After achieving an effective grip, the knife fighter must assume an appropriate combat stance. Advincula teaches Marines to fight from a basic "triangle" stance. Also known as the "fencer's" stance, the triangle posture allows the knife fighter to move in any direction at a moment's notice. This stance also gives the practitioner maximum reach because his knife is held in the hand nearest to the enemy.

Covering

Advincula teaches students to "hide" behind their knife; in other words, keep the weapon between them and the opponent. By keeping the knife

In the "shield hand" technique, the knife fighter places (1) his free hand close to his heart or solar plexus to protect vital areas from his opponent's knife strikes. Or he can use his free hand to parry (2) an opponent's strike, then counterattack.

pointed toward the enemy, you can attack and/or block or parry any thrusts by the opponent. You can also pull the weapon close to your body, leaving your free hand to protect against an opponent's grabbing technique.

Shield Hand

The knife fighter's free hand should be held close to the heart or solar plexus to protect vital areas, such as the heart and throat. Should the enemy's blade get through your defenses, your free hand will hopefully absorb the blade rather than one of your vital organs. This technique is taken from Philippine escrima, in which the hand is used like a shield and is sacrificed, if necessary. According to Advincula, the *escrimador's* credo is: "You can cut my hand, but I will take your life!"

The knife fighter's "shield hand" can also be used to parry, punch, fake a blow, throw objects, distract the opponent, or assist balance in rough terrain. Marines are even taught to grab the opponent's blade, if necessary. It should be noted that your hand can't be cut unless the enemy is able to draw his blade. By grabbing and attacking the opponent, you can prevent him from drawing the weapon and cutting your hand.

Targets

Attacking the right targets is a key to effective knife fighting. The objective is to neutralize the enemy as quickly as possible, but this does not mean always attempting to strike vital points. Because the enemy will generally be defending his vital points, seek the most available target, be it the solar plexus, back, neck, stomach, etc. Drawing first blood is a tremendous psychological advantage. The more you strike your opponent—regardless of where you hit him—the more he will bleed and weaken.

Advincula also teaches students to aim for the opponent's weapon-wielding hand. By disabling the hand that holds his weapon, you neutralize the threat to your safety and gain the advantage. If the enemy has two weapons—say a pistol in one hand and a knife in the other—zero in on the one that presents the most immediate danger to your well-being.

GUERRILLA KNIFE-FIGHTING TACTICS
Unconventional Blade Techniques From Around the World

by David E. Steele • April 1994

G uerrilla fighting refers to unconventional combat. When such combat involves a knife, the rules of engagement can be particularly unpredictable and the outcome particularly violent.

In the United States and in Europe, the knife-fighting method taught to soldiers since World War II is based on Western saber fencing. This style was popularized by William E. Fairbairn in England, and Drexel Biddle, John Styers and Col. Rex Applegate in America. This method is often combined with sentry elimination techniques for use by infantrymen.

The linear movements of the saber method of knife fighting are easy to understand, especially for those with a background in boxing or fencing. Because it is a comparatively simple style to teach, it is a plus in a military environment in which instruction is measured in hours, not years.

The drawback to this conventional type of knife fighting is its popularity. Next to the amateurish ice-pick stab and throat-slashing techniques, the saber method is the most widely practiced knife-fighting style. It therefore does not provide much margin for error against a similarly trained opponent. This is undoubtedly why Asian schools of knife fighting were kept totally secret, because surprise is the best weapon in close combat.

The Criminal Approach

Today's prison convicts have elevated the level of unconventional knife fighting to a science, fashioning everything from pencils to toothbrushes into "shanks" for use against guards as well as inmates. Convicts sometimes tape or tie the shanks to their hands so they won't be lost in a melee. For the same reason, shank handles are sometimes wrapped with rags or sandpaper.

Delinquents also use unconventional knife tactics. In New York City subways, purse snatchers often use knives taped to their hands to cut handbag straps. If a bystander grabs the hoodlum, the former may be surprised to find that the thief has greased his arms with silicone spray or petroleum jelly. Unable to get a hold on the thief, the good Samaritan finds himself the next victim of the taped blade. This sort of attack is virtually impervious to conventional disarming techniques and should be met with armed force.

Knives can also be strapped to wrists, making them virtually undetectable until what appears to be a fist attack becomes a blade cut. Edges can be built into finger rings, as well—another type of fist attack that will open wounds in the opponent. Or razor blades can be taped between the fingers, so a slap becomes a slashing blade cut.

Some criminals choose their blades deliberately for an intimidation effect. As Jack Katz says in his book *Seductions of Crime*, "Just to have these things (ninja stars, switchblades, linoleum knives, etc.), to hold them, inspect them, and observe them swiftly introduced into the focus of the moment is exciting. ... 'Being mean' picks up the evil undertones set off by the display of these objects. Many of these weapons are notable not just for their power, but for their brutish, sadistic character; others, fitted for covert possession, are notably illicit in design."

Since the 1950s, gangs in the United States have used every type of edged weapon, from sharpened belt buckles and spiked golf balls to swords. Leg-

Photo by Dan Fitzgerald

Butterfly swords were generally utilized in pairs and were common among Shaolin monks in China.

125

islation against weapons such as switchblades, throwing stars and "buck" knives has had little effect, because an "illegal" weapon is more attractive to a street culture that specializes in terrorizing the innocent.

Let's take a look at how knife fighting has developed in other countries around the world.

Argentina

Among the world's best knife fighters were the gauchos, Argentine cowboys who carried large knives—called *facon* or *punal*—rather than six-shooters. The knives were used primarily for butchering steers or repairing leather gear but were occasionally employed for self-defense or dueling. Knife duels were common and were traditionally concluded with a slash across the opponent's face. The objective was usually to disfigure

The ancient Japanese ninja warriors threw bladed weapons known as shaken at their enemies to slow their pursuit.

and dishonor the opponent, not kill him.

The facon was often shaped in "Mediterranean dagger" style (i.e., like a thick-bladed chef's knife). The blade was carried at the back of the belt, out of the way, but ready for a fast draw, like the medieval knight's *quillon* dagger. Blade length varied but averaged around 12 inches among antique specimens.

China

Traditional Chinese close combat usually involved the sword and spear. The military tried to keep all weapons in its hands, but peasant revolts were not uncommon. Independent martial arts experts, like the Shaolin monks, were viewed with suspicion by the government. The itinerant monks developed self-defense skills to protect themselves against bandits and rogue soldiers. Some of these techniques involved improvised weapons, like walking sticks. Others required concealed weapons, such as "butterfly knives," hidden in boots. Also known as "butterfly swords" or "butterfly sabers," these knives could be used against staves, spears and swords. Butterfly-knife techniques could also be adapted for use with kitchen shears or short axes, both common weapons among organized crime factions in Hong Kong and old San Francisco.

Japan

The knife-fighting art of feudal Japan was called *tantojutsu*. The *tanto*, literally "half sword," was a single-edged blade 6 to 12 inches in length. Heavier models, called *yoroi-doshi* (armor piercer), were used for grappling in armor. The tanto was distinguished by its full-size *tsuba* (hand guard). Half-guard *(hamidashi)* and guardless versions *(aikuchi)* were also available. Double-edged daggers, known as *himogatana*, also existed but were not preferred by the samurai.

Samurai would carry a two-handed sword (*tachi* or *katana*) as well as a tanto or *wakizashi* (short sword). Unlike the wakizashi, which was worn openly, the tanto was concealed at the waist inside the samurai's kimono. Samurai-class women also carried knives, most often an aikuchi, which was concealed for self-defense or honorable suicide.

The Japanese peasant class was forbidden swords. They could possess only kitchen and utility knives. The samurai fighting styles, on the other hand, commonly featured 18 weapons, with an emphasis on the sword and bow and arrow.

Relatively few styles included the knife because it was rarely used in honorable combat. As a concealed weapon, the knife was given greater status by ninja warriors.

The ninja were also known for throwing utility knives *(kozuka)*, stars *(shaken)* and spikes *(shuriken)* to halt pursuers, and these "shadow warriors" were not averse to tossing caltrops in their opponents' paths. However, because these blades rarely achieved much penetration, they were intended primarily to distract or delay the enemy, not kill him. For killing purposes, ninja would treat a spike with sumac or other poisonous compounds before throwing it.

Modern Japanese gangsters known as *yakuza* think of themselves as the spiritual descendants of medieval warriors. Although illegal, they often carry pistols, swords and knives for use against their enemies. The most common blade employed by the yakuza would be a traditional aikuchi with a plain wooden handle and sheath, carried in the waistband beneath clothing. The scabbard is wedged in by expanding the stomach against the waistband, allowing a quick draw. The yakuza usually draws the blade in an ice-pick grip, edge out, and slashes across the enemy's carotid artery.

Traditional tantojutsu is rarely taught today because of its sinister past.

Indonesia

Indonesia developed more blade shapes than any other country. Each clan seemed to have its own special fighting knife. In farm areas, blades often served a dual purpose as jungle or field knives. In towns and cities, smaller concealment-type knives were common.

The national blade is the *kris*, which may be straight or wavy (always an odd number of waves). The history and lore of the kris fill volumes. Unlike the Philippine kris, which is much heavier, the Indonesian kris is used for thrusts and some light cutting. It is carried today only on ceremonial occasions and is displayed in a special place in the home.

Another popular Indonesian knife is the *golok*, a field knife similar to the Philippine *bolo*. The golok was favored by peasant guerrillas fighting Dutch colonial troops in the 19th century. Today, British commandos carry a jungle knife they call a golok, in memory of operations in the archipelago.

Perhaps the most unique Indonesian knife is the *rentjong*, used by the Atjeh people of Sumatra. The blade's unusual shape has a mystical significance for Muslims. The pistol-grip handle allows for some unusual techniques, such as an ice-pick stab between the ribs accentuated by a twist of the handle to further open the wound. The pistol grip also allows easier withdrawal.

The most dramatic use of the rentjong, however, was with the foot. Practitioners would curl their toes around the grip, with the blade protruding up between the two biggest toes. The rentjong could then be kicked into an opponent. Atjeh patriots used the blade in conjunction with kicks to the groin of Dutch soldiers, after beating aside their bayonets with a golok. This kicking technique compensated for the greater reach of their opponents' musket-mounted bayonets.

Philippines

Philippine guerrillas have used edged weapons throughout modern times. The three most common blade types are the kris, bolo and *balisong*. The kris and bolo were heavy jungle knives. The kris was used for chopping and thrusting, while the bolo was used almost exclusively for chopping. The balisong, often called a "butterfly knife," was a concealment weapon for urban warfare and self-defense.

Philippine long-blade techniques resemble ancient Spanish fencing. Short-knife styles, however, vary widely in method and effectiveness. Some systems model their parries after the sword, but the close distances involved in knife fighting make this hazardous. Other styles, like *pekiti tirsia,* use sidestepping to avoid incoming knife thrusts, which is safer than parrying with a short blade.

*　*　*

Before the development of handguns, the knife was the concealed weapon of choice for defensive as well as offensive purposes. One reason for this is that even untrained individuals can kill or maim an opponent with a knife. The knife, in fact, is the second-most-used weapon in violent crimes in the United States. Whether used conventionally or unconventionally, the knife can be deadly in the hands of both skilled or unskilled fighters.

CAN YOU SURVIVE A KNIFE ATTACK WITHOUT GETTING CUT?
Guidelines for Escaping a Slasher's Blade

by Bud Malmstrom • Photos courtesy of Bud Malmstrom • July 1996

Every martial artist has an idea what he would do if confronted by a knife-wielding assailant. Creating "what if...?" scenarios before such predicaments occur helps you develop a better strategy if and when you need to implement one in a real situation. As you go about your daily activities, look for possible dangers and think of what you would do if a physical threat occurred. While it makes sense to develop a plan of action for a particular dilemma, predetermined tactics don't always pan out in a real fight. However, remaining alert and having a basic plan of action will improve your chances of surviving an attack.

Fighting someone who is armed with a knife is more frightening to most people than trying to disarm a gun-toting assailant. This is probably attributable to the fact that everyone has been cut by a knife, razor blade or piece of glass and has felt that icy nonpain that takes your breath away. It is therefore easier to imagine the pain of being cut in a knife fight. Virtually all edged-weapon attacks occur at such a close distance that the combatants can actually "feel" the rage in their opponent and smell his body odor and breath.

Conversely, being fired on at a distance by a gun-wielding attacker does not place you in direct contact with your adversary. Moreover, a gun has a limited capacity for damage, depending on the number of bullets it carries. After it runs out of bullets, you are left with a small bludgeoning device, and an ineffective one at that. A knife, on the other hand, never runs out of ammunition and never jams.

Your first line of defense against an edged weapon such as a knife is to be aware of the location of your opponent's hands. Always pay close attention to the hand that is holding the knife, and set your distance and angle to him according to where the weapon is. If you can't see his hands, you must assume that he has a weapon.

Your second line of defense is distance. Your assailant can't cut you if he can't reach you. Distance may be all that is necessary to keep him from deciding to attack. If he doubts he can close the distance before you can respond, he may decide not to attack. If you can learn to understand and control the fighting range, your chances of surviving a knife attack, or any physical encounter, are greatly improved.

The first thing that happens when a knife-wielding assailant confronts you is that you lose your mental stability and focus. Expect it—it *will* happen, no matter how much fighting experience you have. How fast you

When faced (1) with a knife-wielding attacker, try to maintain a safe distance from the assailant. Avoid the knife strike by stepping out (2) of the line of attack, then move in and control (3) the knife hand while delivering a punch to the biceps on that same arm. Push the attacker's knife-wielding arm to the side, and deliver (4) a strike to the temple. While continuing to control the knife hand, drop (5) your forward knee onto the assailant's front leg, disrupting his balance as you grab the back of his neck and pull him down (6) to his knees. Step over (7) the fallen attacker, and secure the knife while maintaining an armbar on the opponent.

In this knife-defense sequence, an assailant attempts (1) an overhead stab, but the defender shifts out of the line of attack and uses (2) his forearm to redirect the strike to the outside. The defender then slides (3) his blocking arm over the attacker's striking arm and forces (4) the knife into the assailant's own leg. The defender backs off (5), creating distance while he determines his next course of action.

regain control and refocus on the situation will determine whether you survive. If you have a prior plan of action for such a confrontation, have practiced against knife attacks, have experience defending yourself against knife attacks, or all of the above, your mental recovery period will be much quicker. The mind can focus on only one thing at a time. If it is occupied by "What do I do?" it can't focus on solutions to the problem.

Never defend yourself unarmed against a knife-wielding attacker. If you are not carrying a weapon, there is generally some implement nearby that can be used for your defense. It might be dirt, which can be thrown into the attacker's eyes. Or you can use your shirt to swing at the assailant. A belt, pen or pencil can also be used effectively against an attacker, and you can even slide your shoes over your hands to protect against cuts or use them as projectiles.

The easiest and most natural reaction to a knife attack is to create as much distance as possible between yourself and the assailant. First, take a couple of shuffling steps backward. Then, if possible, turn and run. Just because you are a martial artist doesn't mean you need to prove to anyone how tough you are. If you have to fight, however, do anything it takes to survive. A knife attack is a serious matter and should be dealt with accordingly.

Things tend to happen very quickly in a confrontation, and you may not have time to create enough distance to avoid the assailant's attacks. In this case, your best chance of survival may be to close the distance and

In this scenario, the defender is faced (1) with a knife-wielding assailant who lunges forward to stab him. The defender shifts (2) out of the line of attack, controls the knife hand and initiates a painful elbow-locking technique. He then delivers (3) a front kick to the back of the opponent's knee, sending him (4) facefirst to the ground while still maintaining control of the knife hand. The defender places (5) his left knee on the fallen attacker's shoulder blade for added control, and he uses his right knee to reinforce his hold on the knife hand. Grabbing the assailant's hair gives the defender control of the opponent's head.

fight to win. At this juncture of the confrontation, any level of force you use is reasonable and necessary. Stopping the attacker as quickly as possible is your goal.

There are several important guidelines to follow when faced with this scenario. First, you obviously want to avoid your assailant's stabs and slashes, which will be more difficult now that you have narrowed the fighting distance and are in close quarters with the attacker. If you can thwart the opponent's initial attack, your odds of survival increase dramatically. Your chances improve even more if you can avoid his first attack and remain close enough to get your hands on him. This will enable you to control the weapon, the opponent and, hopefully, the situation. Although you may instinctively want to grab the attacker's knife-wielding arm and remove the weapon from his hand, you should resist this urge. Knife defense is not a contest to see who ends up with the weapon. Your goal is to get control of the attacker without being critically injured. Once you have accomplished this, you have won regardless of whether your attacker is still armed or not. If you stop the attacker, his knife cannot hurt you. Focusing on stopping your opponent rather than his knife is not easy; it takes a lot of training before you can instinctively respond in this manner. Quite often, if the attacker holds on to the knife but is kept from using it, he will concentrate on freeing the weapon for attack and will forget about striking you with his hands, legs, elbows, etc. This is not to say that you should ignore the knife. You must always attempt to control the knife or the hand it is in, but controlling your attacker should be your top priority and the focus of your attention.

*　*　*

Effective knife defense starts with a competent instructor who can teach you proper strategies and practical techniques that will work in a real confrontation. Then, if you are faced with an attacker, visually check for weapons he may have. Also scan the area (and your person) for items you can use as defensive tools. Always be alert. Make your defensive decision, and set your distance and alignment to give you the best advantage. If your adversary produces a knife, quickly create as much distance as you can between yourself and the opponent. If you can't create any distance, get out of the line of attack. Once you have avoided your foe's initial assault, control the knife or the arm wielding it, and stop the attacker as quickly as you can.

MODERN KNIFE FIGHTING
What Martial Artists Need to Know About Using and Defending Against the Blade
by David E. Steele • August 1998

While knife fighting was occasionally mentioned in medieval texts on swordplay, it took an event like World War II for the discipline to earn much attention in military manuals. One of the earliest and most comprehensive writers on this topic was William E. Fairbairn, who penned *All-In Fighting* and *Get Tough* based on the commando course he taught in Scotland.

Fairbairn's personal style was called *defendu*. It was an eclectic system based on his training in *jujutsu* and fencing and his experiences on the mean streets of Shanghai, China. In the 1930s, he was a captain and training officer with the Shanghai Municipal Police, which was responsible for patrolling the international settlement in the city. He went on hundreds of calls and gained a lot of firsthand experience. Although triads like the Green Gang had access to Mauser 1896 pistols and other firearms, a good deal of everyday violence was done with "choppers"—Chinese cleaver-shaped kitchen knives—and other blades. Patrolmen and the flying squads replied with .38- and .45-caliber Colt pistols.

When World War II started, Fairbairn was given army rank and asked to design a course for the newly formed commando units, whose training was conducted at Achnacarry, Scotland. Later, he was placed on detached service to the Office of Strategic Services training center called "Area B," located

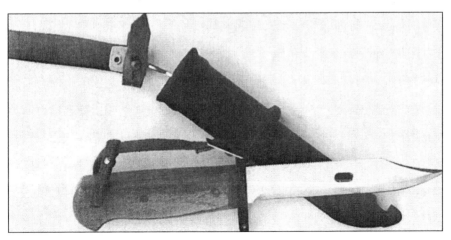

Most modern bayonets, such as this one from the former Soviet Union, were designed to meet a soldier's survival needs rather than his personal combat needs.

135

in Thurmont, Maryland. It was there that he met and influenced Col. Rex Applegate, who later wrote several texts on the subject of knife fighting.

Fairbairn always carried his First Pattern F-S knife sewn into the right-side cargo pocket of his battle dress trousers. Occasionally, however, he carried one on the left. This allowed him to shake someone's hand, then twist the person's arm around jujutsu-fashion, draw the knife and put the tip against the surprised victim's kidney area. This is one of the ways in which he would teach alertness to new students.

Fairbairn always kept his dagger razor sharp, setting another good example for the men. The knife, named for him and "Bill" Sykes (another alumnus of the Shanghai Police, as was Pat O'Neil, hand-to-hand combat instructor for the First Special Service Force) was originally made by Wilkinson Sword in Sheffield, England. However, because of wartime exigencies, the creation of the knife was subcontracted to other, lower-quality Sheffield cutlers. This later gave the F-S a "brittle" reputation.

While no other dagger achieved the fame of the F-S, many other World War II-issue knives developed "stronger" reputations. They included

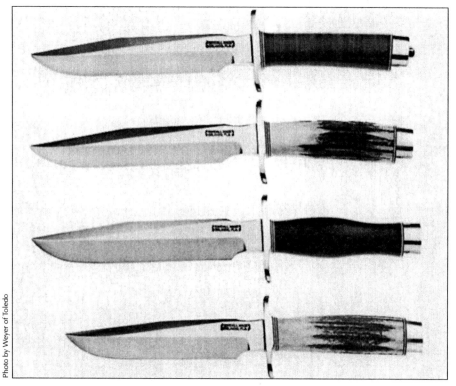

Photo by Weyer of Toledo

The Randall Model 1 fighting knife set the standard by which other combat knives are judged.

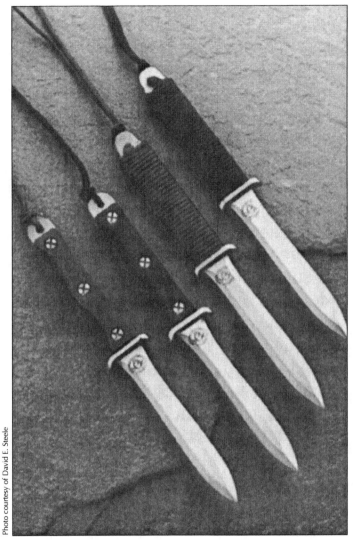

Several variations of the stiletto are produced by Blackjack Knives Ltd.

Photo courtesy of David E. Steele

the Dutch commando dagger, the German trench knife, the V-42 FSSF dagger, the M-3 trench knife, and Ek and Randall stilettos. These knives' reputations were because of their designers and their association with the commandos. In recent years, Applegate resurrected the improved version he had designed with Fairbairn during the war. This Applegate-Fairbairn knife, now made by Blackjack Knives, is as good as a symmetric, double-edged dagger can get.

Fairbairn kept his knife-fighting course simple. In no way was it a complete system like *tantojutsu*. (This is assuming that Fairbairn knew one of the classical Japanese knife systems, because these are rarely taught even to Japanese students, much less to outsiders.) His knife and Smatchet (another larger blade he designed) moves appear to be based on saber-fencing, a style known primarily to British officers and cavalrymen. The F-S handle resembled that of a fencing foil, but it was held thumbs-up like the saber.

Ease of teaching and illustration is the advantage of a fencing method. That is why it has been incorporated into books on hand-to-hand fighting by Fairbairn, Drexel Biddle, Applegate, John Styers and myself. The disadvantage of fencing is that it gives no great edge to the skillful practitioner. The short blade will not allow the user to perform the range of parries possible

Photo courtesy of Imperial War Museum

During World War II, British commandos were issued a machete because a conventional bayonet could not be mounted on the Thompson submachine gun.

with a saber or jungle knife. However, military courses do not provide the time that is required to learn martial arts like tantojutsu or *pentjak silat*.

The rest of Fairbairn's method consisted of sentry-removal techniques and anatomical targets of opportunity. His sentry takeout involved a careful approach, the placing of the left hand over the mouth, and a point strike to the side of the neck. The carotid artery is probably the best target for a short blade because it can cause a fast loss of consciousness. Fairbairn included in his course materials a skeleton chart marked with arteries and vulnerable areas, noting the time required for unconsciousness. I consider these times to be highly speculative, especially the thrust to the heart, which is supposed to cause unconsciousness instantly. Even bullet wounds cannot do this with reliability. For example, on June 9, 1990, Los Angeles Police Department Officer Stacie Lim was shot through the heart with a .357 Magnum. She was able to stay on her feet and return fire with four rounds from her 9 mm Beretta, killing her attacker. She then made it through surgery, recovered and returned to duty. Because knives produce little or no impact shock compared to bullets, traditional martial arts instructors always teach their students to control the enemy's body manually until he becomes unconscious.

Modern Training

Since I wrote *Secrets of Modern Knife Fighting* in 1974, a number of volumes have appeared on the subject of blade fighting, as well as the weapons used. Two recent books are *Combat Use of the Double-Edged Fighting Knife* by Col. Rex Applegate and *Survival Fighting Knives* by Leroy Thompson.

Training films and videos are also available. These depend on the expert, sometimes photogenic, skills of martial artists such as Donald Angier, Ernie Franco or Harold Brosius. Another video, *Surviving Edged Weapons*, has been produced by Calibre Press for police-training purposes.

Practitioners of empty-hand arts such as karate and judo often attend one- or two-day seminars in knife fighting from "name" instructors like Dan Inosanto, Stephen K. Hayes and Chris Kent. Popular styles include Philippine *kali*, Indonesian pentjak silat and Japanese *ninjutsu*. Those whose primary interest is weaponry and who live close to these instructors' schools can spend a lifetime, rather than a two-day seminar, studying these arts.

Military Uses

Military training is broken up into hours, not years. The amount of time is based on the probability of the training being used in modern combat.

Except for special forces, hand-to-hand skills are rarely employed in an era when the average infantrymen carries an assault rifle with 900 rounds of ammunition.

In some armies and some units, hand-to-hand instruction has been dispensed with entirely—even for aggressiveness training—because the statistical chance of its use is almost zero. This reminds me of how some British airfields in North Africa were overrun in the past because the airmen had not been trained to use a rifle.

In contrast, Fairbairn has wisely recommended that all military personnel be given close-quarters and small-arms training. He reasoned that in modern war, any unit could be attacked by guerrillas or commando teams.

While one might disagree with Fairbairn or Applegate concerning the

Photo courtesy of Imperial War Museum

World War II-era British commandos often carried the Fairbairn-Sykes stiletto as a combat knife.

content of their close-combat programs and knife training, the idea of teaching these skills is above reproach. In medieval Japan, samurai were taught to use 18 weapons to cover any eventuality. When I was in the infantry, we still used a full-size battle rifle, the M-14. We practiced bayonet fighting in drills and on the assault course. In addition, we did hand-to-hand fighting in sand pits and attended lectures on the fine points of the garrote, hatchet, knife and improvised blackjack. This was added to regular training with hand grenades, as well as a variety of rifles and pistols.

The M-6 (for the M-14 rifle) and M-7 (for the M-16 rifle) bayonets could be used as a fighting knife, especially because the blade was taken directly from the World War II M-3 trench knife. Of course, most were in poor condition from abuse, oversharpening or deliberate dulling for training use, so soldiers in combat zones quickly came to rely on personal knives. This will likely also be the case with the current, much more expensive, M-9 survival bayonet.

Military training is necessarily brief. The traditional cost-effective method is to select healthy young men and bring them up to a physical and skill standard in the shortest time possible. Close-quarter battle, also known as combat jujutsu, of which knife fighting is a part, is not designed as a lifetime martial art. These skills, part of the honed reflexes of youth, rapidly degrade with age. Those soldiers or veterans who wish to retain their fighting skills must begin the long way of the martial arts, the way that Fairbairn used to acquire his original expertise.

MARTIAL ARTS BEHIND BARS

by Officer Jim Wagner • June 1999

Imagine stepping into a cage with the most violent people of our society, knowing they can turn on you at any moment. This is not the newest "ultimate martial arts tournament" in which winning means you're famous for a month and losing means you have to return to work tomorrow. I'm actually describing a very real arena where you may end up paying the ultimate price—your life. I am talking about the job of a corrections officer.

Every day thousands of corrections officers book, transport and guard America's prisoners. Whether in a city jail or a maximum-security penitentiary, things can turn volatile in an instant. I know because I spent two years as a corrections officer before becoming a cop. Prison is a place where you never turn your back on anyone, where you always double-check locks, and where dropping your guard can mean getting "shanked" (stabbed with an improvised weapon).

I teach a course called Jail and Prison Combatives throughout the United States. Until now, the techniques and tactics of correctional facilities have remained behind closed doors—and bars. In this column, I will reveal some techniques and offer a few pointers to help you survive crisis situations similar to those faced by corrections officers.

Edged-Weapons Defense

Corrections officers know that many prisoners are armed. Some weapons are smuggled in, while others are made on the premises. Criminals with loads of time on their hands quickly learn to be creative when it comes to fabricating weapons out of almost anything—strips of metal, pieces of melted plastic and even paint chips from the wall. That's why the possibility of getting stabbed remains a very real concern to every corrections officer.

I teach a technique called the knife-avoidance exercise, which offers a simple and effective means of defending yourself against cutting weapons. First, outfit your "attacker" with a rubber knife. You, the "victim," will be empty-handed, but you should wear eye protection. The attacker makes a sudden, violent move, slashing and stabbing at your vital areas. When he attacks, place your hands in front of you to guard your centerline. Move out of the way and slap the knife away with both hands. If the attacker is skilled with a knife, you will not be able to get the weapon out of his hand. Therefore, keep dodging and avoiding it in this manner until you can find your own weapon or escape.

Keep in mind that in a real-life situation, you will get cut. You can withstand multiple cuts to your hands and arms and still survive. The hospital can sew you up later. But you won't survive long with wounds to your torso. If you mentally prepare yourself for this in training, you won't be paralyzed with fear if you're cut during a real fight. To make your training more realistic, dip the rubber knife in stage blood. Seeing "blood" will condition your mind to the gore associated with a real knife wound, thus reducing the shock factor.

Another key to remember when it comes to edged-weapons defense is that the average knife fight lasts a mere five seconds and rarely goes beyond 10 seconds. If you are unable to neutralize the attacker or escape within the first four to eight seconds, your chance of surviving will be severely diminished. Thus, you have only moments to observe, orient, decide and act.

Many martial arts instructors teach knife-disarm techniques. They're good to know, but they seldom work. I've attacked hundreds of students—corrections officers, SWAT-team operators, patrol officers and special-forces personnel—in realistic scenarios in which I played the bad guy, and only a handful have survived. Those survivors did so by "shooting" me. Not one student ever disarmed me. (Of course, this test is always conducted at

Photo by Robert W. Young

Just as police and corrections officers prefer not to confront a resisting suspect one-on-one, criminal gangs prefer to attack their victim en masse.

the beginning of my class—before the students learn the knife-avoidance exercise.) In addition, I have survived two real knife attacks, and both times I was unable to disarm the subject—even with years of martial arts training behind me. With that said, let me offer this warning: If you want to live, you're better off using the knife-avoidance technique first.

Back to the Wall

One thing you should never do in a jail or prison is turn your back on an inmate. The moment you turn away or let someone get behind you, you're vulnerable. You immediately lose the tactical advantage, and you could end up getting blindsided. Likewise, whenever you are in a public place where violence can occur, you should position yourself with your back to the wall, if possible, so you can see everything around you.

If a crisis arises, you want to have adequate reaction time. You want to observe the warning signs early on. Scan the area for potential problems so you can be proactive, not just reactive. Being proactive means initiating a response in anticipation of an action. It means getting involved or escaping.

Avoidance

Avoiding a conflict beats fighting any day of the week. Police recruits are taught a demeanor of command presence. In other words, they must appear confident, authoritative and in control. If you have a commanding presence, you can prevent most conflicts. On the other hand, if you are soft-spoken, fail to make eye contact and appear to lack confidence, a crook will exploit those weaknesses in jail or on the street.

The only way to develop command presence—other than owning a God-given gift—is to train. Create fighting scenarios in which you must warn an aggressor to back off. For example, one person plays an aggressive panhandler, and you shout things like, "Get out of my way, or I'm going to call the cops!"

Disturbances

When criminals are cooped up together day in and day out, fights and riots often result. When such a conflict arises, corrections officers often believe they must immediately jump in the middle of it. However, rushing in can be dangerous. That's why they need to remember four rules: First, identify the situation; second, let other officers know that you're checking it out; third, call for backup; and fourth, don't unlock cell doors until it's safe to do so.

If you were to modify those rules for the crisis situations you may face, such as observing your neighbors fighting or seeing a robbery occurring, they would read: First, identify the situation; second, call the police and give them a complete account; third, be a good witness, not a casualty yourself; and fourth, if you are compelled to get involved, make sure the odds are stacked in your favor.

EDGED WEAPONS 101

by Officer Jim Wagner • November 1999

Recently, there's been a resurgence of interest in edged weapons. There are new magazines devoted to it, numerous articles written about it in all kinds of publications, and instructional videos and courses that specialize in it. Yet despite this popularity, many edged-weapons programs are deficient in the full tactical spectrum. This deficiency is not merely the result of the expanding number of practitioners or new "expert" instructors trying to meet the demand but of errant training methods and inferior techniques. In an effort to improve your skills and training methods, I will unveil some little-known facts that are rarely taught in edged-weapons programs.

Psychological Block

Human beings are reluctant to pierce another person's body in combat, and in a self-defense situation, that can prove disastrous. The ancient Romans were aware of this, and it was well documented by the historian Vegetius. Early in the Roman Empire's history, it was observed that most soldiers engaging in close-quarters battle used their sword to slash rather than thrust. Enemy soldiers were wounded but not stopped. (Cuts seldom kill, but penetrating thrusts are often fatal.) The Romans then began an aggressive training program that emphasized a two-inch thrusting technique. The re-education paid off, and the Roman army's exploits became legendary.

As is often the case in history, certain truths must be rediscovered. The advantage of thrusting over slashing had to be learned the hard way. Historians who study the American Civil War, World War I and other conflicts in which bayonet charges were ordered found that the soldiers charged at their enemy well enough and intended to run their targets through, but once they came face to face with the enemy, they chose to use their rifle like a club. Some part of our nature makes us prefer to swing at our opponent rather than to go for the immediate fatal blow.

Modern armies around the world still emphasize stabbing over slashing, and it is part of every combat soldier's basic training. Even in the modern sport of fencing, born out of ancient warfare practices, the rules state that in foil, epee and saber matches, a valid "hit" is a thrust to the torso because such a strike is likely to be fatal. In 1787 fencing master Domenico Angelo, considered the first instructor of modern fencing, wrote, "You cannot practice the thrust too much, it being the most essential and the most superior technique that is made in fencing."

Up Close and Personal

Why do human beings find it difficult to stab an enemy? One reason may be that stabbing is up close and personal. Lt. Col. Dave Grossman, author of *On Killing,* called it "intimate brutality." In modern *kali,* one is taught that the weapon is an extension of the hand. Indeed, the ancient samurai went even further, believing their sword was a symbol of their soul.

In a self-defense situation in which lethal force is justified, most people still find it hard to impale their attacker. Even though more people carry a knife than a gun, guns are the preferred method of self-defense. Yet both weapons are lethal. Guns can intimidate from a distance, whereas knives must be employed at close range. In the 1860s, a French military analyst named Ardant du Picq wrote: "To fight from a distance is instinctive in man. From the first day, he has worked to this end, and he continues to do so."

This truth is evidenced by today's intercontinental ballistic missiles and the expansion of the "less lethal" industries that supply law enforcement with pepper spray, bean-bag projectiles, sting balls, nets, incapacitating foams, etc. Although these products have their uses, there's a growing trend in law enforcement and the military to rely too heavily on them—to the point at which combat training programs are often neglected or discarded. Worst of all, edged-weapons programs are virtually nonexistent in law enforcement and are slowly being phased out in the U.S. armed forces.

The fact that edged weapons can be too "intimate" for some people

When using an edged weapon in combat, people tend to slash rather than stab—even though stabbing is more lethal.

is apparent from FBI case studies on psychopaths. Serial killers who use a knife view it as a phallic symbol, and they feel satisfaction when it penetrates a victim. That's why some bodies are found with a ridiculous number of puncture wounds. It's not the result of overkill but a deliberate act of gratification. Fortunately, the percentage of this type of person in society is extremely low. However, it is believed that 2 percent of the world's military has psychopathic tendencies. These people are referred to as "natural soldiers." I often tell my law-enforcement and military students that if someone attacks them with a knife, they are dealing with a person like this—someone who is not afraid of combat and has the psychological mind-set to back it up.

Overcoming Instinct

For the average person, knowing that there is a natural resistance to stabbing is the first step in overcoming the problem. Greater effectiveness in self-defense can be achieved through proper training. One proven method is called the multiple-stabbing exercise. Student A is armed with a rubber training knife, and student B holds a kicking shield in an upright position. On command, student A pumps the knife into the shield without stopping, pushing student B backward to mimic the aggression and dominance of an attacker. Student B slowly walks backward, absorbing the blows with the shield. As student A has student B on the run, student A continues to thrust and retract the training knife, all the while emitting a fierce war cry. The students will move forward and backward, covering a total distance of 30 to 40 yards. This exercise not only instills the idea of multiple thrusting moves but also develops endurance and the warrior spirit.

Another exercise is called the fatal-fight exercise. As the name implies, it teaches the importance of fatal target areas, or in cop speak, center mass. (Use of the term "fatal" implies stopping, not necessarily killing, the aggressor.) Two students arm themselves with rubber knives and put on eye protection. The goal is to "fatally" strike the opponent with a thrust to the torso or to slash the jugular vein in the neck (which actually is fatal). When the command to start is given, the students defend themselves. For one to win, he must successfully thrust his weapon into his opponent's torso, making the rubber blade bend. After retracting the weapon, he must escape from the danger zone before becoming a casualty himself. When a student loses, he is punished; a "mutual kill" gets both fighters punished. Because my students are strictly law-enforcement, corrections and military personnel, losing is unacceptable. On the streets, in the jails or on the battlefields, it means sacrificing your life. I order losers to go to one side of the room and do tortuous strength exercises.

Never Stop

When students are doing the fatal-fight exercise and a fatal blow occurs, I let them continue for about five seconds. Here's why:

- If you stop students every time there's a fatal blow, they will end up doing the same thing in real life. As they say, you fight the way you train. In a real encounter, you should never stop and give up, and you learn that only through proper training. Even if you think you may be mortally wounded, in pain or frightened, you shouldn't stop. A strike to a fatal area does not mean certain death. However, giving up may very well lead to death.

If your attacker sees you hesitate, stop or give up, his chase instinct will kick in. It tells him to take down anyone who runs. A good example of this is when a vicious dog threatens you. Most of the time you can intimidate the animal and make it back down. But if you start running, even the smallest dog will chase you. The same holds true for humans. Most killing done on ancient battlefields occurred while the enemy was in retreat.

- Immediately stopping a fight after a point is scored gives you a false sense of security and can lead you to believe the conflict is over because you got in a good shot. That is the danger of point sparring as practiced in many martial arts schools and tournaments. Although the participants understand that a match is not a real fight, it conditions the mind and body to act a certain way.

An example of that occurs during the firearms training of soldiers and law-enforcement officers. They are always taught to fire multiple rounds into the bad guy during a firefight because hitting a person with one bullet will not always stop him. Of course, after a police shooting, the question inevitably comes up: Why did the police have to fire so many rounds? It's as if the police had gone on a shooting spree! The reason is that the officers had to guarantee their survival.

Now, if a bullet sometimes fails to stop an attacker, so can a single stab wound in a self-defense situation. Therefore, when you train with edged weapons, you must think in terms of multiple strikes.

- In a real-life situation, an attacker may be capable of fighting even after he sustains a fatal wound. For example, if his jugular vein is cut, he could still have five seconds or more before his brain depletes its blood supply. Thus, he may be able to seriously injure or kill you. The average knife fight lasts only five seconds, so the possibilities are endless. Remember: A knife fight is not over until your attacker is rendered unable to fight.

EDGED WEAPONS 102—DEFENSE

by Officer Jim Wagner • December 1999

If you are attacked by someone with a knife, you will probably not perceive the threat until he is on top of you. During the first few vital seconds, you will be unarmed. Even if you are a law-enforcement officer, it is unlikely that you'll have your weapon in hand at the moment of attack because most officer-related stabbings occur during the pat-down, handcuffing or while the suspect is in custody.

Distance is the key to survival. Twenty-one feet is the minimum safe distance to be from a subject with an edged weapon. A determined person can cover that distance in 1.5 seconds. Known as the Tueller Rule, this observation has been ingrained in officers' minds for years through the popular law-enforcement-only video titled *Surviving Edged Weapons* (Calibre Press). At 21 feet, the officer has time to get his gun out and fire two rounds. Distance, however, is a luxury that few victims of a knife fight ever receive.

Because of the close ranges involved, the average edged-weapons fight lasts less than five seconds. During that time, serious injury or death can result. The most critical portion of the fight is your reaction. If your first move is to disarm the suspect or move in on him—as many self-defense courses teach—your chance of survival will be greatly reduced.

Learning From Experience

I teach a course called Edged-Weapons Defense. Over the years, I've trained thousands of officers, agents and deputies. At the beginning of each class, I have the students wear their gun belt with their duty weapon holstered. I then stand in front of one of them at "interrogation distance"—about six to eight feet away—with my hands in my pockets. I tell the student, "I have a concealed rubber knife, and I will attack you with it sometime during your contact with me. You can hit me, kick me, push me away or simulate shooting me with your gun. Just do what you have to to survive." The student has a tactical advantage because he knows what's coming; on the street, you never know what someone will do.

Gripping his gun, the student approaches and starts interrogating me like he would while on duty. I suddenly pull the knife from my pocket or the small of my back and go for the chest or throat. The results are ugly. Ninety percent of the students are "critically" injured in less than five seconds, unable to even unholster their weapon. Nine percent are able to draw their weapon and get off a round but are cut at the moment of discharge (a "mutual kill"). Only 1 percent are able to survive the encounter and neutralize me with an evasion maneuver and a lethal shot.

If the student has no firearm, the statistics are even worse. The casualties for unarmed corrections personnel are 100 percent when doing this exercise for the first time. However, the tables are turned by the end of my one-day course. More than two-thirds of the students are then able to survive the same brutal attack without sustaining a life-threatening wound.

Disarms Are Dangerous

No student has ever disarmed me in a full-speed, full-contact attack. The closest anyone has ever come was when a huge Marine grabbed hold of my weapon hand like a vice grip. He thought he had me until I used my free hand to pull his baton from his gun belt and whack his head a few times—gently, of course.

Now, I'm not saying I'm "Mr. Hotshot Instructor With So Much Experience That People Can't Disarm Me." The results are the same even when I let inexperienced students play the role of the attacker. The point is, if men and women who have actual street- or jail-fighting experience and who are dedicated to their training can't stop a realistic knife attack, what makes you think you can? The odds are clearly stacked against you.

A disarm maneuver should be your last resort. I'm not saying that just because of my observations of thousands of students; I know it's true from the two times I was attacked by a subject with a knife. The first incident occurred while I was in the Army, and the second occurred while I was on police patrol. I was unable to disarm the attacker both times. The first time, I had no choice but to grab the guy's weapon hand, and it almost resulted in a bowie knife in my Adam's apple. The second time, I had no opportunity to try to disarm the suspect. The attacker came in too fast, and he did not extend his arm at all. All I saw was a flicker of shiny metal moving toward my chest. I did what my instincts told me to do: Jump back and get out of the way. Obviously, it worked.

Evasion Exercise

Although not quite as glamorous or action-packed as a disarm technique, the first move you should do in a surprise attack is evade the blade. To teach students how to avoid the attack, I created the knife-evasion exercise. Your job is to avoid the weapon altogether. The farther you can get from it, the better off you are. While performing this exercise, safety is paramount. The trainer and trainee must wear wraparound eye protection, because even rubber or plastic training knives can injure the eyes. Many instructors train with a wooden or nonpointed metal training knife, but such an implement is not suitable for this exercise because it is done at full speed and with full contact that makes the blade bend backward.

When you are attacked by a suspect with a knife, you should immediately back off and bring your hands up to guard your centerline. Your arms should be extended in front of you, with your elbows slightly bent. They may get cut, but they can always be sewn up once the fight is over. You can't afford to take any slashes or stabs to the torso or head. Penetration of more than 4 centimeters may not be fatal, but it can instantaneously induce shock.

The problem with most law-enforcement officers who have had little or no training in edged weapons is that the first thing they go for during an attack is their sidearm. I've heard many officers joke, "If someone pulls a knife on me, I'll just shoot him." The facts tell a different story. At the last police department in which I worked, an officer was stabbed in the arm with a screwdriver. He could not unholster his weapon during the assault. Afterward, I offered to train my fellow officers on my own time and at my own expense, but the training bureau didn't think that was necessary and declined. It is sad that so few police officers still believe that going for their gun is the best move.

The key to surviving an edged-weapons attack is to get distance between yourself and the knife. You do that by aggressively slapping away the incoming weapon with both hands and sidestepping to get your body out of the line of attack. It's harder for the attacker to move laterally than to pursue you straight back. If you do have to retreat backward, don't go too far without sidestepping or the attacker will overrun you.

Once you have put some space between yourself and your attacker and still can't unholster your gun, kick the attacker in the knee or gouge his eyes. If you still can't get your weapon out, get your hands back in front of your centerline and go through another cycle. If you have no weapon, grab a handful of dirt, a lamp or a jacket and use it. Remember that the longer the fight goes on, the slimmer your chance of survival. Few can last more than 10 seconds without launching a damaging counterattack or running away.

Last Resort

Although disarming an attacker with an edged weapon should be your last resort, you still must master disarming techniques. The general rule of thumb when employing them is: If you can't disarm him in three moves, don't try. Your first move will be to block the weapon hand. Your second move will be to lock or redirect that hand. Your third move will be to deliver a disabling strike. Any more than three moves and things get too complicated and are more likely to fail.

Whatever disarming techniques you practice, you should be able to perform them at full speed and with full contact. Obviously it takes time to build up to that level. Once you're comfortable with the techniques, your trainer should vary the angle of attack. You should be able to adapt to any angular variation and perform successfully whether your partner is right- or left-handed, using an ice-pick grip or a fist grip, or holding his arm extended or retracted.

Disarm Drill

Learning individual disarm techniques has little value unless they are tested in a realistic way. That's why I created the disarm drill.

Place an unarmed student (trainee) in a fighting stance with his eyes closed. Have a trainer with a rubber knife move into a position anywhere around the student. The instructor should clap his hands and make a lot of noise while the trainer gets into position so the trainee cannot hear where he is. On command, the trainee opens his eyes. The trainer immediately launches his attack at close range. The trainee has only a split second to orient himself and attempt the disarm. There is no time to think—only to react. Whether the initial move is effective or not, the trainee should go all the way until the weapon is secured.

The more the disarm drill is practiced, the faster the trainee's reactions become and the fewer mistakes he makes. Of course, the techniques never come out quite as clean as when they are practiced step by step. That's OK. They don't have to look good; they just have to work.

DEVELOPING A WARRIOR ATTITUDE

by Officer Jim Wagner • February 2000

Aggressiveness is a trait martial artists must possess—or at least seek to acquire. Developing aggressive behavior in beginners without discouraging them can be difficult for an instructor—whether he teaches civilians or law-enforcement and military personnel. Although you would expect police officers and soldiers to be more aggressive than the average person, that is not always the case. I often find myself having to cultivate the aggressiveness of my students before I can take them to the next step—learning how to fight.

Even though sparring is a great preparatory drill for real-life threats, beginners and timid newcomers are rarely ready to jump right into it. Therefore, the instructor must have other "tools" in his instructional toolbox to introduce them to physical contact.

Every person has the fight-or-flight instinct, but not everyone possesses a warrior attitude: valor, fortitude, bravery, fearlessness and courage. The instructor's primary goal should be to develop this lifesaving attitude in his students rather than merely to teach them techniques. However, an instructor who pushes students into high-anxiety situations before they are emotionally ready risks evoking the flight response—which usually leads them to drop out of class or, in the case of law enforcement and the military, to develop a negative attitude toward officer safety training.

Even though sparring in a studio is not life threatening, it evokes physiological responses that parallel those of real combat: fear, knotted stomach, paralysis, shallow breathing and even vomiting. Experienced fighters may find themselves going through the same "crisis cycle" when facing a superior opponent.

The best way to get your feet wet is to follow a step-by-step approach that uses slow, methodical conditioning to reduce anxiety. In other words, to get accustomed to violence, you must start with exercises and low-risk drills and gradually increase the intensity from there. To help you accomplish that, I have developed a series of exercises called "contact conditioners."

Knife-Evasion Exercise

If you're like most people, you will not be able to last the first five seconds of a real knife fight without receiving a life-threatening stab or cut to the torso, head or neck. Rarely will you be able to disarm an attacker. Your best hope is to avoid the initial attack long enough to counterattack, go for your own weapon or run.

To perform the knife-evasion exercise, have your partner grasp a rubber knife. You have safety goggles but no weapon. Your partner tries to stab or cut you while charging at full speed. He never gives you a chance to grab his weapon. You keep your hands up and slap your partner's knife hand away to defend yourself. Move from side to side or backward to avoid getting cut. If you can survive for five seconds—the time the average knife fight lasts—you win.

Gladiatorial-Combat Exercise

This exercise instills aggression and the will to survive, and it reinforces the lessons learned in the knife-evasion exercise. You and your partner wear eye protection and grab a soft rubber knife. Each of you then attempts to deliver a fatal blow: a stab to the chest, abdomen or head, or a cut to the neck. Defensive wounds to the hands and arms do not count because they are not usually life threatening. If you are "stabbed" in the arm or leg, you lose the use of that limb. (If it is an arm, it must go behind your back; if it is a leg, you must go down on that knee.)

Even if one of you delivers a fatal blow, the fight continues for another five seconds because in real life, adrenaline-charged fighters rarely go down as soon as they are wounded. They may still have enough life in them to do you in.

Leap-Frog Knife Exercise

Nothing creates more anticipation in a student than the leap-frog knife exercise. It teaches quick reaction and speed, and it incorporates the lessons of the knife-evasion exercise and gladiatorial-combat exercise.

You and your partner lie on the mat facing each other about 25 feet apart. A rubber knife is placed between the two of you. The instructor gives the command to start, and both of you leap for the weapon. The first one to gain control of it, stab the other person in the torso and disengage wins.

Hope for Everyone

The exercises described above work for everyone, from beginners to advanced students. They build confidence by allowing you to engage in limited physical contact one step at a time. When you survive them, you learn a little more about yourself and your limits. In no time, you will be in the ring sparring with the best of them.

THE TACTICAL FOLDING KNIFE
A Self-Defense Alternative for a Violent World
by Kevan W. Matthews • October 2000

As much as we hate to admit it, violence is a prevalent part of American culture. The need to be able to defend yourself is obvious, yet for some people, carrying a concealed handgun may not be the best choice. One often-overlooked alternative is the tactical folding knife. It is small and relatively unobtrusive, but it will allow you to equalize the disparity of force between you and virtually any attacker.

Knife Law

Laws regarding knives differ from state to state, but there are some commonalities. First, anything that was not designed to be used as a weapon can be possessed for its intended purpose. For example, a flashlight is considered a tool—until you hit someone over the head with it. Similarly, a knife can be considered a tool—until you are forced to use it to defend yourself.

Second, carrying an automatic knife (switchblade) or a double-edged knife (dagger) is illegal in most states, and carrying a knife with a serrated blade can get you in trouble in some states. Usually, however, carrying a folding knife with a blade less than 4 inches long is OK provided that you have a legitimate reason; unfortunately, self-defense is generally not considered a good reason. A folder with a blade less than 3 inches long will normally not warrant a second glance. (I've passed through airport security checkpoints to board a plane with my Spyderco Worker knife, which has a 2-inch blade, but I've been denied access to an aircraft because of a *kubotan* on my key ring.)

When an item such as a knife, baseball bat, pair of scissors or flashlight is used in self-defense, it is considered a lethal weapon and is subject to the laws that govern justification for the use of deadly force. Generally, the law allows you to use deadly force to protect yourself and others when you reasonably believe you are threatened with serious bodily injury or death. One other condition must be met: You have to reasonably believe that a lesser degree of force will be insufficient to repel the threat. If you are threatened by an unarmed attacker of the same height and weight who says he's going to punch you in the nose, the use of deadly force will not be justified. Therefore, unless you can prove that you reasonably believed that the threat would result in serious bodily injury or death, you cannot justify introducing a knife into the altercation.

However, slightly altering the circumstances can radically affect the situation. If you are a 110-pound woman and your attacker is a 270-pound man who has just threatened to body-slam and rape you, you might believe that he is capable of carrying out his threat. Therefore, you might be justified to use deadly force.

In many states, you also have a duty to retreat: Before deciding to use deadly force, you have an obligation to avoid any action that could result in the taking of a life by removing yourself from the situation. This obligation generally applies in public places; however, it does not apply in your home or place of business if you own the company. Keep in mind that the right to defend yourself does not extend to property. If a bad guy wants to take your belongings, just give them to him. You can't just whip out your trusty knife and go to work on him to protect your personal effects.

Knife Features

Knives come in essentially two types: fixed blade and folding. The advantages of a fixed-blade knife include superior strength and faster deployment.

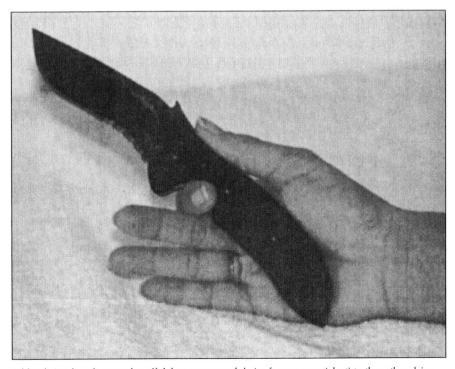

Folding knives have become the self-defense weapon of choice for many martial artists, the author claims.

The advantage of a folding knife is that it's easier to conceal, and that single characteristic makes it the best choice for most martial artists.

When choosing a tactical folding knife, you should examine three features. The first is the locking mechanism. Although there are several ways to secure an open blade, the two most common are the back lock and the liner lock. The back lock holds the blade open with a piece of metal located on the backside of the handle. To close the knife, you must press that piece to disengage the lock. The liner lock uses a piece of the metal lining inside the handle to keep the blade open. It creates a brace beneath the blade, making it remarkably strong and nearly impossible to disengage accidentally.

The second feature is blade type. Just about any kind of steel can be used to make a knife that is suitable for self-defense; however, fighting is not all there is to survival. For example, you may need to use it to cut away clothing or a seat belt in an emergency. Four common types of steel used to make tactical knives are ATS-34, AUS-6, ATS-55 and GIN-1. They have been proved to be strong and durable enough for the needs of most users. Without providing a lesson in metallurgy, one thing to remember is that the higher the carbon content of the steel, the harder the blade will be. This means that it will hold its edge longer but will be more susceptible to corrosion. A knife produced with softer steel might be easier for beginners to sharpen and may hold up better in a humid environment. A knife made of steel that is rated below 440 will be too soft for most tactical purposes.

The third feature is ergonomics. Your knife should feel natural in your hand—like an extension of your arm. It should be light, and the handle should have curves that correspond to the shape of your grip. That will keep

Photo by Kevan Matthews

A tactical folding knife offers several advantages over other types of edged weapons: It fits nicely into a pocket, it clips in place for added security and it snaps open with a flick of the thumb.

your hand—which can get sweaty or blood-soaked—from riding up on the blade if it makes contact with bone. Some knife manufacturers, including Benchmade and Emerson, design their blades with a thumb ramp or a set of thumb grooves to prevent that from happening.

You should choose a blade according to your intended use. For self-defense, many professionals prefer the *tanto* design. Its tip is stronger than that of a conventional knife because it maintains its full thickness almost to the end. Consequently, it has a superior piercing ability. Another virtue of the tanto design is its versatility. For tasks such as skinning and detail cutting, it is not the most highly recommended design, but if it's all that's available, you won't be disappointed.

Knife Skills

To allow for one-handed opening, most tactical knives are designed with either a thumbstud or thumbhole. Better-quality knives are balanced to allow you to deploy them kinetically using a quick, flicking motion.

You should consider owning more than one blade: a primary and a backup. Practice deploying each one quickly from your primary and secondary positions, and using both hands. Also practice under stress without using your thumb. Think about what you would do if you lost your balance, if your clothing interfered with your hands or if your opponent tried to stop you. Use a stopwatch and a partner to hone your ability to deploy your knife under those conditions. Be sure to practice doing it even when you have a less-than-ideal grip.

Most tactical folders come with a clothing clip, and some allow you to mount it on either side of the handle. Choose the position that corresponds to your right-handedness or left-handedness. Remember that the position of the knife in your pocket or on your belt can affect the speed with which you access it. A knife stored in the blade-tip-up position can generally be deployed more quickly than one stored with its tip down. A drawback to using the blade-tip-up position is that it may become exposed and cause accidental injury. As a result, many beginners find the blade-tip-down position simple, safe and effective.

Knife Tactics

In the heat of battle, things don't happen the way they do in the movies, and techniques are never as crisp as they are in practice. However, there are some things you can do to tip the scales in your favor. As with any situation that involves weapons, it helps to have training. Tactical and technical knowledge of edged weapons is only part of the equation. You must also know when to deploy the knife. Your training must be not only situational but also scenario-based. That means you must train to resolve the problem of "If my opponent does this, I should do that" and recognize the signals that precede a lethal encounter.

In the civilian edged-weapon training offered by the Tactical Defense Institute of West Union, Ohio, students learn one of the most important lessons of knife combat: Train for the worst. If you're involved in a fight with a knife-wielding attacker, you will be cut. Your tactics must help you decrease the chance that you will be killed. One of the most important ways to accomplish that goal is to adopt a defensive posture that protects your centerline, along which most of your vital organs and blood vessels are located.

Carl Boockholdt, lead instructor for the institute's defensive knife program, describes three zones of importance with which you should familiarize yourself: the safe zone, the danger zone and the kill zone.

"The safe zone is that distance at which the attacker must take two steps before his blade can reach you," Boockholdt says. "Space equals time. In the safe zone, you have more time to create more distance, deploy your own blade or acquire an improvised weapon.

"The danger zone is that distance at which the attacker's blade can touch you with only one step. In this range, you must concentrate more intently on your attacker's movements.

"The kill zone is that distance within which your attacker's blade can impale you without his taking a single step. If escape is not an option, you must be mobile enough to negotiate the safe and danger zones, then at just the right moment, move into the kill zone to effect your attack before retreating."

Knife Strategy

Once you've made the decision to engage an attacker, you should utilize stealth, deception, surprise, speed and violence to win. If possible, avoid letting your attacker become aware of your skills. Before you attack, try to use non-confrontational body language. Your verbal skills may serve to de-escalate the situation or distract him before you strike. Move when he least expects it. With blinding speed and overkill, attack whatever part of his body he presents. From the outside, start with vascular targets and work your way into structural targets, because they control your attacker's ability to pursue you.

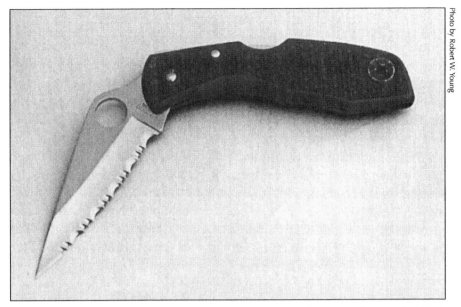

Photo by Robert W. Young

Instead of a thumbstud, some folding knives, such as the Spyderco Delica CLIPIT, feature a thumbhole for rapid deployment.

Recognize that when you are engaged in a conflict in which edged weapons are being used, distance and barriers are your friends. His knife can't hit what it can't touch. You must be able to stay away from his blade as long as necessary.

During an edged-weapon assault, don't concern yourself with complicated disarming techniques. A disarm will occur if you concentrate on immobilizing the threat (weapon), and it will be incidental to the wounds you inflict on the assailant.

If you have read all of this article, you deserve to be congratulated; you have taken the first step in the responsible use of alternative lethal force. Choosing to carry a tactical knife and seeking instruction in the ways in which it ought to be used reflect your desire to conquer all challenges. However, realize that you have taken only the first step. You must train under a qualified instructor, then practice on your own and modify your routine to mimic the types of combat you expect to encounter. Remember the military maxim: Sweat more in training to bleed less in battle.

KNIFE WISDOM FROM WORLD WAR II
Real Self-Defense Never Goes Out of Style!

by Thomas J. Nardi, Ph.D. • *Photos courtesy of John Kary* • *December 2000*

The year was 1940. The Nazi blitzkrieg had conquered Poland, Denmark and Norway. The German panzer division took Luxembourg in one day, Holland in five and Belgium in seven. British Prime Minister Neville Chamberlain resigned because of his misguided policy of appeasement. Winston Churchill became the leader. War was a harsh reality.

The English army had tried to stop the Nazi advance in Belgium, but German military might proved too quick and strong for the British, who were forced to retreat to the sea. From May 29 to June 4, 1940, more than 336,000 British troops were evacuated. They used any vessel they could find—from destroyers to fishing boats—to transport their soldiers out of danger.

Although the troops were safe, the British military arsenal had been abandoned at Dunkirk. The army would not be able to fight again until it was totally rearmed. Before that could happen, France fell to the Nazis, and Britain was defenseless and facing the very real risk of a Nazi airborne invasion.

William E. Fairbairn

It was against this desperate backdrop that William E. Fairbairn emerged. He led the Shanghai Municipal Defender Police from 1927 to 1940. Shanghai had been among the most lawless cities of the world. Vicious armed gangs trained in kung fu kept the city in an almost constant state of riot. Fairbairn managed to restore order to the city by personally intervening in street brawls, shootouts and urban battles. He was an accomplished fighter as well as an instructor in hand-to-hand and close-quarters combat. In 1940, Fairbairn returned to England, where he was commissioned as a captain in the army. Shortly after his departure, Shanghai fell to the Japanese.

Fairbairn was charged with preparing the military and civilian population of Britain to meet—and defeat—the expected German storm-trooper invasion. His task was to instruct a select group of men and women who would go on to teach his fighting methods to others.

Fairbairn's background included training in traditional Asian martial arts. His second-degree black-belt certificate in Kodokan judo was signed by the art's founder, Jigoro Kano. Fairbairn had also studied the Chinese art of pa kua chang under the same master who instructed the bodyguards of the Chinese empress.

 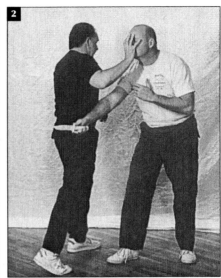

Martial artists should concentrate on learning a few good techniques for self-defense. To illustrate two such moves, John Kary (left) uses his left arm to off-line the assailant's knife thrust (1) before delivering a right palm-heel strike to the face (2).

Fairbairn was proficient in the Western combat arts, including boxing, wrestling and fencing. Perhaps even more important from a pragmatic point of view, he was well-versed in every type of back-alley dirty fighting and gutter trick favored by street thugs. His own personal combat experiences gave him insight into what merely looked good, what would work only with a cooperative partner and what would stop a determined, crazed assailant.

Fairbairn's job was not easy. He had a limited time in which to train those who would be his next-generation instructors. His first class consisted of 12 officers, and he had just 12 weeks to prepare them to teach others.

Lethal Methods

The times demanded that Fairbairn's methods be as lethal as possible. Moreover, they had to be learned easily by the average person, and they had to work against a determined and better-armed combatant. The methods that Fairbairn adopted transformed the typical British civilian, regardless of gender or physical ability, into a worthy match for the expected invaders.

Those close-quarters-combat methods all but disappeared when the war ended. That was partly because many top military officials believed they were too lethal to be taught to a peacetime army. As the military's role leaned more toward policing and peacekeeping, the need for deadly hand-to-hand skills appeared to decline.

The threat from Germany and Japan may have ended nearly a half-century ago, but the need for effective close-quarters-combat skills has not. Indeed, it could be argued that today's street thug is even more ruthless and dangerous than the military enemies of the past.

Fortunately, those original World War II fighting methods have been preserved and passed down by certain people. Foremost among them is John Kary.

Kary is the founder of American combatives, a synthesis of the work of Fairbairn and other World War II-era masters of hand-to-hand combat. A highly decorated Marine Corps veteran of the Vietnam War, Kary has adapted the original methods to meet the needs of contemporary Americans. His approach is ideal for equipping average men and women with formidable survival skills because it emphasizes simple, direct and aggressive techniques.

Fairbairn's Philosophy

"American combatives is not a self-defense art," Kary explains. "We have preserved Fairbairn's philosophy of attacking the assailant rather than defending against him."

Fairbairn emphasized that his students needed to put aside the famous British sense of fair play. He warned about the folly of trying to be sporting when you're facing a vicious attacker.

That wartime philosophy needs to be adopted if you want to survive on the streets today. He challenges many of the so-called self-defense methods currently being taught. In particular, attitudes toward weapons defense illustrate the shortcomings, Kary says. "The knife is one of the most common street weapons, yet most martial artists have no idea how to fight against it. Or worse, they rely on techniques that are pure nonsense."

Kary's knowledge of knife attacks came from several sources. First, he has pored over the teachings of Fairbairn and his contemporaries—men with plenty of firsthand experience with cold steel. Second, Kary has interviewed many military and law-enforcement personnel who have faced knife attacks, and their reports of what works and what doesn't match the teachings of Fairbairn. Finally, while in the Marines, Kary witnessed many blade assaults.

"I've seen real knife fights, and let me tell you, they weren't pretty," he says. "Forget about the fancy moves and fencing techniques. It just doesn't happen that way."

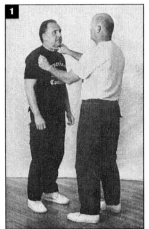

An assailant holds a knife to John Kary's throat (1). Kary uses his left hand to slap the knife hand down and simultaneously raises his right arm (2). He then slams his right palm into the assailant's face (3) and executes an ax hand to the neck (4). To finish the fight, Kary blasts a side kick into the back of the other man's knee (5).

Like Fairbairn, Kary has had plenty of firsthand experience with the reality of hand-to-hand fighting. Shortly after his arrival in Vietnam, he saved a South Vietnamese officer from a Viet Cong assassin. His victory earned him the coveted South Vietnamese Cross of Gallantry. It was the first of many medals, including the Purple Heart, that Kary would receive while in Southeast Asia.

Kary's military service was cut short by a Viet Cong booby trap. While on a jungle patrol near Danang, one of the members of his 12-man reconnaissance team tripped a wire that triggered an explosion. Eight men died instantly. Kary survived, but the explosion cost him his sight. He was also left deaf in one ear and with a severely damaged hip.

Years of rehab plus an indomitable spirit allowed Kary to overcome those physical limitations. He is now recognized as a master instructor in hand-to-hand combat.

Simple and Direct

American combatives instructors advocate simple and direct responses to a knife attack. There are no arm locks, throws or pressure-point tactics. Survivors of actual encounters know that such techniques simply do not work. Kary's philosophy is to teach a few techniques that can be applied to a variety of attacks rather than a large number of different, unrelated techniques.

"At no point during an attack do I think of defense," Kary says. "I'm only concerned with getting the blade off of my body or off-lining it. I want to get at the attacker. My entire focus is on striking the attacker."

Like Fairbairn, Kary emphasizes a limited number of striking techniques—perhaps the most prominent of which is the edge-of-the-hand blow, which he calls the "ax hand."

"The ax hand allows for a very powerful, penetrating blow to be delivered with very little risk of injury to the one striking," Kary says. "We never use a closed-fist punch because experience has shown that you are quite likely to damage your own hand."

Kary also favors palm-heel strikes to the chin, low side kicks to the knee and slaps to the groin. These are simple techniques that can be performed under the high stress of an attack.

"On the street, there are no rounds and no timeouts, so each blow must be decisive," Kary says. "Each one must be capable of ending the attack immediately."

Asian Arts

Many American martial artists seem to forget that there is relatively little street crime in places like Okinawa and Japan. That is because most Asian countries have very strict weapons-control laws, which means that knife attacks are relatively uncommon. As a result, many Asian arts lack a strong foundation in the reality of the blade.

For example, instructors often teach techniques that are based on grabbing the attacker's knife hand. Kary cautions against such a strategy: "Never try to grab or trap the weapon hand. If you do, your mind will focus on the grab and your attention will be diverted from your attack. You'll end up grappling, and against a knife, grappling is a good way to get yourself killed."

"Instead, I teach off-lining the knife with a smooth nudge," Kary continues. "You only need to move it an inch or two. If you try to move it too far, you will rush and miss it altogether."

Many instructors today have precious little awareness of what happens

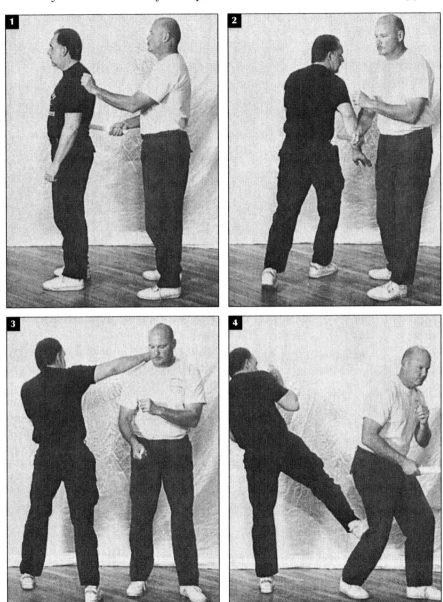

When threatened from behind, John Kary turns clockwise and off-lines the attacker's knife with his right arm (1-2). Kary then cocks his right arm and unleashes an ax hand into the other man's neck (3), followed by a side kick to the back of the knee (4).

during a knife attack. Some even believe that it is acceptable to use a limb as bait, allowing themselves to be cut in order to close on their assailant. Great danger lies along that path, Kary says. "I've personally seen what a knife can do to the human body. A knife cut does not close as neatly as a bullet hole does. Cuts are ugly and frightening. The body goes into shock very quickly when you're cut."

Fantasy Fights

Many of the knife defenses taught in traditional schools are "fantasy defenses," Kary says. They work in the *dojo* (training hall) but would be suicidal on the street.

"A lot of these defenses are predicated on an attacker [who does] not use his free hand to strike," Kary says. "But when someone is serious about killing you, he will be stabbing, striking, kicking, biting and spitting. He is not going to just stick his knife hand out there as if his body is frozen."

Kary teaches his students to move away from the attacker's free hand and use the all-important but often-neglected concept of distancing. "Distance appreciation is crucial when facing a knife," he says. "If the attacker is three or four feet away from you, you really can't do anything other than distract him. I suggest throwing anything available, such as a handkerchief, coins or gravel into his eyes, then attacking. If you simply try to sidestep or move at that distance, the knifer will just follow your movement and stab you."

"In the most common type of knife attack—a mugging—the attacker will put the knife against your body," Kary says. "This makes it somewhat easier for you because you are close and the knife is stationary. Once the knife is in motion, it becomes much more dangerous."

Although the Axis powers no longer threaten peaceable people, street thugs and muggers do. Fortunately for modern martial artists, the combat methods of William E. Fairbairn that proved so effective in war have been preserved by men like John Kary so that they may serve their purpose once again in peace.

REALITY OF THE BLADE
'No Bull' Answers to 13 Questions Black Belt Readers Have Asked About Knife Attacks

by James LaFond • Photos by Khristopher Kramer • January 2001

Author's note: This article is not about the art of using a knife. Its sole purpose is to illustrate the nature and dynamics of edged-weapon encounters, as experienced by more than 75 survivors of such attacks.

Case #13-04: night, 20-30 seconds, eyewitness

Iggy had just turned down a dimly lit alley behind a waterfront bar, where he had parked his Harley earlier in the day. Before he reached his bike, he heard a commotion to his rear. As he turned, he saw three large men silhouetted in the glow of a streetlight, dragging a smaller man into the alley.

The large men were to Iggy's right, half-facing him as they held the smaller man with their left hands and beat him with their right fists. All three attackers used this same tactic. They appeared to be under the influence of cocaine or amphetamines. One man held the victim's right shoulder, one his collar and the other his left shoulder while they punched him in the head, face and body.

Iggy knew the small man—and knew him to be very drunk—but he did not get involved for one very good reason: As the defender was being pummeled and driven farther into the alley, he reached into a pocket and pulled out a *balisong* (butterfly knife). Iggy could see the blade shine under the streetlight. "But they didn't see the blade," he reported. "They must've thought they were getting punched."

The defender drove the blade into the left side of the right-most man at least five times. After every two thrusts into the knife-side man, he stabbed the center man once in the gut. The stabs seemed to sink in beneath the ribs with a smacking thud—the sound of the knifer's fist hitting flesh. Iggy was adamant that the knifer achieved full—about 4 inches—penetration with most of his thrusts.

The attackers seemed oblivious to the blade and successfully completed their assault, driving the defender to the wall and stuffing him headfirst into an empty trash can.

When they backed up so that the smaller man was no longer in their shadow, they could see what Iggy had seen. "When he crawled out of the trash can and stood up, you could see [the knife] under the streetlight," Iggy said. "They did a body check and bolted. He kind of wobbled down the alley."

This encounter certainly was not a typical knife fight. Usually it's one knife-armed aggressor versus one unarmed defender. But Iggy's story does illuminate two common aspects of blade use:

- The blade is often *unseen* and *unfelt*.
- The blade is not always a decisive factor. The knife-armed defender in this situation did not alter the course of the altercation by seriously injuring two of his attackers.

A re-creation of a successful knife defense by a store manager with a purple belt in jujutsu: The martial artist heard the click of the lock-blade but he did not see it, was not cut and did not disarm the attacker. (For illustrative purposes, Arturo Gabriel is shown performing the restraining hold.)

Understanding Violence

Since June 1996, I have interviewed hundreds of survivors of violent attacks. They are a diverse lot: from Iggy, who tends to wind up in the wrong place at the wrong time, to Betty, a secretary who witnessed a fight between two huge young women on the sidewalk beneath her office window.

Interview notes were transferred to a graph-paper index and used to answer eight to 42 questions, depending on the complexity and intensity of the encounter.

As of January 2000, I had recorded 1,600 incidents and done a statistical breakdown of the first 1,000. The edged-weapon stats presented in this article are derived from 256 such encounters involving 512 parties and constituting 275 uses. (Note: Three men stabbing one man equals one act, two parties and three uses.) The following statistics were gleaned from the study:

- 40 percent of all acts of violence involve a weapon.
- 27 percent of armed encounters involve a firearm.
- 44 percent of armed encounters involve one of a host of improvised—and mostly blunt—weapons. The most common is a beer bottle; the most injurious is a baseball bat, pipe or two-by-four; and the most deadly is an automobile. Most martial arts training is more useful against high-commitment blunt weapons than against firearms and edged weapons.
- 11 percent of all violence and 29 percent of armed encounters involve a knife or knifelike weapon, such as a razor or shank. Although these are the preferred weapons of the lone male felon, their practical application is the least understood of all. Knives are also among the most deadly of weapons.

For the purpose of this study, I have ranked edged weapons from most to least common:

1. knives (including fixed and folding blades)
2. razors
3. shanks (prison-made stabbing weapons)
4. swords (including oversize knives and edged tools)

The complete study encompasses 50 photos, 100 stories and 737 statistics. Compressing this information into an article would either distort the picture or put the reader to sleep. So instead of abridging the study here, I will answer the blade-fighting questions posed by eight *Black Belt* readers in hopes that they might address the concerns of thousands more.

Question 1

What type of knife is most often used by an attacker?

Forty-eight percent of knifers use a version of the common folder—a pocket or case knife with a 3- to 5-inch blade that is stabilized by a locking mechanism. The folder is the blade most likely to be used by a member of a group. The second-most common attack knife is the butcher knife; it is used 20 percent of the time.

Question 2

How can you tell whether a knife-armed attacker knows how to use a blade effectively?

The knife is not a distance weapon, like a gun. It is also not a good confrontational midrange weapon, like a club. The knife is most effective when employed in a stealthy manner from within punching range. Shanks are typically used while grappling, often on the floor. Straight razors are most often used in a standing clinch.

Using a jacket or coat as a blade catcher with the knife hand cocked in the ready position is the most successful blade-to-blade fighting tactic. (For illustrative purposes, Arturo Gabriel is shown.)

The competent knifer does not show his weapon unless he is defending himself. Attempts to conceal the dominant hand indicate possession of a weapon. Attempts to close with a concealed hand indicate deployment of an edged weapon. Attempts to corner the victim indicate aggression and awareness. Lack of hesitation is the hallmark of the effective knifer. The more stealthy and aggressive the behavior he demonstrates, the more effective he is likely to be.

Question 3

Is a blade held to the throat—like you see in the movies—really a common tactic?

It is a more common use of the blade than you might think. Nine percent of folding knives, 11 percent of utility knives and 9 percent of straight razors that are deployed are used to threaten with a touch. This tactic is known as "warning."

Question 4

What financial class is the average knife attacker in?

The socioeconomic background of those who attack with edged weapons is tied to the weapons they use. The most common knifer is the working-class man wielding a folder or razor tool. The second-most common assailant is the poor man or woman using a butcher knife, razor or table knife. The toughest demographic is the experienced felon using a prison-made shank or screwdriver. Sword-type weapons are mostly used for home defense. Pencils, switchblades and butterfly knives are favored by adolescent males. "Rambo knives" and other combat blades are generally used by middle-class and working-class men a short distance from their house or automobile.

Question 5

Where and when do these attacks occur?

Two-thirds of shank attacks happen indoors—mostly in prisons, jails and schools—during the day. The rest happen in urban settings at night.

Two-thirds of knife attacks happen at night. Forty percent of those happen indoors, mostly in homes and bars. Fifty-six percent occur on urban sidewalks, lots, streets and alleys—in that order.

Razors are used predominantly outside and at night, with about 40 percent being used indoors (often in the workplace) during the day.

Question 6

What are a person's survival expectations if he is grabbed by a knifer?

Against a razor, 90 percent. (But you will be cut.)

Against a knife, 50 percent. (You will be cut and/or stabbed.)

Against a shank, 30 percent. (You will be stabbed repeatedly.)

Question 7

What does the most damage to the body: stabbing or cutting?

I must preface the answer by establishing the fact that there are two methods of cutting with a hand-held blade: slicing (pressure-cutting) and slashing (impact-cutting).

The various methods of injuring with a blade or shank are listed below from least to most harmful:

6. throwing

5. slashing

4. slicing

3. stabbing

2. slash and stab

1. stab and slice

Question 8

How often do people attack with a knife, and how often do they succeed?

This is the heart of the study. I will limit the scope of the answer to the specific type of blade the reader was referring to: the folding knife.

Sixty-eight percent of those who deployed a folder before or during a violent act adopted an aggressive posture—with the knife hand retracted (in a ready position) or held like an ice pick (in an overhand position).

Eighty-eight percent of those aggressive pocket-knifers attempted to injure the other person.

Eighty-five percent of those injury attempts were successful.

Question 9

Can anyone carry a knife and feel secure that he can protect himself?

First, before carrying a blade for self-protection, you must check state and municipal laws and consult with a police officer about enforcement.

The blade is an offensive weapon. Those defending themselves with it are less than half as likely to succeed than blade-armed aggressors. Furthermore, aggressive defenders fared far better than those who held back. The technical aspects of blade use are less complicated—and less important—than your emotional capacity to cut or stab another human being.

To prevail against a serious antagonist, you must be capable of slashing for effect while maintaining a cool demeanor and staying out of grappling range. To prevail against an armed, crazed, intoxicated and/or group antagonist, you must be capable of applying lethal pressure cuts while grappling and stabbing repeatedly while face to face. Showing the blade is a viable defense, but against certain aggressors, it can be disastrous unless you make good on the visual threat.

Question 10

What kind of knife is best to carry for self-protection?

For pure effect and utility, you want the longest, heaviest, sharpest folding blade that can be practically carried on a day-to-day basis and is simple and quick to deploy. Obviously, the most desirable blades will put you at odds with the law.

Two desirable features are a thumb post and a serrated blade (not sawteeth on the back of the blade). The former facilitates opening, and the latter increases the chance that your antagonist will *know* he has been cut.

Keep in mind that carrying a blade in a visible sheath or belt case will give the aggressor the option of approaching you from the knife side and preventing you

A knife attack is usually facilitated by utilizing a casual approach posture, not by assuming a stance and challenging the opponent.

Typical "edged weapons" include a pencil (the most common shank outside of prison), a box cutter (the most common razor), a cheap lock-blade (the most common knife), a butcher knife (the second-most common knife) and a machete (classified in this study as a sword).

from drawing, or the option of coming from behind and drawing the blade himself. A visible-carry arrangement also allows him to identify you as right-handed or left-handed and to adopt appropriate tactics such as grabbing you from the weak side and jamming your knife-hand shoulder into a wall to prevent you from drawing.

Question 11

How often is a blade drawn during the course of a grappling attack?

Thirty-six percent of blade encounters involve grappling, compared with 38 percent of all violence. The blade is the weapon most likely to be used. Twenty-five percent of blade-grappling situations are defensive draws from the clinch or by a mounted floor-fighter. Most such draws from a belt case or sheath are unsuccessful. Most draws from a pocket result in a success-ful—though not necessarily decisive—use of the blade.

Question 12

What are the most effective unarmed defenses against a blade?

The 23 successful unarmed defenses in the study rank as follows from least to most successful:

- trap: 4 percent
- head butt: 4 percent

- gouge: 4 percent
- verbal: 4 percent
- kick: 9 percent
- punch: 13 percent
- throw: 26 percent
- hold: 35 percent

(Note: The most successful defenses against a blade attack involved an implement, with a hand-held coat or jacket ranking first.)

Question 13

If you attack and injure a person who has drawn a blade, is it safe to walk away, or will he stab you in the back as soon as he gets a chance?

If he is showing the blade from the outset, you can almost certainly walk away. You should do so obliquely, keeping him in sight as long as possible.

If he has cocked or concealed his knife hand, or has attempted a stab, he will most likely persist.

If he is advancing with an ice-pick grip, he will almost certainly pursue you and may strike successfully even while you are running away.

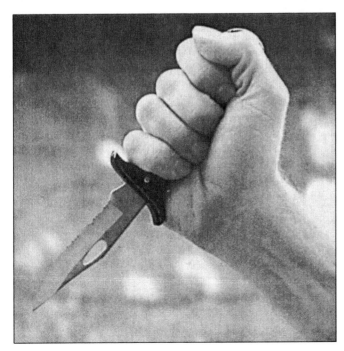

The ice-pick grip (overhand posture) is used on the move and at odd angles by attackers who are often described as enraged. Accounting for 15 percent of edged-weapon deployments, it is often used to stab and/or pursue an unarmed person. There is no record of a knifer slashing with this grip.

177

3-STEP RESPONSE TO A KNIFE ATTACK

by Sgt. Jim Wagner • April 2001

Whenever someone comes at you with a knife and you are empty-handed, you are automatically at a 90-percent tactical disadvantage. Even worse, 99 percent of the disarm techniques taught today are too complicated and unrealistic to be effective in a confrontation. Furthermore, if you do not practice defending against attacks launched at full speed and full power and at the angle of the attacker's choosing, any drill will be merely a choreographed pattern that reinforces a false sense of self-confidence.

After years of mulling over this dilemma, I finally discovered a way to transition from step-by-step practice to full-speed training.

The "Jim Wagner Defense Rule" was born while I was teaching knife disarms to members of the Canadian army. To demonstrate that my reactions were genuine and not part of a prearranged defense that worked only when I knew what was coming, I told one soldier to attack me using any technique he wanted. He lunged immediately, and I had no time to prepare a defense. Without thinking, I caught his knife hand. Before he could wrench the knife free from my grip and launch a second attack, I stepped toward him to deny him the space he needed to cut me, strike me, trip me or even step back. Then I took him down, moved away and drew my pistol. After repeating the drill two more times with the same success, I knew I was onto something.

Since then, I have taught the same course to a mix of law-enforcement officers from different units and countries. Beginners seem to catch on instantly, and advanced students seem to like the system's simplicity. Rather than focusing on 50 techniques to cover all the possibilities of a knife fight, the course has only three components:

• Grab. If a knife-wielding assailant corners you, you must control the knife before he inflicts any damage. Grab his knife hand as if you are clutching at a person's windpipe and do not let go. Remember that in a real attack, blood will make grabbing the weapon even more difficult. It is OK if your hands are not in the perfect position when you grab his hand—especially when you're training at full speed.

• Close. Once you latch on, maintain your grip and immediately close the gap by pressing yourself against the attacker and securing his weapon hand tightly against your own body. From this position, you can execute a takedown to prevent him from escaping. Although you are already in "close combat" (within reach of the opponent) in a knife fight, the attacker still

Jim Wagner's (right) method for stopping a knife attack involves grabbing the opponent's weapon hand (1), closing the gap (2) and taking him to the ground (3).

needs several inches of room to swing his weapon or thrust it into you. While the blade can still cut you, the wound is likely to be superficial.

• Takedown. With your body pressed against his, force your shoulder into his to knock him off-balance, then pivot your body to complete the takedown. If you feel resistance in the direction you intend to take him, immediately switch directions and force him down.

Once the person falls, disengage from him immediately. If you are a civilian, you should escape. If you are a police officer, you should get an adequate distance away from the suspect and draw your gun.

One last warning: Ground combat with a knife-wielding assailant is a no-win situation, and the idea of stripping a knife from somebody's hand while you're down is pure fantasy.

SECRETS OF THE BLADE
20 Essentials You Need to Know About Using and Defending Against Cold Steel
PART 1

by Robert W. Young • April 2001

If there's one part of traditional martial arts training that always seems to get lambasted for being out of date, it's knife fighting. People in the know claim that anachronistic drills like the ever-popular you-do-a-slow-motion-thrust-and-stop-12-inches-from-my-navel-so-I-can-do-an-X-block-and-twist-your-wrist pantomime offer little in the way of realistic skill development. Yet that is precisely what hundreds of thousands of martial artists will depend on if they ever come face to face with a blade.

Lynn Thompson figured that out a long time ago—long before he founded Cold Steel, one of the premier makers of combat knives in the world, in 1980. The knowledge inspired him to embark on a quest to learn the secrets of the blade and the way it is used offensively and defensively on the street. Over the next two decades, he spent countless hours in the *dojo* (training hall) and in makeshift combat arenas around the country to uncover the truth, and he estimates that he continues to drop $20,000 a year on training-related expenses so he can stay on the cutting edge of the business.

All that effort has paid off handsomely. Thompson has transformed himself into one of the most knowledgeable knife experts in the United States, and he routinely earns $400 a pop for his standing-room-only weekend training sessions at his headquarters in Ventura, California. *Black Belt* readers, however, are privileged to get access to the crème de la crème of his findings for the mere price of two magazines: The first 10 of Thomson's teachings are presented below, and the second 10 will appear in the June 2001 issue.

If You're Not Moving, You're Losing

"Knife fights aren't static," Thompson says. "You can seldom rest safely. You can't stand there like a scarecrow and intercept cuts and stabs. Most of the time you need to be moving."

Consequently, he devotes 40 percent to 50 percent of a typical knife seminar to footwork. "Moving appropriately with a knife is different from any other type of footwork," he says. "If you're a really good racquetball or basketball player, none of that counts in knife fighting. The closest thing is probably boxing footwork.

"In knife fighting, you must know how to move quickly and stay balanced. You have to spend a lot of time doing footwork drills before you can move efficiently in sparring."

Once you develop nimble footwork, Thompson says, you can use it as your primary defense. "Mobility allows you to cut him and not be cut," he says. "It's always better to get out of the way than to try to track a knife that's coming at you. Of course, you can't always get out of the way because a strike can come in unexpectedly or at an angle you did not foresee; then you have to intercept the attack with your blade."

Proximity Negates Skill

"If you can get five or 10 feet away from your adversary quickly and you're the one with the skill, you will have an enormous advantage over him," Thompson claims. "You can debilitate him without allowing him a chance to retaliate. He will be in a vulnerable position, and he won't even realize it.

"But if you insist on fighting toe-to-toe and he has the motivation, he will have an excellent chance of maiming or killing you, too. Remember that the closer your adversary is to you, the less your skill counts."

Drop your knife, lose your life: Armed with a heavy blade, Lynn Thompson (right) prepares to attack the knife of instructor Felix Valencia (1). Thompson shifts his body forward and uses the side or back of his blade to strike his opponent's smaller blade (2). Once the opponent drops his weapon, he is in a world of hurt (3).

Start with a basic fighting stance: Lynn Thompson's feet are shoulder-width apart, his knees are bent slightly, the point of his knife is aimed at the enemy's upper body, and his "alive" hand is flat against his left pectoral muscle.

A good knife fighter knows how to fight at close range, but he doesn't like it because he knows proximity gives advantages to even an unskilled opponent, Thompson says. "It's not good to be in a position where he can touch you without even moving. He doesn't need to have power to win; all he needs is the will."

Let a Sharp Knife Do the Work

"If every woman in America carried a sharp knife and knew how to use it, no one would be raped. The knife is the perfect self-defense weapon for women; only a firearm is better," Thompson proclaims.

A sharp blade is also perfect for the elderly, the infirm and the frail, he adds. "All you need is an effective knife and the will. The steel does the work," he says. "You don't have to bring power to it."

An edged weapon stands in stark contrast to empty-hand martial arts techniques, Thompson claims. "If you want to punch me and knock me out, you have to dig in, push off, turn your hips, bend your knee and shoot your fist out. Then you have to hit me on the chin just right. Then I might go down," he says. "But you don't have to do that with a knife. You just touch your opponent with it, and you'll get good results."

An important side note: A serrated edge will seem sharper and more effective than a nonserrated edge because it will cut two to three times deeper, according to Thompson. "If you want to carry a folding knife for self-defense, get a fully serrated edge."

Initiation Beats Reaction

"Bruce Lee said that if you stand toe-to-toe with an opponent and can stop 50 percent of the attacks, you're doing well," Thompson says. "You can absorb the rest of the punches if you're in shape and have the will to fight, but you can't absorb any knife strikes. Some people say, 'I'll just take it on the outside of my arm.' Well, you don't want to take it from a sharp knife on the outside of your arm if you want to use your arm again! Granted, it's better than getting it in the middle of your gut pile, but don't think you can use your arm as a shield."

The only way to deal with a knife attack is to terminate it before it gets off the ground. "When you and your assailant are at extreme close range, it's too easy for him to go cave man on you and attack you with all kinds of weird angles at such a distance that your reaction time is cut down to nothing," Thompson says. "At that range, initiation is faster than reaction. You have a slim chance of emerging unscathed."

Drop Your Knife, Lose Your Life

The first rule of knife fighting ought to be, Don't drop your weapon. "There are many grips you can use to hold your knife securely, but we prefer

Learn to use the point: Lynn Thompson (left) faces Felix Valencia at long range (1). As soon as Valencia exposes his forearm, Thompson lunges to cover the distance and attacks with the point of his blade using a technique called the fleche (2).

a forward grip, which some people call the hammer grip," Thompson says. "We want your four fingers to wrap around the handle and your thumb to lock around your fingers."

The forward grip allows you to put power into slashing, cutting and chopping strokes, and you can use it just as easily for thrusting, Thompson says. "You can go from the forward grip to the thumb-reinforced grip and extend your reach very quickly," he says.

Because many knife novices use an inferior grip, Thompson teaches students a fencing technique called the beat. "If you can't quite muster the courage to go in deep enough to cut your attacker's hand, you can still knock the blade out of his hand," he says. "You use your blade to hit his blade as close to his hand as possible. Even if you beat it and just knock it off-line for a second, you have created an opening to attack."

Start With a Basic Fighting Stance

"There are many different postures that you can adopt in a knife fight; it depends on your skill level and your opponent's," Thompson says. "There's an overhead posture, which is good for a heavy blade. There's a loaded

Don't neglect your nonweapon hand: Lynn Thompson (right) fakes an attack to his opponent's knife hand, then cuts his unprotected empty hand.

posture for use with a thrusting knife. There's a high posture, in which you present the point coming down at the attacker."

But everyone should start out with a basic stance that eliminates any faults that can give their opponent an advantage.

One of the most common mistakes beginners make is to use a boxing stance, Thompson says. "In boxing, you stand in a crouch, cup your shoulders to protect your solar plexus and raise one shoulder to protect your chin," he says. "All that is great when you fight with your fists, but it works against you when you fight with a knife because you tend to move your head away from your knife and out closer to your opponent."

Learn to Use the Point

"A lot of people don't know how to use the point of their knife to hit small targets, but it's important to learn how to do that," Thompson says. "With practice, you can pick the button on the attacker's shirt that you will hit."

Using the point of your weapon can actually increase your safety in a fight, Thompson adds. "If you use it to attack an incoming attack, you can keep your hand four to five inches farther away and still get the job done with a greater margin of safety," he says. "That's important offensively and defensively."

When You Can't Evade, Advance and Attack

If you can't move backward to get out of range of a knife strike, Thompson says, you probably need to move forward into the fray. "If you have no room to maneuver, you should try to end it right away," he says. "As you move forward, you have to intercept and attack almost simultaneously. You can't afford to go forward and block and not do anything.

"When your wife or loved ones have to get away safely and someone is in the way, you have to deal with him immediately. You don't have time to use long-range techniques, which might require you to use 10 or 15 seconds to move him into position where you can do what you want. You have to close immediately and take more risks."

Make Your Opponent Go 'Through' Your Knife

You should position your knife in front of your body between yourself and your opponent. "Forcing him to go 'through' your knife keeps you a lot safer," Thompson says.

"If your knife is in his way, however, he may try to attack the hand

Make your opponent go "through" your knife: Lynn Thompson (right) confronts Felix Valencia, but Thompson cannot close the distance because Valencia's weapon is in the way (1). As soon as Valencia attempts to cut, Thompson evades the strike, detects an opening created when Valencia's knife hand passes his centerline, and lunges so he can reach his opponent's rib cage (2).

holding it," he adds. "So that puts your knife hand at risk. But once you learn some evasion movements for avoiding cuts to your knife hand, you can make it very difficult for him."

In training, Thompson uses hockey gloves to practice attacking and defending against knife-hand cuts. "You quickly learn the importance of keeping your hand in motion, and if you're struck in class, it's not the end of the world," he says.

Don't Neglect Your Nonweapon Hand

"Always remember to use your 'alive hand,' or nonweapon hand, in a fight," Thompson says. "You can use it to effect a stop-hit on the assailant's shoulder or arm. Of course, you have to adapt that hit to the length of his arm and the speed of his attack. If you're late and you try to hit his forearm, his knife's already in your gut. If you're a little slower than you wanted to be in responding, you have to go to the wrist. You might even have to risk hitting the blade itself to avoid being stabbed. But I'd rather be cut on my hand than get seven inches of steel in my stomach."

Thompson says he often encounters *kali* practitioners who employ a substandard method of knife sparring. If he sees their nonweapon hand flopping around or tracing intricate but repetitive patterns, he glances at their knife hand to throw them off, then cuts their alive hand. "Whenever your nonweapon hand gets far from your knife hand, you're vulnerable," he says.

SECRETS OF THE BLADE
20 Essentials Every Martial Artist Needs to Know About Using and Defending Against Cold Steel
PART 2
by Robert W. Young • June 2001

In part one of this article, which appeared in the April 2001 issue of Black Belt, Lynn Thompson explained the first half of his 20 tips for better knife fighting. Here, the founder of Cold Steel finishes the job.

If It's Not in Motion, Hit It

Before you strike, you should identify openings in your opponent's defenses, Lynn Thompson says. One important thing to look for is "still hands."

"Many knife fighters will keep moving around, but their hand will be still," he says. "They may move their hand at first, but once they lose their

If an opponent moves his knife horizontally in front of his body, once it passes his centerline, his forearm will be exposed to an attack. Note how the tip of his knife points away from the imaginary opponent standing in front of him.

When a knife fighter crouches, he makes his face an easy target for a quick thrust.

187

Felix Valencia demonstrates two common knife-fighting mistakes. Left: He uses his empty hand and forearm as a shield to absorb cuts and thrusts—a good way to end up maimed for life. Right: Valencia's stance exposes his hands and leaves his torso open to a quick slash.

concentration, it does not stay in motion all the time. If it's not in motion, you should hit it."

Other opponents will move their hand but not their arm, he says. "Their wrist is turning and their knife is moving two or three inches, but their elbow and forearm are staying in virtually the same spot," he says. "All you have to do is step to a position from which you can avoid the knife but still reach the forearm. And they will never realize they're leaving an opening."

If you come up against an amateur who stands totally still, you can often attack him before he can move because he has to overcome inertia, Thompson says. If he is a little more advanced and gives you a repeating hand pattern—for example, he is moving his knife horizontally—as soon as it passes the center, his forearm is exposed.

"But be careful because experienced knife fighters will sometimes give you a still hand as bait," Thompson cautions. "They want you to attack it because they have already planned their response."

Know the Concept of Mai

"The word *mai* comes from the Japanese art of *kenjutsu*, or sword fighting," Thompson says. "It means you know the exact distance between your weapon and your opponent, and the exact distance between his weapon and you. When you're moving around, you know exactly which parts of his body you can cut and which parts of your body he can cut."

Knowledge of mai teaches you when you're safe and when you're not, as well as when you can and can't rest, Thompson says. "Also, it often allows you to attack your opponent from a range at which he thinks he's safe," he says.

You Can't Cover Against a Knife

"The main thing about knife fighting that people don't realize is that if you haven't done it a lot, you can't keep your concentration up," Thompson warns. "And once your concentration lapses, you can't cover to protect yourself.

"Say your opponent in a boxing ring is attacking you with a flurry of punches. You can take most of them with your elbows and forearms. But against a knife, you can't do that. You have to pick up every stroke and deal with it. You can't afford even a split-second lapse in concentration when you are close enough for your opponent to cut you."

If you ever have to confront a knife fighter in combat, Thompson advises you to look for one of those involuntary lapses in concentration. "The more experienced you get in knife sparring, the more often you'll see (lapses), and they mean that your opponent just isn't ready. And that's when you go," he says.

Exploit Your Opponent's Build

"Being tall is great because you have more reach, but tall guys have to think about their legs," Thompson says. "They tend to stand narrow—with their feet less than shoulder-width apart—and that puts their front leg out for you to attack. You only have to move your center of gravity an inch or two and drop, and you can reach the whole inside of their thigh."

If you're tall, there are several things you can do to minimize your liabilities, Thompson says. "Stand up straight. Don't crouch. Learn how to get full extension, how to turn and how to lean properly to get full reach,"

Defense against a knife attack should never include "passive" blocks because they leave the weapon hand in position for a follow-up attack. Lynn Thompson (right) demonstrates the proper blocking method, in which he slams the knife edge of his left hand into the attacker's forearm (1) and the knife edge of his right hand into his face (2).

he says. "If you're 6 foot 4, you can reach someone eight, nine or 10 feet away. Most people think that if someone is threatening them with a knife six feet away, they're safe. But a tall guy can take one step and cut them."

If You're Empty-Handed, You Must Equalize

Your chances of disarming a good knife fighter are extremely slim, Thompson says. "Your only hope is to run or get a weapon to equalize, to get respect."

"If he's got a knife and you've got a sap, it's still better to have the knife—but he knows that you could kill or seriously injure him, so he respects you," he continues. "If you're just standing there with your hands and feet, you will not be respected—no matter how accomplished you are in the martial arts.

"But if you've got a knife, you're the man. If you don't have a knife, you've got to get something: a bench, a chair, a lamp ... anything."

If Your Knife Isn't Sharp, It's No Good

If your blade isn't sharp enough to shave the hair off your arm, it's not good enough for combat, Thompson says. "A friend of mine witnessed a knife fight in which one person was not injured because his opponent had a dull knife," he says. "The guy who won was the guy whose knife was razor sharp. There was no real difference in skill level.

"A dull knife is like a pointed screwdriver. That limits you because your opportunities to cut are always greater than your opportunities to thrust. Also, you can cut somebody a little bit, but it's hard to stab him a little bit. A cut is usually a less serious attack. In Ventura County, California,

I'm an expert witness on edged weapons. If someone says he cut another person in an altercation but didn't stab him, I'd say he limited the damage he wanted to do. He showed some mercy."

Never Use 'Passive' Blocks

"If you don't have a knife to use against your attacker's knife, you must use your hands as though you did have a knife," Thompson says. "Because the knife is so elusive to face, if you don't think of your hands as a knife, you will always be behind.

"When you block, you have to 'cut' into your opponent's arm with the knife edge of your hand. If you just stick your arm out, it's better than nothing. But as soon as a good knife fighter feels that resistance, he will turn and go for a different target.

Lynn Thompson (right) likes to take advantage of a taller opponent's vulnerabilities—specifically, his lead leg. Thompson faces the attacker (1) and distracts him by raising his arms (2). Once the other man looks up and moves his blade in that direction, Thompson steps forward, drops into a deep squat and attacks the exposed front leg (3).

The vertical whip is one option knife fighters seldom learn in class. To demonstrate, Lynn Thompson (right) exposes his knife arm (1). Felix Valencia begins swinging his blade toward Thompson's hand (2) and accelerates the stroke by flexing his wrist (3). Inset: Contact is made with the end of the blade.

"When you hit his knife arm, you will knock it away for a split second. He can't turn and cut you, and that gives you an opening. If you just block his arm and it stays there, he's free to continue. It's like in boxing: If he is planning to throw a four-punch combination and you just stand and cover, you've got to take all four punches. Once he gets his momentum going, it can overwhelm you."

He's Bleeding and You're Leaving

A popular misconception that exists in the martial arts is that using a knife for self-defense means killing your attacker. But with the proper training, you don't have to be lethal. "If you use a *tanto* to cut the outside of your attacker's elbow, bad things will start happening to his mind," Thompson says. "Maybe it's not the end of the fight, but he's bleeding and you're leaving.

"If someone attacks you with a knife, you don't have to stand there and fight him. If you can't get out of the way immediately, you can cut him and leave. That's what self-defense is."

You Have More Options Than You Think

Success in knife fighting stems from having more techniques in your arsenal than just cutting and stabbing, Thompson claims. That's why he teaches students how to execute the slash, chop, snap cut and vertical whip. "There's also the hacking stroke, a chopping stroke in which you substitute speed and repetition for power," he says. "When you're confined, you just hit your attacker repeatedly in the same spot to accomplish what you would do with one stroke if you had the time and space to put your body weight into it."

Thompson and his associates also show their students how to rake with their weapon. "You can use a raking attack to drive off 10 or 15 people," he says. "They're going to be hurt, but it's unlikely they'll be lethally injured."

You Might Not Be Cut

"In our seminars, we don't say it's inevitable that you will be cut in a knife fight," Thompson says. "Quite often when you're cut, you're maimed for life; and we want people to have a higher survivability rate."

That's why he advocates learning a long-range method of knife fighting in which you use your skill, timing, rhythm and knowledge to incapacitate your attacker while minimizing the chance of injury to yourself.

AGAINST THE BLADE
How to Avoid Misconceptions and Mind-Sets That Could Be Fatal on the Street

by Douglas James Young • Photos courtesy of Craig Deveau • November 2001

Virtually every martial art includes various techniques that are taught as defenses against a knife attack. Many of them, however, are invalid. In large part, that is because most instructors do not know how to fight with a knife. It is virtually impossible to learn how to successfully defend yourself against a knife attack if you have no idea how that attack may occur. If no martial artist in a particular training group has any knowledge of knife fighting, all the defenses the group practices are, by default, based on misunderstandings, false assumptions and lack of knowledge.

Most martial artists who practice edged-weapon defense choose not to train in the use of a knife for several reasons. A core tenet of the traditional martial arts holds that the skills you learn will be used only to defend yourself, not to attack others. Many students naturally have an aversion to practicing how to kill someone using a knife. Furthermore, this type of skill is unlikely to be practiced in a sport- or fitness-oriented martial arts curriculum. Unfortunately, self-defense is not an automatic byproduct of traditional or sport-oriented training.

Although there are no guarantees, clearly if most of the time and energy you spend learning the martial arts is focused on practical and realistic self-

Too many knife defenses are based on unrealistic static attacks, over-committed slashes, straight lunging thrusts and an inactive nonblade hand, the author says.

defense, you will have a greater likelihood of surviving a violent encounter. This is especially true when facing "cold steel."

Gun Defense

Some martial artists supplement their empty-hand self-defense skills by carrying a firearm. They often proudly exclaim, "That's why I have a concealed-weapon permit—so I can bring a gun to a knife fight."

The pertinent question then becomes, Where is the gun when they need it? Is it in their car or locked in the closet at home? Almost inevitably, the people who say this do not carry the weapon all the time. Too often, the "magnum mind-set" leads them to believe that carrying a gun is a panacea that answers the question, What do you do when attacked by someone with a knife?

If you are properly trained, a gun can be a useful self-defense tool in certain situations. However, it will not guarantee your safety in an edged-weapon attack. In fact, reaching for a gun when you're faced with a blade can get you killed. Critical empty-hand knife defenses are necessary to buy the time and distance you need to draw a handgun—or any weapon, for that matter—and use it to stop the attack. Even if you're a quick-draw artist and manage to get a shot off, the result might be a mutual kill. Your success in defending yourself should not be measured by whether you kill your attacker, but by whether you manage to avoid letting him kill you.

Military Service

Some martial artists with military service use their experience to rationalize why they don't need any further training in the use of a knife. In many circles, a tour of duty seems to carry with it the honorific title of "self-defense expert." In reality, recruits—even those in the combat-arms specialties—receive only basic training in hand-to-hand fighting. A small part of that is devoted to edged-weapon training, much of which is also based on false assumptions and a lack of knowledge.

Even if a person is, or was, a member of an elite military unit, much of his edged-weapon training may have little relevance to a civilian street encounter involving a blade. The tactics and techniques that enable a person to silently dispatch a sentry with a knife may not be valid in a face-to-face slash-and-thrust attack in an alley with some gangbanger.

Misunderstandings

Most invalid knife defenses are built on a lack of knowledge in two areas.

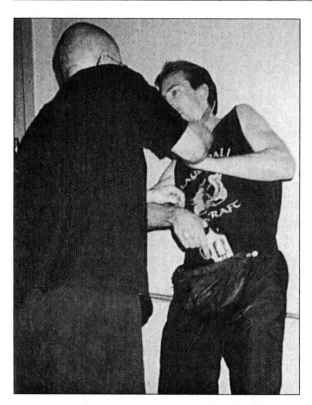

Reaching for a concealed handgun when you are faced with a sudden knife attack can get you killed because it ties up your best defensive weapons: your hands.

First is a general misunderstanding about how a knife is used. Too many response sequences are based on static attacks in a single range from one or two angles. Practicing techniques against over-committed slashes and straight lunging thrusts is an oversimplification of knife-fighting dynamics that can have deadly consequences—and not for your attacker. On the street, where ranges change with the blink of an eye, thrusts from oblique angles and tight elliptical slashes will defeat any defenses that are predicated on long, slow, "hanging" attacks.

Second, and perhaps most disastrous, is the misunderstanding that anybody who has a blade will use it like a crutch. This leads to several false assumptions, which then become the basis for the development of invalid defenses. This is true from both a technique and tactical standpoint.

One of those assumptions is that once you take away the attacker's weapon, the fight is over. If he is disarmed, he might disengage and flee instantly. But then again, he might not. Sticking a knife into somebody takes a great deal of commitment, and any sociopath that has attempted to kill you with a blade will likely continue his committed attack even without his weapon. If you've been cut in the initial attack and you manage to take away his weapon, you may have to continue to defend yourself while partially incapacitated.

Another erroneous assumption is that he will use only his knife in the attack. The blade has a finite number of uses. When utilized in conjunction with a variety of other available weapons—hands, feet, head, elbows, etc.—the knife fighter's potential for destruction expands exponentially. And you need to take that into consideration when you train.

Live Hand

One of the biggest shortcomings of traditional knife defense is the scant amount of attention given to the knifer's nonweapon, or "live," hand. There are many ways his live hand can be used against you. The following are five of the most important:

• A skilled knife fighter will not always begin his attack with his blade. He may opt to "bait" you with an empty-hand lead to exploit any openings

When practicing realistic knife defense, never forget that the attacker has other weapons in addition to his blade and his nonweapon hand.

Knife fighters seldom execute a strike and leave their arm out to be grabbed (1-2). Instead, once their movement is blocked, they transition to a different plan of attack—perhaps using their nonweapon hand to control the blocking arm (3)—and proceed to destroy their victim (4).

created by your reaction.

• A live-hand attack can be devastating when used as an immediate follow-up to a blade attack. This is especially true if the assailant can get you to commit both hands to blocking his knife.

• A knifer can use his live hand to clear your blocking techniques or to check your attempts to block his blade.

• An experienced knife fighter may use his live hand to check any counterattacks you try. Many bad knife defenses that rely on unanswered counters work only against an obliging partner with a "dead" hand.

• An armed assailant may use his live hand to trap your arms to prevent you from blocking his follow-up blade attacks.

Unskilled Attacker

Is it possible you could end up facing an unskilled and unmotivated buffoon with a blade who won't use his live hand, who won't use any other part of his body as a weapon, and who will flee instantly if you manage to disarm him? Certainly.

Is that a best-case scenario that you should count on? Certainly not.

Your ability to defend yourself should carry no caveats. In other words, "I feel I can defend myself except if I'm attacked by someone with a knife" or "I can teach you how to defend yourself but not if you're attacked by a skilled knifer" are not things that should have to be said or heard in the *dojo*.

Ideally, you should seek training in a comprehensive edged-weapon defense system. At the very least, you should test your knife defenses by taking into account the variables discussed above. Free-form sparring with protective gear and training blades is a great way to test the validity of your skills. You will discover that many disarms that work well within the context of the "obliging-partner syndrome" will fail under these conditions.

Learning how to use a knife against a knife attack also has many benefits. You may find that sometimes the only way to beat a knife fighter is to be a better knife fighter. But even if you choose not to carry a knife for self-protection, your empty-hand defenses must be based on a knowledge of knife-fighting techniques and tactics, or you will stand no chance of surviving an edged-weapon attack by a skilled knifer.

GIRL'S BEST FRIEND
A Guide to Knife Training for Women
by Erin Vunak • Photos by Sara Fogan • March 2002

Women who study the martial arts often discover that what they are taught works fine in the *dojo* against a male opponent who doesn't resist too hard, but when they try to use a technique for real, they may find that it is woefully ineffective.

If you are a woman training in a predominantly male environment, you've probably been searching for ways to put yourself on a more equal footing with men. Certainly you should strive to increase your overall body strength and develop your punching and kicking power, but you should also consider a way that will make the most of your natural feminine attributes instead of simply trying to overcome them: Add Philippine weapons training to your workout.

Cutting Edge

The Philippine martial arts were developed by a nation of comparatively smaller people so they could better defend themselves against invaders who were larger and armed with more modern weapons. Strength and power are not major requirements, but coordination, speed and stamina are. Bruce Lee regarded the Philippine fighting methods as quite useful (witness *Enter the Dragon),* and students of *jeet kune do* concepts have embraced them for years.

Philippine knife fighting can help women gain an edge in all aspects of their training. As a self-defense equalizer, the knife is unmatched. As a fitness-enhancing tool, weapons sparring forces quick, agile movement and provides a phenomenal workout. And as a physical, mental and spiritual enhancement, knife fighting offers such a wealth of information and training concepts that no one could possibly learn them all in one lifetime.

Women who take up the blade develop attributes that will make them more effective martial artists: timing, agility, speed, catlike footwork, and the ability to draw and intercept an opponent. These attributes don't apply to just knife work; they will also improve your training and sparring under any conditions.

This article presents four basic exercises that will jump-start your edged-weapons training. For maximum safety, you will need to obtain a training knife before you begin. To protect your hands, boxing or bag gloves work just fine, but hockey gloves are also good. If you plan to spar with intensity or if you just want to be extra safe, eye protection should also be worn.

Before you tackle the exercises described below, take a moment to think about the principle of "defanging the snake." A cornerstone of the Philippine martial arts, it teaches that rather than trying to get close to your attacker so you can cut his body, you should strive to cut his weapon hand as he tries to strike. Once you have done that, his weapon and his attack will be nullified. You will then have the choice of finishing off the snake or letting it go while you make your escape. From a tactical and legal point of view, defanging the snake is the best strategy for self-defense with a blade.

Defang Drill

This exercise introduces the concept of defanging the snake. You and your partner should each have a training knife and a glove for your knife hand. Your partner moves first by stepping in and feeding you an attack along one angle. Your mission is to cut the incoming limb (aim for the glove) while backing away. The footwork is crucial: Don't just stand in place and cut. If you happen to miss with your knife and you stay planted, your opponent's next cut will most likely reach a vital part of your body.

Run through the exercise slowly at the beginning, then speed it up as you become comfortable. Feed your partner different lines of attack—in some sort of order at first but then at random. The following are five basic angles of attack you can use:

- Angle 1: Forehand slash or thrust, high (neck); angle downward
- Angle 2: Backhand slash, high; angle downward

Defang drill No. 1: Jim Moseley delivers an angle 1 (downward diagonal forehand slash), and Erin Vunak cuts his arm as she backs away.

Defang drill No. 2: The partner (right) executes an angle 2 (downward backhand diagonal slash), and Erin Vunak meets it with an angle 2 of her own.

Defang drill No. 3. The opponent (right) feeds Erin Vunak an angle 3 (horizontal forehand slash), and she responds by moving her body backward and cutting his knife hand.

Defang drill No. 4: As Jim Moseley attacks with an angle 4 (horizontal backhand slash), Erin Vunak backs away and slices his knife hand.

- Angle 3: Forehand slash to body; horizontal (rib area)
- Angle 4: Backhand slash to body; horizontal
- Angle 5: Straight thrust to abdomen

Your partner should feed you all five angles, then you do the same for him. This is not a sparring drill in which you and your partner try to attack and defend simultaneously, nor is it a "flow" drill in which each person alternates attacking and defending. Instead, one person defends while the other acts as a coach.

This exercise is called the *largo mano* drill because as the defender, you are trying to stay just close enough to cut his hand. As stated above, footwork is vital. Step backward, zone to the side, change your elevation—but keep moving. You may discover that against certain angles of attack, certain cuts work better while others get you cut. The important thing is to find what works for you.

Cut-and-Check Drill

This exercise familiarizes you with close-range blade work. It is not a preferred method of knife fighting per se, but it is an invaluable self-perfection exercise for sharpening your body mechanics, sensitivity and knife-handling ability. For simplicity, refer to the above-mentioned five basic angles of attack. Your partner feeds those five angles first, and you defend. Your checking hand should ensure that once you cut your opponent's

Defang drill No. 5: The partner (left) executes an angle 5 (straight thrust to the abdomen), and Erin Vunak moves to the left as she cuts his knife hand.

weapon hand, it doesn't come back for another swipe.

• Against angle 1: Cut the attacking arm with a forehand slash, and check your partner's knife hand with your free hand. Release your check before your partner goes on to the next strike.

• Against angle 2: Cut the arm with a backhand strike, and check the knife hand with your left hand.

• Against angle 3: Pass your partner's knife hand to the right (across his body) as you cut the arm with an angle 3.

• Against angle 4: Pass your partner's knife hand to the left as you cut the arm with an angle 4. (Note that your passing hand is also your checking

Cut-and-check drill No. 1: James Wilks executes an angle 1 (downward diagonal forehand slash), and Erin Vunak cuts the inside of his arm while using her free hand to check that arm.

Cut-and-check drill No. 2: The opponent (left) feeds Erin Vunak an angle 2 (downward backhand diagonal slash), and she attacks the outside of his arm.

Cut-and-check drill No. 3: The partner (left) tries an angle 3 (horizontal forehand slash to the midsection), which causes Erin Vunak to check with her free hand as she passes to the outside and cuts the arm.

Cut-and-check drill No. 4: Erin Vunak is confronted with an angle 4 (horizontal backhand slash), so she checks with her free hand, passes the knife and, instead of cutting the arm, opts for the neck.

Cut-and-check drill No. 5: James Wilks attacks with an angle 5 (straight thrust to the abdomen), and Erin Vunak responds by stepping off-line to her left and executing a forehand horizontal slash.

hand; it should be monitoring what your partner's weapon is doing.)

• Against angle 5: Move your body to either side out of the path of the knife as you cut the attacker's arm with an angle 3.

You will find that your ability to avoid being cut, while at the same time cutting and controlling your partner's weapon hand, can be greatly enhanced by using proper body mechanics. Twist left when you cut against an angle 1, and twist right when you cut and deflect an angle 2. Imagine that you are performing this exercise with razor-sharp knives, and think about what you would do to avoid being cut.

Knife Sparring

This is a fun drill that gives you a great workout while drawing out your killer instinct. Your objective is similar to that of the largo mano drill: Cut your opponent's hand as he tries to cut you. The difference is that no one is feeding strikes; you're both going for it. If a cut to the body happens to present itself, do it but don't chase it. Try to stay in the relative safety of long range, making your opponent's hand your primary target. Footwork and timing are essential elements, so be light on your feet.

You can intensify the workout by adding calisthenics or plyometric exercises such as the jump-squat. Spar for one three-minute round, then do 20 jump-squats and spar a few more rounds.

You will learn a lot if you spar with different people, especially those who are more experienced. A beginner is typically the easiest opponent because he will probably use mostly simple direct attacks. A veteran knife fighter will attack with combinations and, therefore, be more difficult to deal with. Make sure to maintain your distance and put together your own combinations.

Knife-Defense Drill

This is one of the best drills for learning to defend yourself with a blade because it forces you to use a training knife to fend off multiple opponents. The attackers are decked out in goggles, boxing gloves, elbow pads and, if desired, groin protection and shin pads.

Start with a single opponent. He moves toward you with obviously bad intentions. Try not to let him touch you. Attack the body part that is closest to you—his arms if he's trying to grab you. As soon as you get one or two good cuts, he should pull back for two to five seconds to simulate what would happen if you actually cut him in an encounter. After the pause, he should come in again for another attempt. Continue for one to three minutes.

When you feel comfortable with this, add another attacker. It is important that no matter how many people are opposing you, they attack with conviction. This will trigger an adrenaline rush in you, and you should learn how to deal with its effect on your fine-motor movements.

Keep the following points in mind:

• Do not focus exclusively on your attacker. Use your peripheral vision to determine whether more bad guys are approaching. Look for a safe place to run to.

• Keep moving. Use your footwork to keep someone from sneaking up behind you. Get your back to a wall, if possible. Do not run into the middle of two or three attackers because they will swarm you. Keep maneuvering so you must deal with only one at a time.

• Don't panic. While the attack is happening, extend your awareness so you can tell where the attackers are without turning to look.

Joy of Discovery

There is so much more to knife fighting than could ever be presented in one article. The four exercises here could keep you busy for years. Remember that the purpose of edged-weapons training is not necessarily to learn a lot of techniques with the knife. It is more about embracing the concept of equalizing the odds. Whether or not you decide to carry a blade for self-defense, the principles and concepts of knife fighting will give you a tremendous edge in all areas of your life.

RAPID DEPLOYMENT
9 Essential Drills for Martial Artists Who Carry a Tactical Folding Knife

by Kevan W. Matthews • June 2002

Volumes have been written about the best ways to use a tactical folder in close-quarters combat because it's the glamorous part of knife fighting. Relatively little has been written about the best ways to deploy a knife under the stress that is always present in a lethal encounter. And that's a pity because to be proficient with a blade in any situation, you first have to surmount the obstacles that stand between you and the successful deployment of your weapon.

It's easy to believe that your knife will be available when you need it. It's easy to think that by exercising situational awareness and anticipating the threat, you will be able to silently take it out and open it and then engage the enemy. In a perfect world, that might be the case, but in the heat of battle, you can experience any number of setbacks:

- You may be ambushed.
- You may be forced to fight on the ground.
- You may be in a position in which your strong arm is occupied or injured.
- You may slip on snow or wet grass.
- You may experience a loss of dexterity because of the cold.
- You may extract your weapon but fail to acquire the necessary grip to deploy the blade completely.
- You may be exhausted.
- You may find that your clothing restricts your hand movement.
- You may be disarmed.

I call these factors "combat stress indicators," or CSIs. You can never really eliminate them. However, if you make your training resemble combat as much as possible, you can boost your ability to work through the challenges they pose.

This article will present nine stress-deployment drills designed to help you overcome the CSIs and deploy your knife under less-than-ideal conditions. Instead of the adrenaline-induced stresses of combat, physical exercise will be used to bring about the dexterity loss and muscular fatigue you would experience during an actual encounter.

Photos by Robert W. Young

Prone-deployment drill: The practitioner performs a set of push-ups to fatigue his muscles, thus simulating the effects of adrenaline (1-3). He then remains in the up position as he extracts his knife from his pocket (4) and deploys the blade (5-6).

Timed-Deployment Drill

Your partner blows a whistle to signal you to begin and activates his stopwatch to time your reaction. You respond by extracting your knife and opening the blade. The clicking sound the locking mechanism makes when the blade is fully open signals your partner to stop the watch. With the clock providing the only CSI, a time of 1.6 seconds should not be difficult to achieve.

Standing-Deployment Drill

To introduce more stress, this drill has you beginning with the "10-count bodybuilder exercise." After completing one cycle of the exercise, your partner signals you to deploy your blade and records the time. Your goal is to complete two sets of 12 cycles of the movement, deploying the knife 12 times with each side. Observe how a time of 1.6 seconds becomes more difficult to attain as the stress increases.

Prone-Deployment Drill

Now you must perform after you complete a set of push-ups at 50 percent of your point of muscular failure. (For example, if you can do 100 push-ups but fail at 101, your threshold is 100. So for this drill, you would perform sets of 50.) After completing the final rep, stay in the up position until your partner signals you to deploy your blade. Strive to keep your legs straight and support your body on the balls of your feet and one arm. Once you deploy your knife and your partner records the time, place the

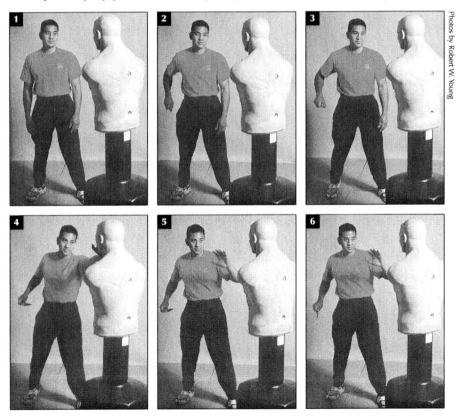

Photos by Robert W. Young

Deployment-malfunction drill: When faced with an imminent attack (1), the practitioner reaches for his knife (2). He attempts to deploy the blade, but stress and perspiration cause him to fail (3). He then executes his preplanned empty-hand technique or combination (4) to buy time to attempt to open the blade again (5). With the knife now fully deployed, the practitioner can defend himself (6).

Deployment-of-backup drill: The partner threatens the practitioner (1). The practitioner takes out his primary knife (2), and the partner seizes the weapon hand (3) and disarms him (4). Meanwhile, the practitioner deploys his backup weapon and prepares to counter-attack (5). Note: This drill should not be interpreted as advocating the use of a knife against an unarmed assailant.

weapon on the ground and recover safely. Be sure to drill with your strong and weak sides. A good time to shoot for is two seconds.

This drill is designed to simulate a tactical need to deploy your knife while engaged in a ground struggle in which you are compromised from behind. You can keep the drill fresh and discover new ways to add stress by varying the types of push-ups you perform. Try fingertip push-ups to stress your digits more and provide you with extreme dexterity loss.

Moving-Threat Drill

Because sometimes you need more time to take out your weapon, you should practice putting distance between your attacker and yourself. To assist you, the moving-threat drill takes the prone-deployment drill one step further in that it develops your ability to ready your weapon on the move, thus buying you a few extra seconds.

Instead of drawing your knife after the final push-up, upon hearing the whistle, you spring from the up position and sprint across the room while doing it. The moment your blade is out, turn to face your partner and assume a ready position. Practice with your strong and weak sides.

Deployment-Malfunction Drill

This drill prepares you for the eventuality that your blade might partially open or fail to open. First, visualize what you would do if that happened in combat. When your partner gives you the signal, extract your weapon and deploy it as described in the timed-deployment drill—but this time you will not be timed. Continue to kinetically deploy the blade until you experience a failure, then execute your preconceived striking or distraction technique. Immediately try to open the blade again. Your goal is to improve your ability to immediately recognize the problem and work through it.

Deployment-of-Backup Drill

An extension of the deployment-malfunction drill, this exercise trains you to rely on your backup weapon in the event that your primary is lost. Start by taping the blade of your primary weapon closed for added safety. Then face your partner and extract the weapon. He attacks your weapon hand and disarms you. You must then deploy your backup. Stop as soon as it is opened.

Grappling-Deployment Drill

This drill teaches you how to exploit your opponent's weaknesses and deploy your weapon by creating an opportunity. You and your partner begin by facing each other on your hands and knees. When he makes physical contact, you must extract your weapon (with its blade taped closed for safety) while he tries to stop you. Practice with your strong and weak sides.

Arm-Immobilization-Deployment Drill

To develop your ability to extract and deploy your knife with your weak side while you are being choked and restrained, begin by facing away from your partner. He then places you in a choke hold while immobilizing one of your arms. Your goal is to take out your (taped) weapon before he can maximize his hold and force you to submit. The drill continues until you extract your weapon or he makes you tap.

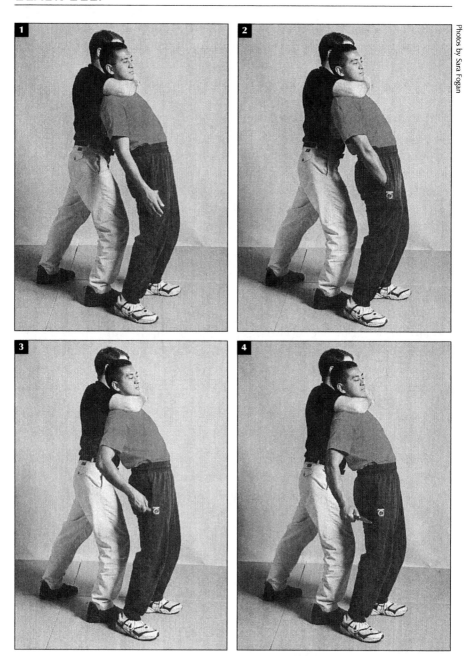

Photos by Sara Fogan

Arm-immobilization-deployment drill: The partner uses his right arm to choke the practitioner and his left arm to lock the practitioner's left arm behind his back (1). The practitioner must then ignore the choke or protect himself from its effects long enough to access his knife (2) and open it (3-4).

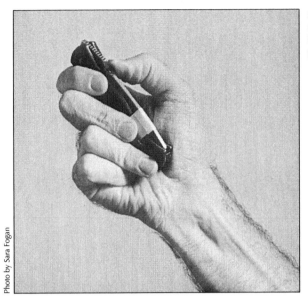

If a training knife is not available, use a length of tape to secure the blade so it won't open during partner drills.

Photo by Sara Fogan

Threat-Closing Deployment

The final drill forces you to think tactically. Face your partner as he stands about 21 feet away. He closes the distance as quickly as he can while keeping track of the time with a stopwatch. You must deploy your (taped) knife while you step into a defensive posture. Your options include the following:

- stepping forward while deploying your blade
- stepping backward while deploying it
- attacking and deploying it
- distracting him and deploying it
- combining tactics and deploying it

Your choice should not be based on your favorite technique but on your partner's actions. For example, if he takes one step and then stops after seeing your weapon, you probably will not want to chase him down with your knife. Or if you have a wall behind you, you will be forced away from certain options and toward others.

Practice and Survive

Feel free to modify these drills to suit your tactical needs and challenge yourself in training. Then, if you ever lock eyes with an attacker, there will be no doubt in your mind. You will be resolute, your spirit will be indomitable and you will be trained for that moment. Your weapon will be more than just a decoration.

REALITY OF THE STAB
Uses of the Ice-Pick Grip in Actual Knife and Shank Attacks

by James LaFond • Photos courtesy of James LaFond • September 2002

Author's note: This article is not about the art of wielding a knife. Rather, it is a study of 41 real-world uses of a blade or shank gripped in the reverse, or ice-pick, posture.

Cases #65-01/02: daytime, one second/one minute, eyewitness/first-person aggressor

Mac is a highly placed law-enforcement official who related the following story concerning his time as an undercover narcotics agent with a big-city police department on the East Coast:

"I was sitting in court in front of a witness we brought in—for some reason, the accused had been seated behind the witness—when I heard this popping sound behind me. I turned around and saw the witness. He was seated on the bench. I'll never forget the look on his face. His eyes were bugged out real wide, and his mouth was opened in an O-shape. All he could do was stare straight ahead and shake like a leaf. Definitely in shock. There was a pencil sticking out of the top of his head! And behind him—jumping up and down on the bench and waving his arms was the accused—screaming, 'Die, &%#@, die!'

"For a split second, there was this stunned silence. But there were about 20 of us [police officers], and we were on this guy in a heartbeat. Now, there were these nonviolent people there to take care of the witness, so we concentrated on the accused. The judge, he was a real wimp. He just dove down behind the bench and cowered there until it was all over—didn't see a thing. A good thing, too.

"We really went to town on this guy: grabbed him, punched him to the ground and stomped him.

"A pencil? You got to love that. Can't stop that at the metal detector."

* * *

As bizarre as that incident sounds, it represents in many ways a typical use of the reverse grip:

• It is almost exclusively used as a means of attacking a victim, as opposed to combating an opponent. It is never used in blade-to-blade encounters and rarely in fights.

- A shank, or improvised stabbing weapon, is commonly used with the reverse grip.
- A reverse-grip attack is usually a come-from-behind attack.
- An overhand stab is five times more likely than other stabs to strike the head or face.
- About 97 percent of reverse-grip stabbing attempts succeed in injuring the victim. About 68 percent of those attempts result in an incapacitated victim.
- Virtually all reverse-grip aggressions occur indoors.

Mac's story also represents two atypical uses of the reverse grip. First, it was not a multiple stabbing. In reality, between five and 15 wounds are typical in incidents in which the reverse grip is used.

Second, the aggressor used a two-handed grip for a vicious downward stroke. Such a tactic was duplicated in only one other case out of the 41 cases studied.

Three Myths

The purpose of this article is to provide martial artists with information about the parameters of blade and shank use from the reverse grip. Before demonstrating the seven reverse-grip strokes employed by the untrained knifer—98 percent of blade users are untrained in any fighting system, and 99 percent are untrained with the blade—it is necessary to expose the three myths that pertain to reverse-grip blade and shank use:

Lethal Martial Arts Myth No. 1: The full-commitment, stiff-armed, one-handed, stepping, linear, downward stroke by a zombie aggressor.

There is no record of such an attack. The only purpose served by it is to make martial arts masters look good in self-defense demonstrations. Reverse-grip attacks are never stiff-armed, are rarely linear unless delivered two-handed, are rarely full-commitment strokes, and are always

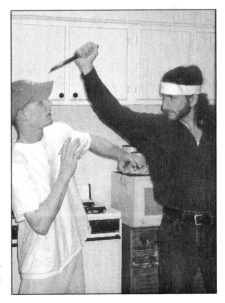

Myth No. 1: The full-commitment, one-handed linear attack. There is no point in training for a scenario that never happens, the author says.

employed by highly motivated aggressors with a predatory mind-set.

Purge this scenario from your training regimen.

Lethal Martial Arts Myth No. 2: The one-handed knife-hand grab.

Although grabbing the knife arm has saved more unarmed defenders than any other tactic, only one successful one-handed grab has been documented (by a professional wrestler who crushed the wrist of the knife hand as the knifer attempted to withdraw his stiletto from the wrestler's left kidney—which was lost). All unsuccessful knife-hand grabs have been one-handed, and most resulted in a maimed right hand for the defender.

It requires two hands to immobilize the knife arm and wrist. This is even more true in a reverse-grip attack because the reverse-grip knifer is the only one who is likely to be stronger than his victim. (The typical knifer is smaller than his prey.) Furthermore, the breakout cut with the reverse grip can threaten the vitals of the defender more quickly than the twirl of the natural-grip knifer.

Breaking out of the one-handed grab with a crosscut is more of a power move than the twirl is. It is appropriate and natural for the more offensive-minded reverse-grip knifer.

Most people can use a wrist twirl to slice the holding hand of even their biggest sparring partner. How could a woman or boy trust a one-handed grab against an adrenaline-primed man?

Purge the one-handed grab from your anti-knife arsenal.

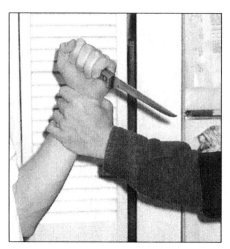 

Myth No. 2: The one-handed knife-hand grab. If you try it, you are likely to face a redirected blade that slices your wrist.

Lethal Martial Arts Myth No. 3: Slashing from the reverse grip.

A fighting style that is built around the reverse slash is seldom used by the untrained knifer. Therefore, training to deal with a slash attack from the reverse grip should focus on learning how to spot a trained knifer based on subtle visual cues—and then how to run away. Too many self-defense teachers assume their students will know how to flee, and as such, they do not teach fleeing tactics.

Unlucky Seven: The First Four

The Grab and Stab: This attack is usually launched against men seated at a bar and against those who have just turned to walk away from an

argument. It is the most common reverse-grip attack, with strikes usually falling on the right shoulder and neck. These attacks are fatal only when perpetrated by members of a group.

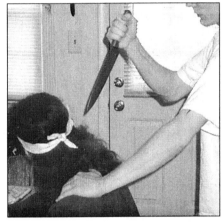

The Grab and Stab: It is often used to attack someone who is seated or has turned away from an argument.

The Woodpecker: The second most common reverse-grip attack consists of multiple low-commitment stabs (issued from the elbow) to the head, neck and shoulders of a fleeing or dodging defender.

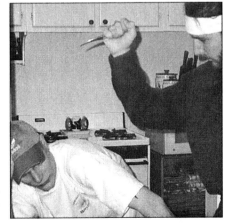

The Woodpecker: It consists of a series of low-intensity stabs that rely primarily on the motion of the forearm.

The Ripper: In the study, this rare come-from-behind attack was used twice: by a butcher and a retired Navy SEAL. The blade is held with the edge toward the knifer, and it is plunged into the trapezius muscle. The victim's back is sliced 12 inches to 30 inches, with the blade exiting at the armpit or hip.

The Ripper: It positions the edge of the blade toward the attacker and can result in a long cut down the back.

The Lung Piercer: This is the rarest stroke (used once in the 41 cases studied) and was instantly decisive. The blade enters under the rib cage with the knife hand severely supinated for an upward stab.

The Lung Piercer: It plunges the blade upward from underneath the rib cage.

218

The Frontal Attacks

The Backhand: This, the most deadly stroke, was used three times, causing three one-strike knockouts (and two instant deaths). It is a full-commitment stroke delivered on the move with a lateral step or while rising from a chair. It is used against standing or seated victims, and it targets the chest and face.

The Backhand: It is delivered on the move using a full-commitment motion aimed at the chest or face.

The Spike: This is a defensive stroke used in the clinch to strike the kidney, chest or thigh of a larger opponent. This stroke is usually the result of an escalation during a brawl and is something larger fighters—especially bouncers—should be wary of.

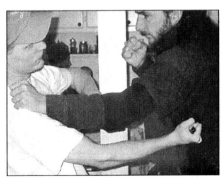

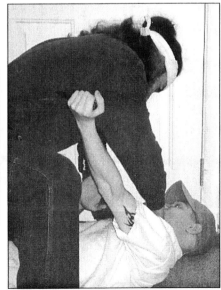

The Spike: It can be used on the ground (right) or in a clinch (left) and frequently crops up when an encounter escalates.

219

The Baby Bates: One of the rarest and most bad-intentioned knife strokes is the lateral or slightly diagonal downward stroke to the left side of the defender's neck. Of the two attempts recorded in this study, one, with a 7-inch blade, missed its mark, resulting in an indecisive grappling match; the other, with a pair of scissors, found its mark repeatedly, resulting in death.

The Baby Bates: It is a lateral or diagonal downward stroke that targets the left side of the neck.

Conclusion

Overall, reverse-grip blade and shank uses were nearly twice as deadly as stealthy uses from the natural grip and 30 times more lethal than lead-hand blade deployments. The weapons employed were usually butcher knifes, other fixed-blade knives or pointed tools. Only a few folding knives were used in this manner.

The higher incidence of injury, knockout and death can be attributed to four factors:

- Larger than normal blade and shank users
- Higher percentage of fixed blades and screwdrivers
- Confined locations
- The mechanics of running (They prevent a pursuer from striking effectively with a blade from the natural grip without breaking his stride. They do, however, permit the reverse-grip knifer to pump short-arm strokes on the run.)

Hopefully, the information presented in this article will help martial artists develop self-defense skills that are better attuned to reality.

TRIPLE THREAT
Escrima's Fighting Forms Promise the Utmost in Baton, Knife and Empty-Hand Versatility!
by Bob Orlando • Photos courtesy of Bob Orlando • March 2003

Two for the price of one! Most people will jump at a chance to snap up such a bargain in a department store. But what if you could get a deal like that in your martial arts training? Better yet, what if you could get access to a three-for-one special?

If you think it's too good to be true, you're mistaken. The Philippine martial art of *escrima* includes training drills called *sombrada* that are designed to impart all the skills you need to swing a baton, wield a knife and fight with your empty hands. And best of all, you learn all three fighting methods at the same time.

Sombrada drills are believed to take their name from *sombra,* the Spanish word for shadow. Defined as movements that function within the range of your shadow, they are an integral part of escrima and, in a slightly modified form, of the related arts of *kali* and *arnis.*

Ordinarily performed with swords, batons and knives, sombrada drills repeat short sequences of movement over and over. They constitute an efficient training method that facilitates quicker internalization of combination-based responses to a variety of attacks.

There is, however, another benefit to practicing such drills, one that is often overlooked in a society that values specialization. That would be versatility. With only minor adjustments, a single sombrada-range drill can be remarkably well-suited for use with—and against—a variety of weapons. This article will explore three sections of one of those drills.

First Couplet: Baton

Player B (on the right in the photo sequences) begins the drill by advancing with his right foot and attacking with a high right-hand strike that descends vertically toward player A's head (called a "12-line" in most Philippine arts). Using that as the starting point, the drill progresses through a series of couplets, or linked pairs. Each couplet begins with an initial defensive action followed by a counterattack.

Player A's defense begins when he steps back with his right foot. As he does, his left hand intercepts B's right forearm. Simultaneously, A's baton smashes his foe's right elbow. As the weapon strikes while rising diagonally from left to right, A's left hand moves B's right arm to the left. This dual action increases the impact of the baton by accelerating A's arm into the blow.

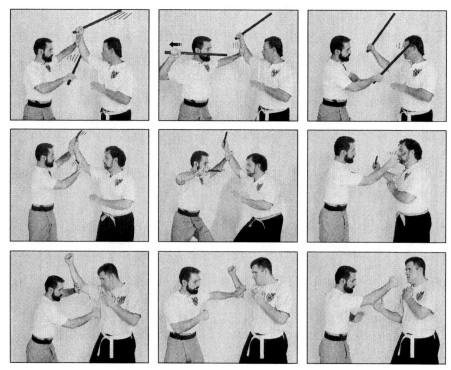

The initial couplet of the sombrada drill is performed first with a baton, then with a training knife and the empty hands.

Player A's defense here ends with his baton pointed toward his opponent, about six inches away from his face. Player A's counterattack is a diagonally descending right-to-left strike (called a "1-line") to the left side of B's face. Obviously, the blow can be directed to the collarbone or any other suitable area. What is important is the line of attack, not the target. Understand and master the line, and you can follow it to the target of your choice. The counterattack concludes the first couplet.

The second couplet begins with B's defense and subsequent counterattack, but before continuing, it is useful to repeat this first movement using a training knife.

First Couplet: Knife

The drill begins with B (right) advancing with his right foot and attacking with a high right-hand strike that descends vertically to A's head. Admittedly, such an attack with a blade is weak and almost as dangerous for the attacker as for the opponent; however, exchange the knife for a beer bottle, club or screwdriver, and its weakness fades away.

Once again, A's defense begins with a step back with his right foot while his left hand intercepts B's right forearm. Simultaneously, A's training knife slashes across his attacker's right forearm. Player A's blade travels from left to right while his left hand carries B's right arm aside, thereby increasing the effectiveness of the cut and directing the attacker's weapon away. Player A ends his defense here with his practice knife pointed at his opponent, about six inches in front of A's face.

Player A's counterattack is a diagonally descending right-to-left cut to the left side of B's face. Again, what is important here is the line of attack, not the target. Player A's counter concludes the first knife couplet and allows us to compare this action to the same maneuver performed without a weapon.

First Couplet: Empty Hands

The drill begins with B advancing with his right foot and attacking with a high right-hand strike that descends vertically to A's head. An empty-hand attack of this sort is weak, but as was emphasized above, the line is the important element. As in the other drills, A's defense begins with a step back with his right foot while his left hand intercepts B's right arm near the elbow. Simultaneously, A punches his attacker in the ribs. As he strikes, he uses his left hand to clear away B's attacking right arm from right to left. Player A ends his defense with his right fist pointed toward his opponent. Player A's counterattack is a right vertical punch to the face.

This concludes the first couplet. To maintain continuity, we will stay with the empty-hand version as we move on to the second couplet.

Second Couplet: Empty Hands

Player B's defense is to parry A's right forearm with a two-hand movement called "strike-left." Player B's right hand makes the initial interception of the punch, and his left follows it immediately, striking A in the face. With this movement, B practically climbs his partner's arm to his face as he moves in for his counterattack.

Completing the second couplet, B counters with a right backhand to A's groin. Because B moves inside his opponent's right arm with his strong side forward, this relaxed strike is as unexpected as it is effective. Now let's see how this action might be performed with a weapon.

Second Couplet: Baton

Player B's defense against A's attack to his head is a strike to A's right hand

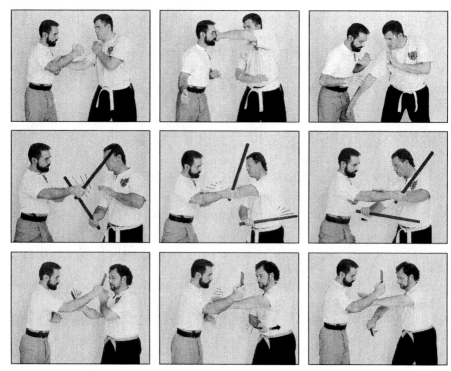

The second couplet of the drill continues from the first couplet. It is shown first with the empty hands, then with a baton and a training knife.

or wrist. Like the preceding empty-hand movement, this defense is also a two-count movement: B's baton striking A's limb is the first count, and B's left hand striking (not checking) his opponent's right forearm is the second. This is important because if the baton strike (the first count) is unsuccessful, the defender is still in danger of being injured unless, of course, he keeps the attacker's baton away. The second strike does exactly that.

Completing the second couplet, B counters with a horizontal left-to-right strike (a "4-line") to A's midsection. It may be executed with either end of the baton; the butt can be used to hit the torso, and the striking end can be used for the legs.

Second Couplet: Knife

Using a training knife, B's initial defense is not a block. Instead, it is a downward cut across the inside of A's right forearm. This is another two-count movement: The cut is the first count, and the displacement of A's right knife hand with B's striking left hand is the second. Again, this two-step movement is important because even if the cut is successful, the defender may still retain the knife—albeit with a weak grip. In that case, a sharp follow-up blow to the injured arm has an excellent chance of dislodging the weapon.

Completing the second couplet, B counters with a horizontal left-to-right 4-line slash across A's abdomen. A successful cut weakens the attacker because abdominal support must be provided by smaller secondary muscles like the psoas, which parallels the abs but is located on the inside of the spine. For continuity, we'll stay with the knife drill while we continue to the third couplet.

Third Couplet: Knife

Player A's defense against B's last counterattack is a simple one: He drops his left arm over his opponent's arm as he moves his abdomen back out of harm's way. Simultaneously, A's right hand slashes out with a horizontal right-to-left motion aimed at the closest target.

Checking the attack with his left hand might seem like it's a better move; however, such a check requires greater precision than a fast-moving knife attack allows. Simply extending the left arm over and dropping it onto the attacking arm effectively redirects the attack. The assailant's weapon arm naturally follows the line of least resistance (to the defender's midsection); however, with a slight outward movement of his left arm, the defender easily redirects the attack.

As A guides B's knife hand to his left, he brings his training blade quickly back to the right, cutting across his attacker's lower arm motion and stopping at A's right side, poised for his counterattack. Concluding the third couplet is a thrust of A's blade toward B's torso, also known as a "5-line."

Third Couplet: Empty Hands

Player A's defense against B's last empty-hand counterattack, a backhand strike to the groin, is a simple one: He drops his left arm over his opponent's attacking arm while he simultaneously pulls his hips back and redirects the backhand away from his groin. Simultaneously, A fires off a right-to-left palm strike to the side of B's face. The blow continues past his face and returns left to right as a hammerfist strike to the right elbow. Player A's left hand works in conjunction with the attack to B's elbow by simultaneously accelerating B's right arm from right to left against the blow. Completing the couplet, A slams a vertical right punch into B's diaphragm.

Now let's look at how this part of the drill plays out with the baton.

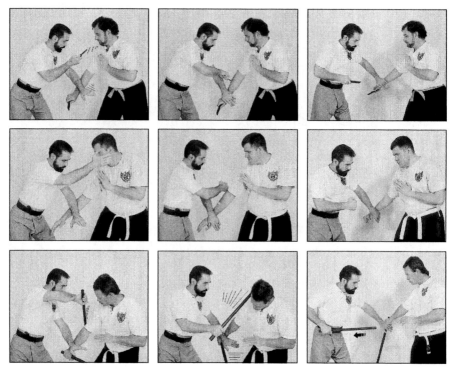

The third couplet continues from the second. It is shown first with a training knife, then with the empty hands and a baton.

Third Couplet: Baton

Player A's initial response to B's counter—a strike to A's body with the butt of the baton—is similar to the knife and empty-hand actions described above: He simply drops his left arm over his opponent's attacking arm while he simultaneously withdraws his hips and redirects his opponent's baton downward and to the left. At the same time, he executes a counterclockwise *abaniko* (fan) strike that races from 3 o'clock to 6 o'clock, where it smashes the outside of B's right hand, wrist or elbow.

Mounting his counterattack, A executes a left-to-right downward diagonal backhand strike (a 2-line) through B's collarbone or face, terminating in a chambered position at his right side. Concluding the third couplet is a thrust of A's baton into his partner's torso.

Conclusion

Obviously, this portion of the sombrada drill—along with the baton, knife and empty-hand applications presented above—cannot address every possible attack or every possible counter. Moreover, the article's abbreviated length prohibits a discussion of other elements like angling and footwork. A qualified instructor will have to show you that.

The article does, however, show you how a variety of effective tactics can be developed quickly, even against several different baton, knife and empty-hand attacks. With just one basic pattern, you can learn defensive tactics against three common weapons, all coming at you from common lines of attack. It truly is three for the price of one.

CUTTING EDGE
Self-Defense Expert Andy Stanford Reveals Everything You Need to Know to Survive a Knife Attack—or Initiate One!

by E. Lawrence • June 2003

The martial arts community is replete with self-proclaimed experts who insist they know everything there is to know about knife fighting and knife defense. But close examination of their techniques reveals just how unrealistic and ineffective many of them are. Their routines are often filled with complicated moves that would be more at home on the set of the next Jackie Chan film, while the oversize blades they like to defend against could have been lifted from a *Crocodile Dundee* movie.

Enter Andy Stanford, a man who has dedicated himself to remedying those shortcomings. The head instructor for the Sebring, Florida-based Options for Personal Security, he strives to impart practical knife skills by focusing on techniques the average person can apply under stress. His weapon of choice is a folding knife with a 3- to 5-inch blade. "The only place where you will see two people going at each other with 12-inch knives is on a pirate ship," he says, smiling.

Stanford divides knife knowledge into three areas: how to use a blade to defend against unarmed assailants, how to use it to fight against another knife, and how to defend against one using only your empty hands. This article will address all three areas.

Eminently Qualified

Stanford cut his teeth in the self-defense world when he worked as a firearms instructor and later as a weapons and tactics analyst for the U.S. Department of Defense. During the ensuing years, he completed a host of shooting, knife-fighting, survival and unarmed-combat courses. He now holds a black belt in combat *hapkido* and possesses extensive experience in *jeet kune do,* the Philippine martial arts, and the acclaimed Model Mugging program.

When he set about creating his own knife system, he chose to emphasize straightforward and practical techniques. Although he drew from the work of such notables as Eric Remmen, James Keating, Michael Janich, Gregg Hamilton and Lynn Thompson, the end product is a unique synthesis that is definitely his own.

To make his system available to the largest possible audience, Stanford condensed it into a two-day seminar. Unlike some knife courses, it is not simply about exposing students to two days out of a 20-year path to mastery, he says. Instead, it is about guiding them through a comprehensive self-contained module. Participants can use the techniques and principles they learn as soon as they walk out the door.

Common Sense

Stanford says your No. 1 option for personal security with or without a knife should be a commitment to avoid trouble. Unfortunately, many martial artists fail to realize that. A fair number of the violent encounters reported on the news, he says, are the result of stupidity: keeping company with stupid people, hanging out in stupid places or doing stupid things.

On occasions when bad situations simply cannot be avoided, you must be prepared to deal with flashing steel. As soon as a blade appears in a fight, be it by the defender or the attacker, it becomes a deadly force situation. A knife is just as serious as a gun and should be drawn only in the face of impending death or serious bodily injury, he says.

Techniques and Equipment

If you are a civilian learning how to use a knife, know that your goals are different from those of the military—which is the source of much of the Western world's knowledge of knife fighting. You should strive to use the least amount of force that will enable you to escape unharmed, he says. On the other hand, a soldier's mission is to eliminate the enemy, and that can involve doing things that are inappropriate for civilians.

Likewise, the knives chosen by members of the armed services are not necessarily suitable for you—for tactical as well as legal reasons. The military tends to rely on large fixed-blade models, and Stanford acknowledges that for combat, they are superior to folding knives. They are always

A fixed-blade knife such as SOG's Tsunami (left) may be more effective in combat, but a tactical folder such as Cold Steel's Recon 1 (right) is easier to conceal and more likely to be legal to carry.

"open" and ready for action, and you never have to worry that a locking mechanism might fail. But as a civilian, you will probably find that a tactical folding knife is best. It is more likely to be legal to carry concealed, and it will be much more convenient to slip into your pocket. For these reasons, his courses emphasize folding knives.

Because getting your knife into play is half the battle, Stanford says

Knife expert Andy Stanford prepares to defend himself against an armed attacker clad in FIST protective gear (1). He reacts to the thrust by moving his trunk out of the way and using both hands to jam the attacking arm (2). Stanford then wraps his left arm around the upper part of the other man's knife arm and locks it against his body (3). Next, he drives a palm strike into the assailant's face (4) and slams a knee thrust into his midsection (5).

Photos by Dee Shepard

you should devote a significant amount of training time to opening your weapon. Do it from a variety of positions with your dominant hand and your weak hand. Do it with both hands while trying to minimize the noise it makes. No matter how proficient you become, he says, know that the stress of combat can so devastate your dexterity and coordination that you may have to use both hands whether you want to or not.

Tough Training

To mirror reality, knife training must be intense. Stanford suggests a drill in which you deliver four quick strikes on a focus mitt before you draw your weapon. The purpose is to simulate deploying a knife in a struggle. For safety, only training knives should be used, he says.

A more dynamic drill begins with you and a partner donning white T-shirts and holding magic markers. Using the pens to simulate knives, you try to cut each other without getting cut. Afterward, the number and location of the marks on your arms and shirt will convey just how difficult it is to engage a knife-wielding attacker without sustaining any damage.

Another type of training Stanford favors involves sparring with rubber knives and eye protection. Your goal is to target your opponent's weapon-bearing hand or destroy his vision using a quick slash or snap cut.

In most of the drills he has concocted, he says the goal is to gain an understanding of striking range and experience firsthand how a knife can move. You quickly learn that facing a blade-whirling foe is radically different from facing an opponent who stands in one place and attacks with a single slash or thrust.

Best Defense

The likelihood that you will ever be required to use a knife to defend against a knife is low, Stanford says. In fact, it is difficult to find any substantiated accounts of modern duels in which the participants were armed with blades. On the street, an experienced knifer will not give you an opportunity to draw your weapon—and that is precisely why unarmed knife defense is so important.

For maximum realism, Stanford says, your unarmed knife defense must not be limited to techniques that work against only slow-motion thrusts and slashes, and it should not be done with foreknowledge of which offensive methodology your partner will use next. It must revolve around an opponent who strikes at random and keeps his weapon in constant motion, and that is obviously a tall order. The late Capt. Stephen Stavers, a Marine Corps hand-to-hand combat instructor during World War II, once said: "No barehanded disarming technique is dependable even against a fair knife fighter. Trying to disarm a truly scientific knife fighter would be like trying to stop a propeller with bare hands."

Stanford insists it's not quite so hopeless most of the time. When you are unarmed and facing a knife, he says your best bet is to run—provided you have sufficient time and space. If escape isn't possible, you should try to maneuver until a large object is between yourself and your attacker. Grab an improvised weapon if you can.

As a last resort, Stanford teaches a simple but effective unarmed defense against a blade assault. Developed by a British police officer named Peter Boatman, it involves avoiding the strikes until you can grab the attacker's knife arm. You then wrap your arm around his upper arm, pulling it tight against your body and applying maximum leverage to immobilize the limb. Finish by striking—with your free hand, knees, elbows or any other natural weapon—until he is out of commission.

Always use both arms or hands to jam the knife-bearing arm, Stanford says. Realize that seizing the arm may require several attempts and result in multiple cuts, but it is necessary because the last thing you want to do is allow him to keep his weapon so he can strike at will. The exact method you employ to capture the arm and incapacitate the assailant will vary because of the fluid nature of knife fights, he adds.

Stanford's final message echoes the words of the World War II vet: Do not expect the Boatman technique or any other defensive maneuver to work reliably against an experienced knife fighter. In a way, that directs you back to

the wisdom of his first bit of advice: Avoid trouble whenever you can. That simple philosophy will work wonders to keep you out of jail and out of the emergency room.

Andy Stanford watches as two students prepare to spar with rubber knives. Note the use of eye, head and hand protection.

BATTLE BLADE
The Hottest Edged Weapon of the 21st Century Has Roots That Stretch Back Hundreds of Years!

by Ernest Emerson • Photos courtesy of Ernest Emerson • February 2004

How many martial arts fads have you seen come and go? I've been in this game for more than three decades, and I've witnessed quite a few. Sometimes they've involved weapons, gadgets and tools. Other times they've been about entire fighting systems. It's rare that a fad will catch on and stick around for more than a few years, so when one does, it's worth taking note. The *karambit* knife from Southeast Asia has the potential to be included in that elite group.

Brief History

Over the past 4,000 years, mankind has effected thousands of variations in the design of swords, knives and impact weapons. The major influences in their evolutionary path are related to three triggers. The most profound one has been the discovery of new materials or the ability to process old materials into a more usable form. Human beings progressed from sharp sticks to stones, then to copper, bronze, iron and steel implements. Each discovery caused a major leap in weapon design and tactics.

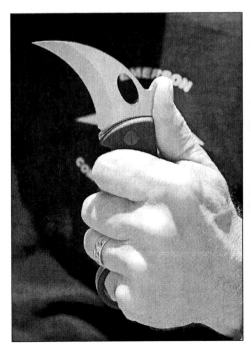

The design of the karambit allows the user to insert his pinkie (left) or his index finger (right) into the hole in the butt of the handle, resulting in two entirely different ways to grip the weapon.

233

For knife aficionados, an appealing feature of the karambit is the ability to spin it using the finger hole in the handle. (Practicing the spinning technique with a sharp blade is not recommended.)

The second trigger has been the clash of cultures. Every time there was a physical shift of cultures—whether because of famine, natural disaster or invasion—an opportunity to learn from the successes and failures of the enemy ensued. Inevitably, each side would adapt, modify or copy the weapons and applications that appealed to its people.

The third trigger has been invention and innovation. Whenever there was an advance in armor, weapon design or tactics, the development of the key needed to defeat it inevitably followed. Those that didn't evolve quickly enough faded into obscurity or died off.

Is it, then, safe to say that just because something has been surpassed by modern technology, it's no longer effective? Far from it. Once when I was teaching a course to the military, an adjunct instructor formerly with Britain's famed SAS forces explained how he had neutralized an enemy with a sharp stick. "If I didn't have the stick," he said, "I would've used a rock."

It would seem that what was effective 2,000 years ago is just as effective today, given the right circumstances. For example, the weapon of choice for some German street gangs is the baseball bat—which is nothing more than a club. A citizen can't even possess one unless he's playing baseball or on his way to or from a game. They're restricted because they're effective.

Design Advantages

How does all that relate to the karambit? Well, the aforementioned principles apply here, too. Consider: Why has the Japanese sword been around for more than a millennium? Why has the Nepalese *kukri,* or Gurkha knife, been used since the time of Alexander the Great? Why has the bow and arrow been in existence for 4,000 to 5,000 years? Because they all boast efficient designs that get the job done.

The karambit is in the same boat. If its design did not have merit, it also would have been relegated to the dustbin of history's failures. The bottom line is, it was a good knife then, and it's even better now because of 21st-century manufacturing methods.

The origin of the karambit is shrouded in mystery and controversy, but it's fairly certain that it was devised in Indonesia many centuries ago. It has become popular among modern martial artists mainly because of the increasing interest practitioners are showing in the Indonesian fighting arts and because of the subsequent proliferation of schools that teach them. Thus, the karambit has started finding its way into the mainstream.

In combat, the karambit can be used to attack the most vulnerable targets of the body—even if they are located on the back side of a limb.

235

The modern karambit comes in two styles, with numerous variations within each one. The fixed-blade karambit is the traditional version. It has all the features that fixed blades are prized for: strength, rigidity and a lack of moving parts. The folding-blade karambit is the more modern version of the ancient knife. It can be made reasonably strong, but it will never be as solid as a fixed blade.

When you're ready to cough up your hard-earned bucks for one style or the other, remember that you may train with a fixed blade, but chances

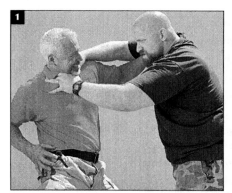

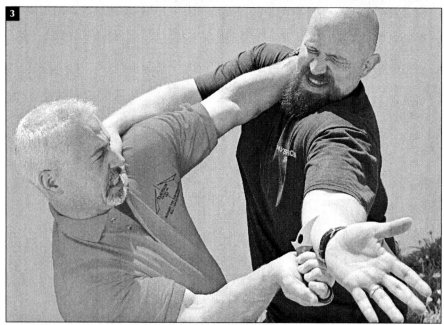

Ernest Emerson (left) is choked by an assailant (1). He deploys a karambit knife from his pocket and opens it with one hand (2). He then uses the curved blade to slice his attacker's arm as he directs it away from his neck (3).

are, you'll carry a folder. So if you're in the market for a self-defense tool, that should weigh heavily on your decision. Of course, if you're a member of the military or a law-enforcement unit that issues fixed-blade knives as part of its duty gear, you may want to opt for a fixed blade.

Either way, the karambit is lightweight and efficient. Because of its minimal mass, it can be wielded almost as rapidly as you can move your hand. Its inwardly curved blade mimics the claw of a tiger or, if you look further back in history, a velociraptor. The shape of the blade enables even a rank beginner to effectively employ it simply by slapping forward and downward in a pawing motion.

Some say the karambit is a cutting tool, not a stabbing tool. But anyone with any amount of experience with the weapon will attest that it can be driven into a target right up to its hilt with very little effort.

Most karambit knives, but not all, have a hole in the butt of the handle, and it's by far one of the finest features of the weapon. When you insert a digit—either your index finger or your pinkie, depending on the grip you prefer—you create a durable hold on the knife and make it virtually impossible for an opponent to dislodge it. Furthermore, if you were to lose your balance and splay your fingers to break your fall, the knife would still remain securely under your control.

Combat Method

When it comes to combat, the karambit has characteristics that are not found in other knife designs. Cerebral martial artists will forever debate distance and range, but reality is reality. In a real life-or-death struggle, things are up close and personal—and almost always destined to end on the ground. There's no dueling and no dancing around. And that is where the design of the karambit shines.

Its unique grip and clawlike blade enable you to use it with simple punching motions, and the finger ring permits you to grab an object or an opponent's limb while still holding the knife. You can also use it to execute a myriad of devastating takedowns that will disable your opponent as he falls, thus opening a new range of combat that might be termed "knife grappling."

To top it all off, the karambit works perfectly when you attempt to execute virtually any traditional move derived from the Philippine slashing and cutting arts.

One final characteristic makes the karambit unique in the world of bladed weapons: You can spin it around your finger like a tiny buzz saw.

Few knife experts would recommend trying any sort of spinning, twirling or extended gripping in a real fight—just as you wouldn't flip your *balisong* knife in a street battle. However, just like with the balisong, manipulating the weapon at blurring speed is half the fun of owning one. Just make sure you use a training knife—or at least apply a liberal covering of thick tape to the edge and the point if all you have is the real thing.

Your Decision

In the end, martial artists like you will decide whether the karambit is a fad or an ultra-efficient tool Americans will embrace for decades to come. For what it's worth, I've evaluated plenty of designs during the 25 years I've been in the knife-making and knife-design business, and the karambit is the one I carry. It's also the knife I would use if I had to protect my life or the life of a loved one.

AGAINST THE ODDS

by Richard Ryan • Photo by Robert W. Young • April 2004

Most people severely underestimate how deadly a knife attack can be. The rule of thumb is, if a blade can touch you, it can hurt you. A lot of martial artists must not know that, however, because I frequently come across masters teaching questionable knife-defense methods and am often left wondering if they've ever tried to use their techniques in real life—or even in the *dojo* against an uncooperative partner.

The hard truth is that you're unlikely to ever control someone who's armed with a knife. You'll never grab or trap the knife hand, you'll never lock or break the arm or wrist, and you'll most certainly never take a knife away from all but the most incompetent attackers. It's almost as if the average knife-defense technique should come with a warning: Attempting this can be severely harmful to your ability to continue breathing.

There's a reason the blade has been the weapon of choice since man first learned to make tools to ensure his survival. Of all our interpersonal weapons—short of a hand grenade or gun—it has the most advantages and the fewest disadvantages, especially when it comes to close-quarters combat.

The first advantage is that a knife is a multidirectional touch weapon, meaning it can harm its victim by contact alone, and it can "touch" that person from any direction and almost from any position. The second is that, unlike in unarmed combat in which precise technique is required to be effective, a knife doesn't need exact body mechanics to achieve the desired effect. The third is that a knife is a "forgiving" weapon in the sense that the person wielding it can be physically inferior and still take out his enemy in a heartbeat.

Therefore, the greatest challenge in neutralizing a knife attack lies in acquiring the ability to react instantaneously to a sudden and often deceptive assault. The problem is that doing so requires that you perceive where, when and how the attacker will try to slash or stab you. After all, you can't stop what you cannot see—or more precisely, you can't stop what you cannot perceive. You have to see the blade to react to it, and of all the weapons, the knife is the most difficult to see and predict.

Those facts make catch-and-control defenses difficult, if not impossible, to pull off in the real world. Unless your attacker telegraphs his intention or delivers the clichéd overhand "psycho stab," you stand little chance of discerning the exact line of engagement. Consequently, you have almost no chance of intercepting, catching, controlling or manipulating the blade without literally risking life and limb.

At every knife-survival seminar I conduct, before teaching any techniques or tactics, I pair off the students and give them protective gear and a single training blade. Then I tell them that they each have 10 minutes to choose and practice any technique they wish to use to defend against a prearranged attack, usually a basic straight thrust to the torso.

At the end of the time, we gather around and watch each student demonstrate his method. The most common techniques include those mentioned above, as well as some counterkicks and interceptions. With some skill, such techniques can appear to be effective, especially when you know exactly where, when and how the attack will come. But that's the catch: In the real world, you *don't* know exactly where, when and how it will happen, and even slight variations on the theme will wreak havoc on any attempt to control the blade. It's a problem of compound stimulus and response.

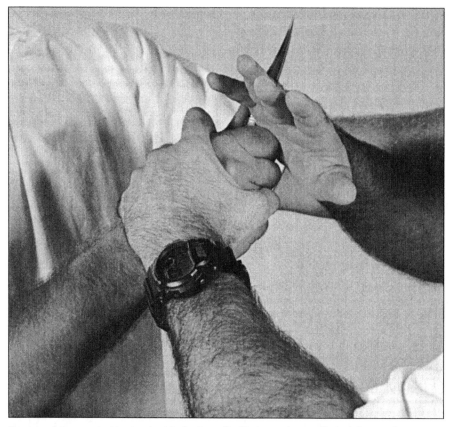

Because of the complexities involved in fending off a blade attack, most knife-defense techniques are likely to fail if attempted on the street, the author says.

To illustrate that point, I suit up and take on each student. I explain that I'll strike either at his heart or throat, but this time, he doesn't know which one will be targeted or when. I also explain that I'll change the angle of attack ever so slightly from a slash to a stab, and I might change my timing, commitment and rhythm a bit. So far, no one has ever stopped my attacks. Every student gets cut, and in the real world, every one would have been killed.

Now, if you imagine that situation being complicated by a factor of 10 or 100—because of multiple lines of engagement—you'll realize that even if you could quantify every possible line of attack, you would never be able to predict your opponent's timing and movements with any accuracy. If he were allowed to strike anywhere at any time—like in the real world—the complexity would soar astronomically. Add to that broken rhythm, feints, footwork, strikes with the free hand or foot and, well, you get the picture.

The edged weapon truly is the ultimate equalizer. In the hands of a novice, it's exceedingly dangerous. In the hands of an expert, you'd better pray that luck is on your side regardless of how good a martial artist you are. The knife offers no margin for error, so unless your attacker is an idiot, your chances of recognizing, intercepting and controlling him—or his weapon—are about as good as your chances of winning the lottery.

UNARMED AGAINST A KNIFE

by Richard Ryan • June 2004

In the April 2004 installment of this column, I discussed the extreme difficulties involved in surviving a blade attack using conventional blocks, grabs, traps and takeaways. I painted a pretty bleak picture of knife defense, but I didn't mean to imply it's hopeless. Presented below is the best strategy I've come across. It may not be pretty, but it's all we have.

Edged weapons are lightning fast and cruelly deceptive. The best defense against them is avoidance. If you can escape by leaping over a car, wall or table, do it. Get out of there so you can fight another day. If you can't escape, try to level the playing field by accessing a weapon yourself. Pick up a chair and use it as a shield. Throw a rock, bottle or telephone at the assailant and sprint in the opposite direction.

One of the most effective defenses against a knife attack is a gun. Remember the scene from *Raiders of the Lost Ark* in which Indiana Jones comes face to face with a man who's slicing and dicing the air with two scimitars? He pulls out his pistol and shoots the guy. Only a fool fights fair when his opponent possesses an overwhelming advantage, because in the real world, there are no retakes.

If you end up empty-handed in a battle with an armed assailant, don't expect to tie him up in knots and leave him for the police. Even if he's the most incompetent attacker in the world, you probably won't escape injury. Instead, you should focus on escaping death. Once you've accepted that notion, you'll be psychologically prepared to deal with the situation and concentrate on doing whatever it takes to end it as quickly as possible. That's the only way to minimize damage to life and limb—by ending the fight as soon as possible.

Try to take him out before he gets a chance to organize his attack and overwhelm you. Get low and small. Make your body compact to reduce the size of the target you present to him. Shield your vital areas as you move forward to strike. Once you're in the kill zone, execute rapid-fire blows with everything you've got, blasting over and over into his most sensitive targets until he no longer poses a threat. This advice runs against conventional wisdom, but in the real world, it's the only way. To survive, you have to take the fight to him and make him worry about his own safety instead of about cutting you.

One last tip: Unless you have a clear path to flee from your assailant, you have no reason to back up. Retreating only prolongs the fight and allows him to build momentum and courage before re-engaging you. Anytime you step backward, you risk paying a heavy price. Forge ahead. Stop the attack and stop the attacker. Then be thankful you're still alive and get to the emergency room.

AIKIDO UNDER ATTACK
Morihei Uyeshiba's Peaceful Art Takes on the 5 Angles of the Knife

by Lynn Seiser, Ph.D. • Photos courtesy of Lynn Sciser, Ph.D. • November 2004

Every day as we read the paper and watch the news on television, we see violence. And more violence. It comes in many guises and employs many weapons, perhaps the most common of which is the knife.

Few people, martial artists included, understand the real dangers of a knife attack. Only those who have faced cold steel in combat know the emotions that emerge when a person is assaulted by stabs and slashes. The intensity of the situation demands that the defender prepares himself to the best of his ability if he is to survive. Unfortunately, with the exception of the Philippine martial arts, very few schools of self-defense teach effective methods for countering blade attacks. If you believe some gaps exist in your training, this article will help you fill them in.

The Aikido Advantage

Aikido is a nonviolent, noncompetitive Japanese martial art that has gained popularity around the world. Morihei Uyeshiba created it after a lifetime of training in other arts. Aikido originally included strikes, but they were later eliminated to keep it congruent with the art's philosophies of compassion and peace. Its knife defenses, which have been part of the curriculum from the get-go, have escaped those reductionist efforts and are as elegant and effective as they ever were.

Awareness and good manners are aikido's first line of self-defense. Violence is progressive, and signs of it can often be picked up early in a confrontation in the form of probing verbal contact, posturing or positioning. Therefore, it's taught that one way to forestall an attack is through politeness. It's amazing what kind words can do.

When it comes time to get physical, aikido techniques generally follow a four-step process:

First, you enter with the simple footwork of shuffling *(tsugi-ashi)* or walking *(ayumi-ashi)*. Then you blend by performing a step-and-turn movement *(tenkan-ashi)*, which repositions your body off the line of attack and often leaves you facing the same direction as your attacker. The blending establishes a unity or oneness between the body, mind and spirit of both parties. This action, unique to aikido, is the physical basis for its philosophical emphasis on harmony and peace.

Dang Thong Phong, an aikido master based in Westminster, California, emphasizes the directness of entering and blending by matching his attacker's pace and momentum. He says you can accompany your entering and blending action with an inhalation, creating a breath vacuum to further pull your opponent into your sphere of influence.

Second, you redirect and off-balance him using full-body circular motions such as pivoting or turning *(tenkan-ashi)*. It's important not to engage in a strength contest but to apply the power of your whole body in a circular, screwing-type motion.

Third, you either throw the attacker or control him by pinning his body to the ground with a joint lock. You extend your *ki* (internal energy) through his center toward his balance point while you exhale. Phong believes that the elusive and controversial ki is developed naturally through technical proficiency and training. Because the attacker is already off-balance, it's easy to accomplish.

Finally, you let go and move on without inflicting undue harm on the other person. Phong advises making sure your adversary is no longer an immediate threat by quickly moving out of range of any further attack.

Angles of the Knife

Aikido contains numerous techniques derived from sword movements. Consequently, its practitioners are used to defending against knife attacks delivered along comparatively larger angles. The three most common of these are the downward strike *(shomen-uchi)*, the oblique-angled attack to the neck *(yokomen-uchi)* and the straight thrust *(mune-tsuki)*. For the purpose of this article, though, we'll focus on the five angles of attack taught in most Philippine martial arts because they have a wider acceptance and appeal.

Angle No. 1 is a downward diagonal slash from the right shoulder to the left hip. Angle No. 2 is a downward diagonal slash from the left shoulder to the right hip. Combining them produces a downward figure-8 or, if reversed, an upward figure-8. Note that slashes on angles No. 1 and No. 2 can also travel down and back up along the same line of attack.

Angle No. 3 is a horizontal slash from the right hip to the left hip. Angle No. 4 is a horizontal slash from the left hip to the right hip. They can be combined into horizontal-downward and horizontal-upward figure-8s. Notice that four of the five angles are slicing or slashing movements that exploit the damage potential of the blade.

Angle No. 5 is a straight-in stab at stomach height. A variation of it involves making rapid jabs to inflict multiple puncture wounds. This type of attack, called "shanking," is common in prisons. The opposite hand is usually active, constantly checking, countering, controlling, concealing and assisting with the movement of the blade.

While there are other numbering methods and angles of attack in knife fighting, it's easiest to begin with these five. Note that once you learn how to deal with them, you'll be able to handle any weapon that's used along the same paths of attack, be it a sword, stick, bat, hand or foot. The main difference in the way you respond will be the distance.

Three C's

Aikido's three C's of weapons defense are clear, control and counter. The first step is to clear the path of the weapon before you enter and blend. In knife fighting, it's essential to develop a "blade consciousness," which tells you where the cutting edge is at all times. Without it, it's all too easy to get cut.

In training, it's recommended that you start with a rubber knife that has yellow tape along the edge of the blade. That bright color will aid in retinal detection and retention, and it will clearly show you where not to touch. Later, you can transition to a wooden knife, a dull metal training knife and finally a training weapon that has inked edges so you and your partner can tell when you've failed to evade a slash.

Once cleared, you control the weapon using redirecting and off-balancing techniques until the attacker cannot assault you again.

Only after the knife has been cleared and controlled can you begin to counter. In aikido, that counter might be a throw or a joint lock and disarm. It doesn't have to be a counterstrike. The art teaches that it's possible to defend yourself without hurting your adversary. Remember that your goal is to stop the knife attack and help your assailant "re-evaluate" his intentions and actions.

Angle No. 1

The opponent initiates an angle No. 1 attack. You retreat as required to maintain a safe distance from the knife as it completes its motion. Then you immediately enter using a shuffling technique and jam the man's knife arm while controlling his elbow. Next, you shift your center by turning your hips, after which you begin your counter: an aikido wrist throw known as *kotogaeshi*, which sends him airborne. When he lands, you turn his body, pin his arm, lock his wrist and take away the weapon.

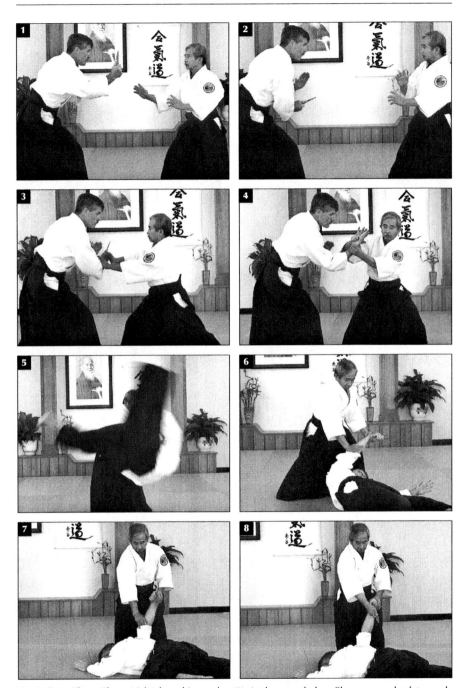

No. 1: Dang Thong Phong (right) faces his attacker (1). As the man slashes, Phong moves back to evade the blade (2), then shuffles forward and seizes the knife arm (3). Maintaining his hold on the man's wrist, the aikido expert turns (4) and launches his foe into the air (5). Once he lands (6), Phong rolls the man's body, pins his arm and locks his wrist (7). He then removes the knife from his grasp (8).

Angle No. 2

As your assailant launches an angle No. 2 attack, you maintain a neutral stance at a safe distance. When the blade is close enough, you intercept the motion of the knife arm and blend with the path of attack. Then you

No. 2: Aikido master Dang Thong Phong (left) confronts an assailant who's ready to execute a diagonal slash (1). When the knife is extended, Phong repositions his body and intercepts the arm (2). Next, he spins under the attacker's trapped limb and applies a wrist lock (3). Phong spins again and snatches the knife (4), after which he executes a butt-end strike to the torso (5). The defender finishes by forcing his opponent down (6) and using the knife handle to exert pressure on his elbow (7).

redirect it by spinning under his arm and seizing control using a *sankyo* wrist lock. Maintaining the hold, you spin once again and take away the knife. Further off-balancing the attacker, you follow up with a strike to the heart or solar plexus using the butt end of the weapon. To finish, you control him by applying pressure to his elbow with the knife handle as you pin him facedown on the mat.

Angle No. 3

Your foe attacks with an angle No. 3 to the stomach. As soon as possible, you blend with and intercept the strike. Then you scrape your wrist bone down his arm and pull slightly to off-balance and control him. Next, you reverse direction while controlling his elbow and applying an *ikkyo* wrist lock, after which you step forward and transition into an elbow lock. You finish with a disarm.

No. 3: As soon as the aggressor slashes at Dang Thong Phong (left), Phong blends with the motion and intercepts the attack (1). He then scrapes his wrist bone along the opponent's arm while pulling to upset his balance (2). Phong quickly reverses direction as he effects a wrist lock (3). To finish, he moves forward and applies an elbow lock (4), then completes the disarm (5).

249

Angle No. 4

When your adversary commences an angle No. 4 attack, you maintain a neutral stance at a safe distance before entering and controlling his knife arm. Your next task is to blend by stepping behind him with the angle of attack, then redirect and control his elbow. Continuing your circular footwork, you apply downward pressure on his arm and follow through with a takedown. To finish, you effect an arm lock and snatch the knife from his hand.

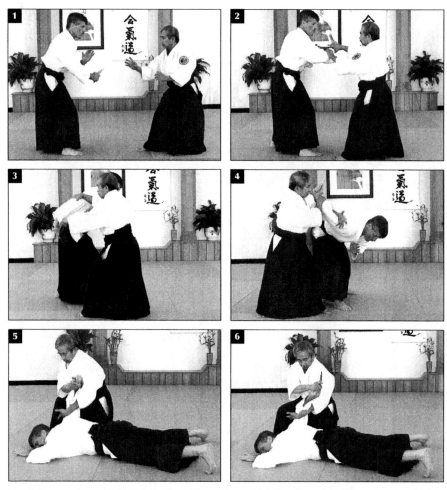

No. 4: An armed attacker (left) faces Dang Thong Phong (1). When he strikes, Phong enters and takes control of the weapon arm (2). He follows up by scooting behind the man and redirecting his elbow (3). Phong continues his circular footwork as he applies pressure on the trapped arm (4), causing the opponent to fall (5). The aikido instructor locks the limb and finally takes away the knife (6).

Angle No. 5

The enemy attacks with an angle No. 5 thrust, and in response, you adopt a neutral stance out of range. You then enter and redirect his knife hand before striking him in the face. Continuing your forward momentum, you disrupt his balance, then follow up with a takedown. Once he's grounded, you control him by using your knee to apply pressure to his elbow, after which you take away the weapon.

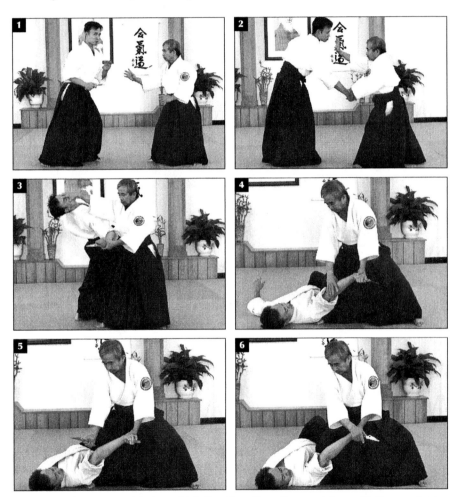

No. 5: When the opponent (left) thrusts his knife at Dang Thong Phong's abdomen (1), Phong maintains his stance at a safe distance before entering and redirecting the weapon (2). Once the knife is under control, the aikido master strikes his assailant's face (3) and breaks his balance to force him to the ground (4). Phong then applies pressure against the elbow with his knee (5) so he can use his free hand to grab the weapon (6).

Final Advice

Remember that the effectiveness of any knife-defense technique depends more on your proficiency than on the style you practice. Ultimately, aikido sequences described above are a fine place to start, but ultimately, success will depend on the effort you put into your training.

RED WARRIOR SYSTEM
Resurrected American-Indian Martial Art Teaches More Than Just Blade Fighting!

by Dr. Robert G. Rose • Photos courtesy of Adrian Roman • December 2004

Some years ago, Adrian "Chief" Roman, already well-known within *kenpo* karate circles, began working on a fighting system to honor his native Choctaw people and, indeed, all American Indians. He faced more than a few challenges.

He knew that the Indians were great fighters in terms of archery, lance throwing and so on. He did not, however, know much of their hand-to-hand techniques. Because every culture possesses empty-hand fighting methods, it would make little sense to suppose that America's many Indian tribes did not. Unfortunately, the details of much of their culture, including hand-to-hand fighting, were lost when waves of settlers from Europe migrated west.

Adrian "Chief" Roman (left) founded the red warrior system of self-defense after learning grappling and striking techniques from his family members and conducting research into the lost combat methods of his ancestors.

253

Roman wasn't discouraged. He drew on two sources to develop the system that would eventually be called *tushkahoma,* which is Choctaw for "red warrior." First, he learned grappling and striking techniques passed down to him by his father and uncles. For the most part, however, he knew he would have to recreate the lost fighting systems based on the Indian way of life.

It All Starts With the Knife

Indians carried knives as customarily as modern Americans carry a driver's license. It was an all-purpose tool as well as a weapon. If a close-quarters altercation began, it's reasonable to assume that the combatants did not put down their weapons.

Once you imagine a fight with knives, a system begins to emerge. A system is not a hodgepodge of techniques but a set of moves unified by reasonable assumptions and a short but essential list of underlying principles.

Assumption No. 1: Knife fighting exists in reality. All of Roman's training is reality-focused, and that's especially true for the red warrior system. Many martial arts neglect hand-to-knife combat based on the very reasonable assumption that it's virtually impossible to even the odds in a fight against an armed assailant. Because most arts are sport-based, you wouldn't pit an unarmed person against a person with a knife any more than you would put a lightweight in the ring with a heavyweight.

In the reality of the American Indian, however, there were no doubt occasions when one person lost his knife during an altercation. Did the unarmed person at that point simply bare his throat and wait for the end? Certainly not. In a world where everyone was packing a blade, might martial arts teachers have thought about the eventuality of losing one's weapon? Certainly.

Reality involves virtually no margin for error. In sport, you can take a strong but wild swing; it's a calculated risk based on your vulnerability to being counterattacked. You may get hit by that counter, and the worst case will be that the ref wakes you up to fight another day. In life-or-death situations, however, extreme caution is called for. If you get shanked, you probably won't get up.

In reality, there's no rest break and no bell at the end of three minutes. Your fight may last 10 seconds or 10 minutes. Every second counts against you. Exhaustion has the same skill-numbing effect as alcohol or drugs. Try staying away from someone swinging a knife at you in a closed room. He'll expend virtually no energy, and you'll be hopping all over the place. Your physical strength and conditioning may be greater than his; but sooner than you imagine, you'll be cornered with no energy left to defend yourself.

Assumption No. 2: A warrior escapes from the encounter when possible. One of the hallmarks of reality-based self-defense is retreat. In a street fight, a weak ego with false pride may consider it necessary to "hold one's ground." In life-and-death warfare, there's a logical dictate to avoid defeat and secure victory. Frequently that goal calls for retreat, even by the bravest and best. SEALs and Green Berets don't fight against the odds if there's no need to do so. They're not out to prove anything.

In the same way, only the most foolhardy of Indian braves would have fought unarmed against a knife if there was any possibility of escape. Note that escape isn't always synonymous with running away—for example, fleeing isn't an option if it involves leaving a loved one behind or if you're slower than your attacker.

Underlying Principles

The practitioner of the red warrior system understands that knife fighting is life or death, and when faced with an unavoidable duel with a blade-wielding assailant, he follows five basic principles.

Principle No. 1: Establish your base. All training emphasizes a strong base whether you're on your feet or on the ground. (Roman prefers standing because rolling around on the ground when a knife is present can be deadly.) Establishing that base means getting out of the way of the weapon in a manner that gives your body firm support.

Opponents of knife defense point out, somewhat smugly, that you'll get cut if you fight back. That's like telling a boxer he'll get hit if he enters the ring: It's true, it's obvious and so what? The boxer still needs to defend himself to the best of his ability. Of course, there's a high likelihood of getting cut or stabbed in a knife fight, but quickly creating a strong base out of the path of the weapon can diminish that danger.

Principle No. 2: Intercept the weapon. This edict makes many students shake their heads. Establishing a safe base sounds like "backing away," but that's not the case. You must get close to the attacker, track the weapon and parry the hand that holds it. By intercepting the weapon, you build in a margin for error. Even if your technique fails—and every technique does fail sometimes—you will have moved the knife to where you want it to be.

Principle No. 3: Control the weapon. Now the logic of the first two principles becomes even more apparent. Controlling the weapon is the

third, sequentially, but the primary one when it comes to importance. With a firm base and an interception, you're in position to control. Once the weapon is controlled, you have at least a temporary respite and a chance to exercise your options. As long as you control it—which, in the case of the knife, means seizing the hand that holds it—you're safe.

Principle No. 4: Take away the weapon. Acting on the assumption that your opponent knows what he's doing, your control will not last long. You must disarm him, and that's easier said than done. Because your opponent is no amateur, he knows he has to hold the knife tightly. A great deal of practice and finesse is required for the disarm, as well as an anticipation of cause and effect. He won't be passive while you disarm him. For this reason, the number of techniques in the red warrior system is limited, but they're modularized so they can be assembled in hundreds of combinations.

Principle No. 5: Neutralize your opponent. That usually involves doing physical damage to him. While it might sound vengeful, it's not. It's common

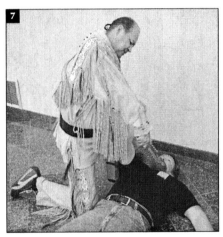

The dance of war: The opponent (right) thrusts his knife toward the abdomen of Adrian "Chief" Roman (1). Roman zones to his left, creating a solid base and anchoring his elbow, while simultaneously intercepting the weapon and twisting the wrist (2). Anticipating the man's most probable response—pulling the knife away horizontally across his body—Roman advances and takes away the weapon (3). He then steps and turns—thereby rotating the opponent counterclockwise—and executes a slash to the ribs to neutralize the threat (4). Next, the tushkahoma stylist drops to his knee and forces the man to the ground (5-6), where he restrains him at knifepoint (7).

sense. He has tried to kill you once; if he gains access to another weapon, isn't he likely to try to harm you again?

The Dance of War

The aforementioned principles are also steps that must be followed, and they must be done in a flowing fashion, one moving seamlessly into the other. As the opponent thrusts his knife with his right hand, you zone to your left into a strong stance—a solid base—parallel to and outside of his line of thrust. Simultaneously, you use your left hand to contact and then grab, or intercept, the knife hand at the wrist/hand juncture, with your left elbow anchored at your side.

The need for a strong base becomes apparent because without it, you cannot turn the contact into a firm grasp of the wrist. A one-handed wrist grab isn't a strong hold—until you rotate your opponent's wrist counterclockwise to destroy his grip strength. Once that rotation is done, you're temporarily in control of the knife hand. His grip is now weak enough for you to strip away the knife, but cause and effect says he'll try his only avenue of escape—swinging the knife across his body and breaking your grip on the weak (thumb) side.

Thus, you step forward with his motion and strip the knife with your right hand. But you haven't finished until you circle under his arm to effect a lock and drop to your left knee, pulling him down. Then you take steps to neutralize him.

Transcending the Knife

The red warrior system has many counter-knife techniques, but it also has club-to-club methods, unarmed defenses against the club, and a range of defensive moves, including bare hand vs. bare hand. All of them follow the logic of the knife.

As you read the principles above, one thing becomes clear: They apply to all effective techniques of self-defense. It's only when you're faced with a lethal edged weapon that you realize the need to show the proper balance of caution and aggressiveness that you should show in all fights. It bears reiterating:

• First, always assume that your fight is taking place in the real world. In competition, a touch to the stomach may score a point and a touch to the head may bag two points. That's fine for tournaments, but on the street, if a small person hits a larger and stronger attacker in the stomach, it will likely have no effect. If that same small person slams a knuckle fist into the thug's temple, it may be all the "points" needed.

• In the real world, you should avoid conflict even if it means enduring insults. If you wind up fighting, you may have to deal with legal hassles afterward as you argue that you attempted to avoid combat.

• In the case of a knife fight, you know your opponent is superior and potentially lethal. Assume that in every fight. Your opponent may be as skilled in a martial art as you are, and his kick may be able to cripple you as surely as a bullet. Forget the "invincible warrior" hype teachers may have given you. If Ken Shamrock, Royce Gracie, Muhammad Ali and Lennox Lewis can suffer defeats, how can you imagine that you're invincible?

• If you must fight, establish a firm base. Try standing on one foot and boxing—silly, isn't it? Yet some martial artists pay so little attention to stance that they might as well be standing on one foot. A firm base doesn't mean staying still; instead, it means striving to keep your balance even while moving.

- Intercept the weapon. A parry is often better than a hard block. You can redirect even a powerful strike with a well-timed parry. On the other hand, a block effected against a powerful blow may not be effective and might even break a bone in your arm.

- Control the weapon. In the red warrior system, you usually take your opponent to the ground by locking an arm or leg in such a way that he cannot strike.

- Disarm the opponent. He'll likely strike again once you release your lock, so you must take away his weapon immediately. This disarming action may involve hyperextending his arm to traumatize the joint, striking him or causing excruciating pain. You must do whatever is necessary to render him harmless.

- Neutralize the opponent. In sport, a submission ends the fight. In reality, he may submit and then begin fighting again. There's a fine line between defense and counter-aggression. If the fight is halted, your assailant is neutralized even if you haven't "paid him back." But equally important, remember that you cannot take a chance on letting him resume his violent acts before you're able to escape.

TACTICAL FOLDER FIGHTING
Cold Steel Founder Lynn Thompson Unveils the Truth Behind Knife Self-Defense!
PART 1

Interview by Robert W. Young • Photos by Rick Hustead • February 2005

*F*ew people in the martial arts industry are more dedicated than Lynn Thompson. In the Ventura, California, headquarters of his company, Cold Steel, he's constructed a 2,600-square-foot gymnasium that would be the envy of any martial artist. On any given day, he puts in two-and-a-half hours to three-and-a-half hours of sweat to hone his skills in kali, silat, kickboxing and shootfighting. In his free time, he travels the world in search of knowledge of little-known weapons of war, and whatever he uncovers, he studies. In this exclusive interview, the master of the blade reveals some of the wisdom he's acquired over the years.

—Editor

Black Belt: What is the status of the self-defense knife in the United States?

Lynn Thompson: The most commonly carried knife for self-defense is the tactical folder. Twenty-five years ago, a lot of people carried boot knives, but fixed-blade knives are becoming more and more politically incorrect. The tactical folding knife started getting popular during Desert Storm. Servicemen were carrying their own fighting knives, especially

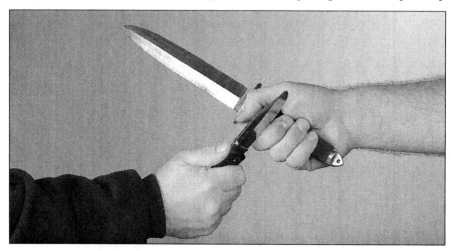

Although a tactical folder (left) offers plenty of advantages in a self-defense encounter, it isn't as effective as a fixed-blade knife such as Cold Steel's Tai Pan (right) because of the former's limited reach.

the bigger models, [but their commanding officers] didn't want them to look so fierce—you know, with bowie knives and all that stuff. There was a particular general in the Middle East who was out of joint because men were carrying fighting knives, so some of them started carrying weapons that were more unobtrusive. That's when the tactical folder really started to take off.

BB: Are the two types of weapons equally effective for combat?

Thompson: No. A sheath knife is much more effective than a folding knife for any type of work you want to do. Folding knives are designed for small jobs, but because of the political climate, people are trying to use them for jobs that require a bigger knife. Self-defense with a tactical folder is better than fingernails, but it's not optimal by any means.

BB: An instructor recently visited the Black Belt offices and said women shouldn't be taught to rely on a knife for self-defense because it's an assassin's tool, not a fighter's tool. What do you think?

Thompson: I don't agree. Throughout history, the knife was always the woman's weapon. If you look back at all the Nordic people, the women used to carry knives. Women carried sheath knives all through the Middle Ages. And the dirk or dagger was the woman's weapon up to the advent of firearms. In Brazil where I grew up, women used to promenade into the major Amazon towns in the evening with a dagger in their hand clear into the '60s.

BB: You would think placing a knife in the hand of anyone—man or woman—would be a great deterrent.

Thompson: [A friend of mine] tells a story about a police officer who saw a woman being accosted by three guys at a train station. He was on the upper level, so he couldn't possibly get to her to help. He was yelling at them to stop. She just had a box cutter, and when they went to grab her, she cut everybody that came close. And after a few times, they all ran away screaming curse words at her, holding their wounds. What could she have done with a full-on dagger?

BB: We also hear martial artists say they're afraid to carry a knife because the bad guy might take it away and use it against them.

Thompson: Once you know how to use a knife, it's really difficult to have it taken away. I'd pay anyone $10,000 if they could take a double-edge Tai Pan [knife] away from me. It's very difficult. Now, if the guy's totally untrained, you might do it. Dan Inosanto says, "Disarms are accidental, if not incidental." If you see it, you take it; but you can't really try for it. If your main thing is to take the knife away from your assailant without

State law generally permits a person to use a knife against an unarmed attacker if he's larger and/or stronger. Here, Lynn Thompson (left) faces Robert Vaughn (1). Rather than wait for the taller assailant to start pummeling him, Thompson uses his training weapon to debilitate the man's lead hand as soon as he extends it (2). The defender then flees (3).

some heavy offense directed against him, you're probably going to be unsuccessful.

Once you understand how to use a knife, no one can beat you unless they have a weapon with greater reach and greater power. Or they have an enormous skill advantage over you—there's probably only 100 people on the planet that have that kind of skill, and I'm not one of them. It's like they say: Defending yourself against someone who's skilled with a knife, you can extend your life 10 or maybe 15 seconds. If they really want to get you and you can't get away or get an equalizer, you're probably not going to be successful. Now, if they don't know what they're doing and they're just swinging away, you might have a chance.

BB: Is the best strategy to try to control the weapon and then punch?

Thompson: You have to go on the offensive, and you have to lay traps for him. In other words, you give him targets you want him to go for. I often extend my hand and get ready to move it out of the way. If he hits,

I use an evasive move, then try to enter into that space and put a hurt on him big enough to enable me to run. Somebody once asked me what steps I would take if an attacker came after me with a knife, and I said, "Big ones." I'll take the biggest steps I can because there isn't any good unarmed defense against it.

Even if you have your own knife, there's no advantage to getting in a knife fight. No one's going to take out an ad in the *Los Angeles Times* and say, "Lynn Thompson vanquished three scumbags with a knife in Oxnard last night." There's nothing in it for you. You only fight with a knife when you have no other recourse or when your duty requires it.

With that said, a knife, even a tactical folder, is a very comforting thing to have, and it can be very useful, especially in disparity-of-force situations where you're under attack by someone who's superior because of his height, weight, reach, strength, age or physical condition, all of which can negate your skill.

BB: Is it ever a good idea to take out a knife to prevent a fight when you're threatened by someone who is basically your physical equal?

Thompson: That's called brandishing. Under California law, you'd be the aggressor. If he's threatening you and you up the ante by pulling out a knife, you're not responding in kind. You're bringing it up to a whole other level. You're using deadly force to repel a simple assault, and that's not allowed by law. Simple brandishing of a weapon is a misdemeanor. If you say, "I'm going to cut you," that's assault with a deadly weapon. You don't have to complete the assault; you just have to threaten it within a range that you could deliver it.

BB: What is it about tactical folders that appeals to so many martial artists concerned with self-defense?

Thompson: The biggest advantage is their weight—usually 2, 3 or 4 ounces. Most are compact—a 4-inch blade will seldom be more than 5-1/2 inches closed. And they're flat—very few are more than a half-inch thick. Because they're so convenient, they can be carried 24 hours a day. And they're relatively safe. With pepper spray and stuff like that, you have to be careful you don't dislodge the safety; you don't want one going off in your pocket. But with a tactical folder, there's no way the blade can punch through anything—it's folded up inside the handle.

Folding knives are also politically correct because most people see them as tools, which, in fact, they are. Ninety-nine percent of the people who carry a knife use it as a tool; only a small fraction will ever use it for self-defense.

BB: How do you rate the effectiveness of the tactical folder?

Thompson: They're harder to use, but there's no denying they can make a horrendous slashing wound and a very deep penetrating wound.

Folding knife vs. stick: To overcome the disparity in weapon size, Lynn Thompson (left) advances as soon as his opponent raises his stick (1-2). He blocks the weapon arm with his forearm (3), then shifts and turns his body to lock the limb (4). Once the opponent has been doubled over by the pressure on his elbow, Thompson simulates cutting his triceps with his training weapon (5).

I've done some research on tactical folders in South Africa. Probably more people are killed with folding knives there than anywhere else in the world. There's a knife that's almost standard carry for everybody over there called the *okapi*. It has a simple lock activated by a ring. Everyone has their own secret opening and hiding techniques ... the knife fighting isn't very sophisticated, but it's brutal.

BB: And the disadvantages of the folder?

Thompson: The biggest one is the lack of reach. Most have a blade 4 inches or shorter, and that's a drawback if you're facing a longer weapon. The main problem is, if you've got 3 or 4 inches of the folding knife sticking out of your fist, when you're really excited and go to cut someone, you might hit him with your fist instead of the blade. Every time I train somebody and we're sparring with small knives, they find out that quite often you hit the opponent with your fist before the blade, or you hit him with the flat of the blade.

The longer the blade, the greater the margin for error. You can be off a couple inches and still get the edge on target. But when you've only got 3 inches sticking out of your fist, your accuracy has to be perfect. That's a disadvantage when it comes to engaging an incoming weapon arm and because you have no reach to get to your opponent. [If you have short arms,] you'll have a hard time leading with a tactical folder. And if you don't lead, if you're not aggressive, an opponent with a longer weapon will overrun you. If you can't put some fear into him and [generate] some respect for yourself, you'll lose right away.

BB: Do you think that the less-lethal nature of a shorter-bladed folding knife is why we have laws that permit people to carry, say, a 4-inch knife but not a 5-inch one?

Thompson: I don't think [lawmakers] are sophisticated enough to know that. I think they're saying the longer the blade, the more lethal it is if you get stuck with it. Basically that's true, although the Romans used to say 2 inches of steel in the right place will kill anybody. I think that's probably the reason they limit blade length. Plus, the shorter the blade, the more likely it's going to be used for utility purposes.

BB: What's the truth behind serrated edges? Will the fact that they're claimed to be more effective at cutting eventually lead to their being outlawed?

Thompson: I hope they're never outlawed because they're extremely useful—for example, during a rescue operation when you need to cut something quickly. A serrated edge is like gasoline: It's a wonderfully useful

Carrying a larger tactical folder will enable a martial artist to use more complicated maneuvers without sacrificing his chances of success. Here, Lynn Thompson (left) confronts his attacker (1). When the man lunges and thrusts, Thompson darts off to his right as he shifts his training weapon to his left hand (2). While still within range, he issues a left-hand cut to the forearm (3).

thing, but it can also be very destructive. Anything powerful can be used for good or evil. But if you're going to carry a tactical folder, a full serrated edge is the way to go. It'll increase your cutting power exponentially.

TACTICAL FOLDER FIGHTING
Cold Steel Founder Lynn Thompson Unveils the Truth Behind Knife Self-Defense!
PART 2

Interview by Robert W. Young • Photos by Rick Hustead • March 2005

In part one of this article, Lynn Thompson outlined the basic concepts of knife fighting and discussed the limitations of using a folding knife instead of a fixed blade. Here, he concludes with his thoughts on the various design elements of folders and how well they stack up against other weapons.

—Editor

Black Belt: How much of a liability is the hinge on a tactical folder?

Lynn Thompson: It makes them inherently weaker than a fixed blade. It's unlikely, but you could have a knife and be facing someone with a stick and he goes after you with nonstop rapping motions. One of the things we teach in our cane and walking-stick course is to attack the knife hand. If your folding knife gets hit hard on top of the blade, the strikes could conceivably fold it by overcoming the lock. A lot of the big-name custom makers would see their knives slam shut after five or six hits on the back of the blade.

BB: But Cold Steel stress-tests all its designs, doesn't it?

Thompson: Yes, of course. We show ours taking 40 to 50 hits as hard as we can strike. In fact, in 1999 at the tactical knife symposium held at the Gunsite Academy, we showed a demonstration of our 4-inch Voyager being struck as hard as we could on the edge of a table. There wasn't any other knife we tested that went more than five. So that's something to be aware of when you're fighting with a tactical folder: You don't necessarily want to let him hit your blade.

BB: How bad is it when a locking mechanism fails?

Thompson: There are advantages and disadvantages to every lock design. The rocker lock is very simple. It can be extremely strong when it's done right. It's a little bit vulnerable to lint in the locking mechanism—or getting crud or blood in there if you use it as a hunting knife. You have to keep that channel clean. But if it fails, it fails catastrophically. In other words, if you exceed its lock strength, it slams shut on your fingers. It's the same thing with a compression lock or an axis lock. The only knife that doesn't do that is an extremely well-made liner lock or leaf-spring lock. When one of those fails, the leaf spring crumples and it bends to the point

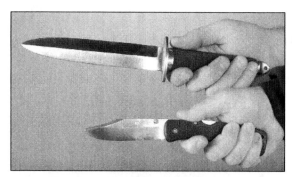

Left: The forward grip offers the user a good hold on a folding knife, but with a short weapon, reach is sacrificed. Below: The palm-reinforced grip affords the martial artist a more secure grip and extended reach, making the folder functionally closer in length to the fixed blade.

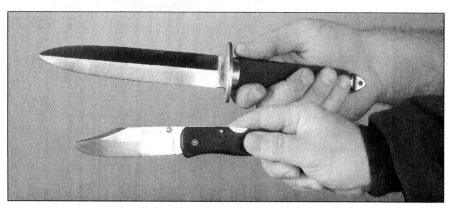

that it blocks the progress of the blade, making it virtually impossible to get cut. We've put 800 foot-pounds on our Scimitar, and we've never been able to crush that spring enough that you'd be cut.

BB: What are some of the trade-offs of the other designs?

Thompson: Any design that has little openings means there's more spaces for pocket lint and all that stuff to collect. There's more maintenance.

BB: Do you recommend washing the lint off and maybe scrubbing the knife with an old toothbrush once a month?

Thompson: With any design, you have to look carefully to make sure there's no lint or gunk, and if you use one as a hunting knife, make sure there's no blood or fat or anything that can congeal and maybe foul up the mechanism. And you shouldn't be constantly assembling and disassembling your knife because eventually you're not going to do it right and it'll fail.

BB: Should martial artists be concerned about carrying a folding knife that doesn't have any kind of protrusion to keep their hand from sliding up the blade?

Thompson: That's a good point. Tactical folders seldom have a good enough guard. Some people think a thumb ramp will stop their hand from going forward—absolute fantasy. If you stab hard, there's no way your thumb is going to impede the forward progress of your hand on that handle. With a tactical folder, [you should consider] switching to a palm-reinforced grip or a reverse grip. Let's say you're in a forward grip and you're slashing and you see an opportunity to thrust. You can switch to a palm-reinforced grip without even thinking about it. Or you can go to a thumb-reinforced reverse grip, capping the back with your thumb so it stops your hand from going down the handle.

What you don't want to do is stab harder than your grip strength allows. You normally don't have to stab that tremendously hard, and in a knife fight you won't have much opportunity to generate a lot of power until you've got his weapon on the ground. Before that, it'll usually take too much preparatory time, and you'll be telegraphing. It's the same thing when you want to throw a cross. If you're going to put any power into it, even without telegraphing, you're going to have to dig in with your feet. You're going to have to load with your legs. That's why landing a good cross or overhand right is a little harder to do than a jab—it takes more

If you don't have access to a training knife, you can fabricate one from a cylindrical length of foam. Make it as long as your preferred self-defense weapon, and use a marker to draw a line where the edge would be.

269

Footwork and balance play important roles in knife fighting. To illustrate, Lynn Thompson (left) confronts Robert Vaughn (1). When the opponent attacks, Thompson simulates cutting the back of his hand with a training knife (2), then charges in with his left arm positioned defensively (3). He continues advancing to disrupt the assailant's balance and knock him to the ground (4). Had he deemed it necessary, Thompson could have used his weapon to attack the man's torso.

preparatory time. And loading those muscles for the big effort shows in the way you move.

BB: Let's talk about weapon-vs.-weapon situations. How might a martial artist with a 3-inch folder confront an attacker who's holding a big Maglite?

Thompson: I'd put the knife out in front and make him not want to get cut with it. If you put the knife back here, he's going to hit you on the side. Realize that you're bringing a 3-inch knife to a potentially lethal altercation where the guy has a superior weapon. You're probably not going to get out of there unscathed. But the advantage you have is that he's armed with an impact weapon—the flashlight or a stick or whatever—and he's got to get a good hit on your head or neck to knock you out. Or he has to take you out with multiple blows. If you get your edge on him in the right place, you can finish him. The Filipinos that are honest will tell you the knife is much more deadly than the stick.

BB: Is there any way to give a quick ranking of the continuum of weapons available for self-defense, from a gun all the way down to empty hands?

Thompson: Sure, I can give you my opinion. In fact, I'm actually doing a DVD series about that—every lethal weapon you can acquire or improvise. It'll be called *Never Unarmed*—I've worked on it since 1983. At the highest level of force are the battle rifle and shotgun. Those are what you take to a fight. Then you go down to the carbine and the machine pistol, then the handgun. A handgun is something you carry when you don't know you're going to be attacked because it's more convenient than carrying a rifle or shotgun. From the handgun, it goes to the sword.

BB: A full-size sword, like a *katana*?

Thompson: Right. A two-handed sword or a saber. Under that would be a club of some type.

BB: Why does a club rank so high?

Thompson: There's a whole family of clubs. You've got a quarterstaff, which John Silver, a 16th-century master of defense, said was the king of all weapons. And you've got a spear. Then you've got the heavy club, medium-size club and short club. Then would be a walking staff or hiking staff. Shorter than that would be a cane, and then you'd have maybe a five- or six-cell flashlight. And even shorter than that would be a lead-filled sap.

BB: Would a sap rank above a knife for effectiveness?

Thompson: No. The knife would probably be equal to the club—clear up there with the walking stick or cane, if not higher. So a 4-foot-long blunt-ended weapon would equal a knife.

BB: Are you talking about a large fixed blade, or does that pertain to a tactical folder, as well?

Thompson: A full-size fighting knife. The bigger the knife is, the more damage it can do. But you have to remember that things aren't so simple. The sword has a hard time dealing with the quarterstaff because of the reach. It's a little bit better at dealing with a big, heavy club. If you ever try to fight sword against spear, you'll find that the spear man will win probably seven out of 10 engagements. The Japanese found that it took a very skilled swordsman to go up against somebody with a spear.

BB: At the bottom of the continuum would be something like a *kubotan*?

Thompson: Yes, what we call a pocket stick. And at the bottom of the knife continuum would be a key-chain knife—one of those small push knives or a small fixed-blade knife. Even with those, if you know what you're doing, you can do an awful lot of damage, but they're a far cry from a 4- or 5-inch tactical folder or a fixed blade. The middle of the continuum of force for a knife would be a sheath knife, then a combat knife, then a *kukri* or a large bowie knife with a 10- or 11-inch blade. After 12 inches, you start getting into sword lengths. It gets harder to wear on your belt, it sticks out and catches on things, etc.

BB: With the rising popularity of American designs for all those self-defense implements, do you foresee a trend in your industry away from Asian weapons and toward Western weapons?

Thompson: Right now, most Americans are still more interested in Japanese swords. I mean, our Japanese swords outsell our other swords 6-to-1. But I'm trying to change that because I also have an affinity for Western martial arts. A lot of people think that swordsmanship is all Oriental. What they forget is that when the Portuguese showed up in Japan, there were a number of duels where Portuguese swordsmen equaled or bested Japanese swordsmen. There's a huge martial tradition associated with Western swords. A lot of that knowledge has been lost because it was never written down, so I'm going to help spread what little I can bring back and what little I can contribute.

Using a knife for self-defense does not always involve face-to-face dueling. Many nonlethal targets can be attacked from a variety of angles and even while you're fleeing.

ANATOMY OF A KNIFE FIGHT
Learn How to Handle the Three Most-Common Assaults

by Ernest Emerson • Photos courtesy of Ernest Emerson • May 2005

Can you really defend yourself against a knife attack? Can you even survive one? If you're honest, your answers will probably be, "Maybe." It would be great if there were three magical techniques that would work every time. Unfortunately, there aren't, and anyone who tells you otherwise isn't being truthful.

Fortunately, there are plenty of things you can do to increase your chances of surviving a knife attack and decrease the likelihood that you'll be severely injured. It doesn't matter whether you're a beginner or an expert; you'll benefit from learning about three basic ways things can unfold. As you'll see, they're quite different from what most martial artists practice.

Three Attacks

The first scenario is the surprise attack. The most vicious and deadly, it's exactly what its name implies: an ambush. The assailant's goal is your death; in fact, he's already decided to kill you. He may be standing in front of you when it begins, or he may attack you from behind. The surprise attack is the hardest one to prepare for and defend against because the aggressor can usually get in three or four strikes before you even know what's happening—and he'll probably aim for your neck and chest. This type of assault often results in the victim exhibiting defensive wounds to his hands and arms because of his efforts to block the strikes.

The second scenario is the escalation attack. You're confronted by one or more people who are giving you a hard time, perhaps while under the influence of alcohol. A fight erupts, and you trade punches with one of the thugs. He grabs you, and before you know it, you're rolling on the floor and getting punched in the ribs. Suddenly, your left side goes weak, and you can't catch your breath. You let go, and he jumps up and runs away. When the paramedics get there, you learn you've got nine puncture wounds in the left side of your torso.

The third scenario is the opportunity attack. It starts when you're alone, perhaps in a parking lot, and someone approaches you. He brandishes a knife and demands your wallet. You hesitate, and he lunges. It wasn't premeditated or planned; the knife was intended to threaten, not necessarily to injure. However, the dynamics of the altercation turn it into an attack,

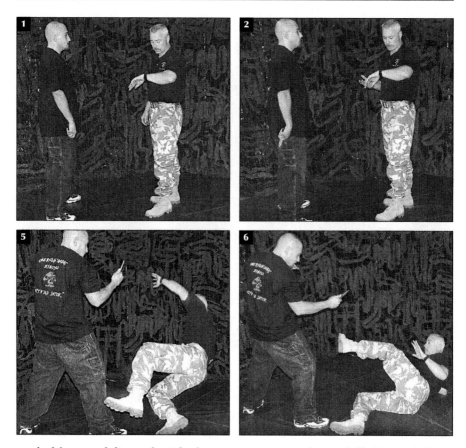

probably one delivered with the intent to wound, not kill. Nevertheless, your life is in danger.

How do you prepare to deal with these three scenarios? Not by squaring off and sparring knife against knife. Note that in each of the attacks described above, the good guy never had a knife in his hand. Practicing knife sparring is fine because it can develop timing, range and footwork, but it's not realistic. I've trained thousands of military and law-enforcement personnel and hundreds of civilians, and not once has a student reported that he'd been in a knife-against-knife confrontation. Plenty had been in confrontations in which a knife was used, but only three were the party with the weapon.

The first lesson to be learned is this: If you train for reality, you need to practice defending against a knife attack while you're unarmed. In reality, "knife fights" don't exist. The second is, there's still a lot you can do to stack the odds in your favor. The following principles, concepts and techniques

Surprise attack: Mike Sakata (left) distracts Ernest Emerson by asking the time (1). While Emerson checks his watch (2), the attacker strikes, triggering the startle-response in the defender (3). The assailant manages to execute two slashes before the victim realizes what's happening (4). Emerson immediately throws himself to the ground to introduce the element of surprise and, hopefully, break the momentum of the attack (5). From his improved position, Emerson can protect his face and neck (6) while he kicks (7).

have been culled from the Black Course I teach to the military. The course will never be taught to civilians, but the techniques and drills listed here are still lifesavers.

Counter to the Surprise Attack

Unfortunately, there's no simple solution to this problem. People like to say, "If you're in a knife fight, prepare to get cut." Well, in this case, you should prepare to get hammered. You'll probably be hit three to five times before you even realize what's happening. It doesn't matter how good your reflexes are or how extensive your training is because it takes you time to process information and respond, and during that interval, even an untrained person can usually fire off several shots unopposed. You'll probably never see the knife.

The key is to respond instead of react. Respond means you receive a stimulus, analyze it and choose to answer with an action. When you react,

The escalation attack takes place when the two combatants are engaged in a fight and one clandestinely draws his knife.

your body executes a nonthinking action that's caused by a stimulus. Touch a hot stove, and your hand jerks back. The signal for pain doesn't even reach your brain; it just hits your lower spine and back. A surprise attack will trigger the startle response. Your legs will flex slightly, your abdominal muscles will contract, your shoulders will hunch and your elbows will draw in. Furthermore, your arms will raise and your fingers will splay at approximately eye level. This reaction marks the beginning of the fight-or-flight mechanism: You protect the vital areas of your body as you prepare to move quickly. (Using the right drills, you can develop the startle response to make it more effective and transform it into a viable fighting stance.)

The following is a defensive scenario I use in my classes. The opponent initiates the attack, and you react by raising your hands as quickly as possible to protect your vitals. At that point, your best course of action is to go to the ground. You can fall, jump or roll—it doesn't matter. If you stand there, trying to formulate some type of defense, you'll die.

Going to the ground also introduces the element of the unexpected. The bad guy has to react to you, not you to him. He has to decide what to do. You'll have bought yourself time and created distance. Furthermore, you can mount a fairly solid defense from that position. His first choice won't be to leap on you. Bolster your defenses by using your feet and any natural obstacles that are nearby. Throw things at him if you can.

Drill No. 1 Practice jumping into the startle-response position from a relaxed stance, then throw two to three hard strikes as quickly as possible. Repeat 15 to 25 times a day. The next time someone tries to scare you or when you're genuinely startled, you'll be surprised at how you react.

Drill No. 2 Have your opponent don protective gear, then stand in the middle of the training area and close your eyes. Instruct him to move around you quietly and scream as he initiates his attack. He should begin from just outside of arm's reach, about three feet to four feet away. If he's wearing boxing gloves, he can punch you. If he's not, he can grab you or stab you with a rubber knife. Don't think; just react. Get your hands up

Left: The partner dons boxing gloves and attacks with a barrage of punches, while the defender protects himself and tries to deploy his training knife.

Bottom: On the ground, the partner assumes a 90-degree cross mount on the defender, then attempts to stop him from accessing his training knife.

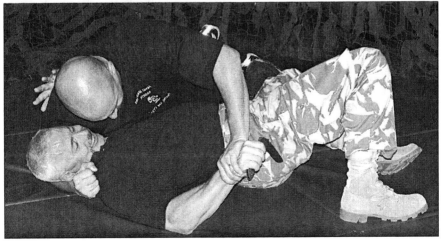

An advanced knife drill begins with both parties on their knees (1). Once the grappling starts, they must concentrate on three objectives: defending themselves against their opponent's assault, accessing their own knife and stopping their opponent from accessing his (2-3).

and throw a couple of strikes, then hit the deck and defend yourself from the floor. As you advance in this drill, draw your own training knife once you're on the ground and attack if he tries to reach for you.

Counter to the Escalation Attack

This knife scenario is also tough to prepare for because it's not evident at the outset that a knife will be involved. It's best to assume that every attack, every fight, every physical confrontation is a deadly threat. Because you never know what your assailant intends to do, you have to respond, counterattack or pre-emptively strike with such force that you neutralize his ability to harm you. By doing so, you'll prevent him from gaining access to his knife and deploying it against you. Your goal is to take away the distance and destroy his balance, then injure him with a choke, armbar, shoulder lock or similar technique that will cause him to react defensively. By employing overwhelming firepower with no letup, you increase the chance that you'll disable him. Don't forget to eye-gouge and bite, if need be.

Drill No. 3 To help you understand just how difficult—or easy—accessing a knife can be, you should obtain a training blade, preferably a folder, and put it where you usually carry your real one. Have your partner stand in front of you and attack. Try to ward off his technique, then counterattack or take him down while trying to open your knife. Have him really put the pressure on while wearing boxing gloves or holding a padded stick. The drill will teach you the importance of defending against the attack before trying to access your knife. If you go for it too soon, you'll get pounded.

Drill No. 4 This exercise will introduce you to knife grappling. Have your partner put a training knife in his pocket and lie on his stomach, then mount him at a 90-degree angle. Once a third person gives the command, your opponent tries to access and deploy his knife, and you try to prevent it. Use any technique—a choke, lock or strike—to stop him. Vary the starting position, sometimes with him on his back and sometimes with you on the

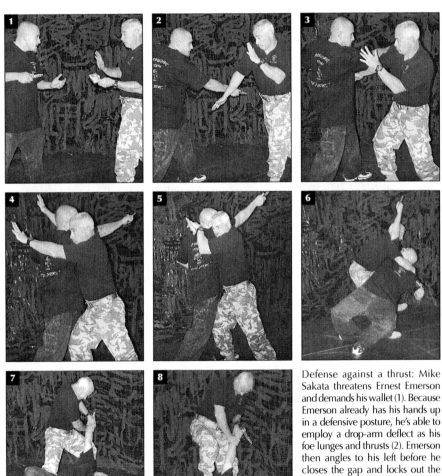

Defense against a thrust: Mike Sakata threatens Ernest Emerson and demands his wallet (1). Because Emerson already has his hands up in a defensive posture, he's able to employ a drop-arm deflect as his foe lunges and thrusts (2). Emerson then angles to his left before he closes the gap and locks out the attacker's knife arm (3). Next, the martial artist wraps his arms around the man's right shoulder and neck (4-5) and spins counterclockwise to take him down (6). From there, Emerson can disarm him (7) and attack with his feet (8).

bottom. Switch roles so you can feel what it's like to go for your knife.

Drill No. 5 This knife-grappling drill starts with you on your knees on the mat, facing your partner. When the command is issued, begin normal grappling. When a second command is given, you try to get to your training knife while preventing him from getting to his, and he does the same. The first few times you try it, you'll both stop grappling, and it'll be a race to see who can get his weapon out first. Strive to transcend this stage and maintain your grappling composure. Learn how to access your blade without presenting your foe with an opening.

Counter to the Opportunity Attack

This is the knife attack you have the best chance of defending against. With that said, remember that no knife assault is easy to negate and no scenario involving a knife should ever be taken lightly.

Because you know you're in danger and can see his knife, your first thought should be to escape. If you can't—perhaps your wife and 4-year-old daughter are standing next to you—you'll have to fight. Even though it might escalate the situation, you should immediately begin preparing. While maintaining eye contact, raise your hands in a "calm down" position, which doesn't appear to pose a threat but is very similar to the ready position.

Speak calmly to keep his attention focused. You might say: "Hey man, you want my wallet? You can have it. Honey, give me your purse and take Jennifer around the car."

Precise word choice is the key to strategically maintaining control. You assure the bad guy that he'll get what he wants, and you give direction to your wife—not by directly telling her to move away but by using your child's name to disguise your plan. Thus, it doesn't appear that he's losing control. The moment the strike comes, you'll be as ready as you can be. Your plan should mirror the military's: parry, stun, take down and finish.

Remember that the overall strategy of this defense, as well as those listed above, is not to fight your attacker but to finish him.

8 TIPS FOR BETTER KNIFE DEFENSE

by Joel Huncar • Photos by Rick Hustead • October 2005

If you watch the news on television or read the statistics in the newspaper, you're bound to notice that more and more criminals are using weapons. Consequently, more and more martial artists are focusing on self-defense techniques that enable them to fend off armed attacks. If you're one of them, this article will help you polish your counter-knife skills. If you're not, it may whet your appetite enough to inspire you to begin learning effective knife defense.

Before beginning, however, it must be stated that fighting empty-handed against a blade is extremely difficult. In fact, it's so dangerous that only the possibility of saving a human life—whether yours or someone else's—can make taking such a risk worthwhile. And that's exactly why you should learn knife defense.

The other essential caveat is that no matter how honed your knife defense is, you should always remember that avoidance is recommended over conflict. If you sense danger, move away from it. Only when a safe retreat isn't possible should you rely on your physical skills to stay alive.

Focus on Strategy

Good strategy can sometimes overcome superior strength, skill and speed. If you trick an assailant into thinking you're too frightened to defend

When it comes to knife defense, a disarm is fine if you can execute it, but the attacker can still be taken out of action even if you don't strip him of his weapon. (For illustrative purposes, John Pellegrini is shown.)

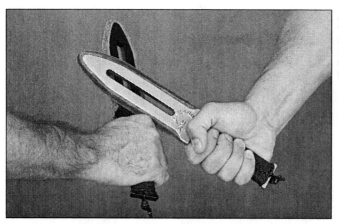

A knife is invaluable when you're forced to confront an armed attacker, but improvised striking and throwing weapons can be just as useful.

yourself, you may be able to blitz him before he knows what's happening. Another ploy might involve throwing a blunt object at him while you're still at a safe distance. The course of action you select depends on your environment, the position of your attacker(s), the terrain, and your physical and mental state.

Good strategy comes from drilling, sparring and conducting research. Drill in seemingly impossible situations, such as when you're facing multiple opponents, when you have an injured arm (simulated by tying it to your body) or when you're held by one opponent while another attacks you. Spar with objects—including focus mitts, kicking shields and foam sticks—strewn across the floor to simulate improvised weapons and obstacles. Read what reality-fighting experts such as Marc MacYoung, James Keating, Kelly S. Worden, Jim Wagner, W. Hock Hochheim and Jim Grover have to say about knife attacks. Also peruse classic texts such as Sun Tzu's *The Art of War* and European fencing manuals.

Keep Your Hands Back

If you raise your guard in a classic karate, kickboxing or boxing stance, you can expect to have your hands cut. An experienced knife wielder will slice up anything you extend and expose. Keep your hands close to your body with the backs of your forearms facing outward. That way, if one of your arms does get cut, you'll be less likely to have an artery severed.

Don't interpret this advice on stance to mean you should assume a static position. Instead, you should be mobile as you try to gain control of your attacker and his weapon. Your hands will be in motion, and your body will be maneuvering. A benefit of employing this type of defense is that it forces your opponent to commit to reach you. That will lure him in close, making it easier for you to control him. Once he's there, counter his attacks viciously until you can safely escape or you've incapacitated him.

Develop a Tool-User's Attitude

It's always better to fend off a blade attack when you have a tool in your hand. A knife is fine, but even an improvised weapon can extend your reach and keep an assailant at bay. Also, improvised distractions—such as a drink or a cigarette that's thrown his eyes—can buy you time to flee. The effectiveness of more massive objects—bottles, chairs, dishes and so on—is even better. They can inflict grievous injury without requiring you to get within range of his knife.

It's essential to disregard any notions you might have about the shame of fighting dirty. Anything that can help you should be used without hesitation. Remember that knives are reputed to be the No. 2 murder weapon in the United States and the No. 1 murder weapon in Canada. You should feel justified in using anything you can to stop such an attack.

To fine-tune your tool-user's attitude, train with sticks, knives, staffs and swords. Most improvised weapons will function in a way that's similar to one of them. You may want to practice throwing rocks, bottles and glasses. Get used to working with all kinds of weapons, then experiment with objects in your house to see how you would use them.

To cover all the bases, knife-defense practice should include weapons of all sizes, not just the standard 6-inch-long blade. For illustrative purposes, Gary Alexander (left) is shown.

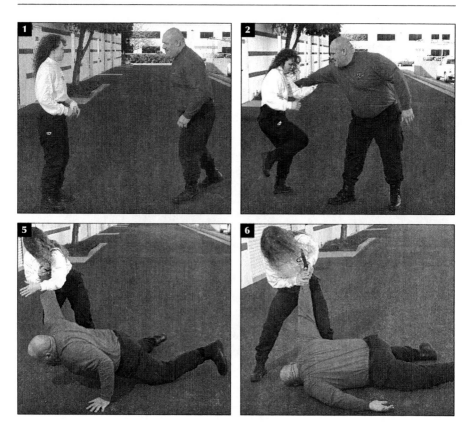

Fight the Man, Not the Weapon

Don't focus solely on the attacker's weapon. If you do, you could miss that kick or punch he throws while you're fixated on his blade. Even worse, he could flash a knife in his right hand while using his left to plunge a hidden dagger into your stomach. Or he could have an accomplice waiting to take you out from behind. Be wary of the blade but aware of what's going on around you.

In training, incorporate kicks and punches into your knife drills and sparring. Devote the occasional workout to fending off multiple attackers, some of whom are armed. Make things as unpredictable as you can while ensuring the safety of your classmates and maintaining your focus on the skills you're trying to develop.

Control the Weapon in Close Range

If your foe gets into close range, you must seize his weapon hand. Strive to control it long enough to negate his attack and escape without

Strategy is essential in knife defense. To illustrate, Kathy Long feigns helplessness in front of her assailant (1). That lures the man into overcommitting to his attack, which Long traps (2). She then kicks his lead shin (3) and leverages him to the ground (4-5). To finish, she takes away his weapon (6) and eliminates the threat (7).

being killed. It's not an easy task; he'll probably be twisting, struggling and striking you with his empty hand. If possible, mimic that behavior in your workouts.

To see how challenging it can be, try to control your partner's knife hand. As you experiment to find the best ways to do it, try closing the distance after you execute a strike or throw an object, then grab his weapon hand. When you have a secure grip on it, pin his trapped limb against his body while you attack him or execute a disarm or lock. Otherwise, he may yank his hand out of yours and cut you.

A good way to develop this skill is by doing sticking drills. Have a partner slash at you in a prearranged pattern, such as with a downward X-technique, and parry the knife on each strike. Once you get good at this, stick to his arm with at least one limb while he attacks. The exercise will develop a soft control that can lead to a proper grip or grab. When you get good, change the attack angles and throw in some disarms, counterstrikes and takedowns.

Make It Fast and Devastating

When you're up against an armed assailant, you must terminate the encounter as quickly as possible. The longer the struggle lasts, the more likely it is that you'll be cut. You must cultivate a no-holds-barred attitude, one that allows you to attack vital points, rip out eyes, destroy limbs and do whatever else it may take to put the attacker down quickly.

Practice until your responses become second nature. Human beings have a natural tendency to not want to maim other people in a conflict. It's a healthy attitude in society, but it's counterproductive in weapons defense.

When you work out on a heavy bag—or on tires if you're a stick fighter—strike with full power. That's the best way to teach yourself to not hold back in a real fight. Sparring has its place in your training, but too

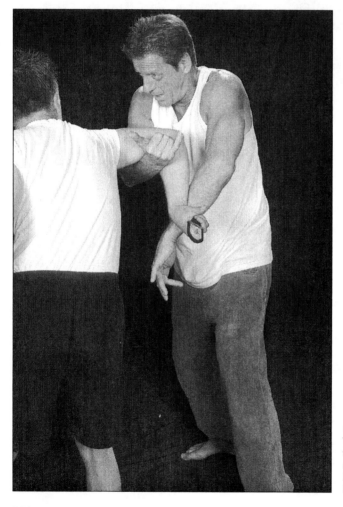

Knife experts like Paul Vunak know it's crucial to focus on fighting the man who's threatening him, not just the weapon he's using.

much of it can adversely affect your self-defense ability. No matter how "full contact" it is, it's still controlled. It's obviously important, but doing too much of it can leave you with a sparring mind-set, which is limiting in real-world self-defense.

Work Out With Large and Small Training Knives

Most aluminum training weapons and rubber knives have at least a 6-inch-long blade, but most folding knives have a blade 3 inches to 4 inches in length. The extra size can make it easier for you to perform a disarming or controlling technique, thus instilling a false sense of confidence. To avoid the pitfall, strive for variety in your workouts. Use training versions of stubby pocket knives as well as rubber machetes.

Don't Make Disarms Your Main Focus

Disarming is probably one of the most overtrained aspects of knife defense. While it's important to know how to disarm an attacker, you shouldn't focus on it in the *dojo*. The reason is simple: Disarms are tough to pull off in a high-speed knife assault. They are, as Hochheim says, "both accidental and incidental" to the conflict. In other words, learn how to do them because the opportunity might present itself, but know that they cannot be made to happen.

A second problem related to disarming is that both your hands are usually required to control the attacker's weapon hand. That leaves his other hand free to attack you. In the time it might take you to execute a disarm, you could perform a nasty wrist dislocation or throw.

A third is that if you're dealing with a small knife, it's extremely difficult to get the leverage you need to strip it out of your attacker's hand. You might even injure yourself during the attempt.

The best way to practice disarms is as part of a sticking drill, a flow drill or a sparring combination. In this way, you'll develop more functional skills than you would if you were to practice only static disarms.

As you train to keep your knife-defense skills sharp, try the eight tips mentioned above. Experiment with each one, and if it works for you and fits in with your art, incorporate it into your arsenal. It may take some time, but you'll be safer in the long run.

THE CODE HAS BEEN CRACKED!
8 Steps to the Ultimate Edged-Weapons Defense
by Hank Hayes • Photos by Rick Hustead • August 2006

This article is designed for high-risk operators who encounter life-threatening situations on a daily basis. It's for those who need to acquire skills that reflect what happens on the street when they face an attacker who's committed to inflicting severe bodily injury with an edged weapon.

The article is also different in that it's interactive. At several points, you'll be asked for responses to issues that pertain to knife defense. Answering honestly—on paper—will make you rethink your current survival training and, hopefully, begin a crash course to improve it.

—H.H.

In *Sharpening the Warrior's Edge: The Psychology and Science of Training,* Bruce K. Siddle writes: "Research has indicated that gross motor skills are performed at optimal levels under high-stress conditions. In contrast, fine and complex motor skills deteriorate under high-stress conditions."

In other words, techniques that involve major muscle groups performing basic movements are your best bet for self-defense. Intricate moves, especially ones that are strung together in elaborate sequences, will most likely be doomed to failure.

Once you accept those statements, you'll want to seek instruction that transcends what's normally taught in knife-defense courses. To fill in the gaps that exist in most *dojo* training, you should look to the reality-based programs that are meeting the needs of military and law-enforcement groups around the world. One such program is the No Lie Blades curriculum. In this article, I'll examine an essential part of it: the eight components of knife defense.

Step 1
Know What You're Up Against
Interactive work: Answer the following questions truthfully.

- Have you ever been attacked by someone who was committed to killing you with a knife?
- Do you know someone who has been attacked in such a manner?
- Have you seen firsthand what a human body looks like after it's been stabbed, hacked or slashed multiple times?
- Do you know how much blood you can lose before your hand-eye coordination diminishes, before you get dizzy and pass out, and before you die?

If you answered no to any of those questions, do yourself a favor and find someone who has the answers. That act alone will boost your knowledge base, elevate your skill set and help you start laying the groundwork for a solid edged-weapons program.

To better understand what actually happens during a knife attack, examine the accompanying photo sequences. When coupled with knowledge of the role an elevated heart rate plays when you're losing blood—up to three shot glasses' worth per severed artery per second—the photos will motivate you to learn how to neutralize an attacker as soon as possible.

Step 2
Have a Way to Measure Your Combat Skill Set

In his seminal text *Kill or Get Killed,* Col. Rex Applegate writes: "Any individual can test the efficacy of any combat methods and holds by asking himself a simple question: Will this work so that I can use it instinctively

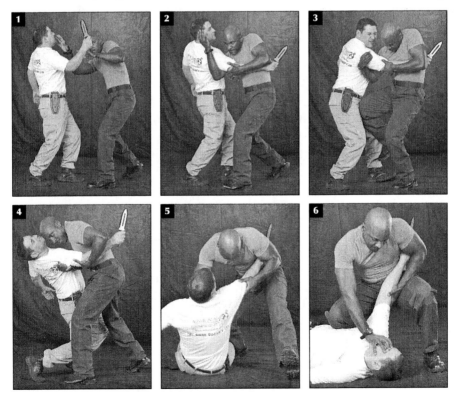

Sequence A: The opponent begins a high-line knife attack, which causes Hank Hayes to block the arm and strike the eyes (1). Hayes wraps his left arm over the man's right arm and secures it from underneath using his own right arm (2). He follows up with a knee thrust to the groin (3) and a head butt to the face (4). The finish begins with a takedown (5) and ends with a neutralizing eye strike (6).

in vital combat against an opponent who is determined to prevent me from doing so?"

Most martial artists will agree with Applegate's wisdom because they know that the price they'll pay otherwise is far too high. The hard part is finding a method for evaluating your combat skill set because purposefully getting into life-or-death fights obviously isn't a good idea. This is where an experienced instructor and motivated training partner come in.

Once you've built the foundation with the first two steps, it's time to delve into the preferred methods for neutralizing a knife attack. All of them have withstood the test of time, during which they've been fine-tuned by numerous high-risk operators in combat environments.

Step 3
Develop the Will to Win—and Live

It's self-explanatory, but in case you need a little inspiration, here's some interactive work: List the top three reasons you have for staying alive.

Step 4
Create a Superior Mind-Set

In his classic book *On Combat*, Lt. Col. Dave Grossman writes: "Napoleon said that in war, 'The moral is to the physical as three is to one.' That is, the psychological factors are three times more important than the physical."

Interactive work: List the top three "successes" you've had—obstacles you've overcome that resulted in a strengthened mind-set.

Step 5
Focus on Proven Combat Methods

"Research ... provides two clear messages about why people place themselves in bad tactical situations," writes Officer Darren Laur in *Edged Weapons Tactics and Counter Tactics*. "The common phenomenon of backing away under survival stress results from the visual system's deterioration of the peripheral field to attain more information regarding threat stimulus."

Interactive work: List three techniques, methods or tactics you'd use to maintain a position of advantage and ultimately win a fight, then discuss them with your partner and instructor.

To maximize your combat capabilities and performance, you must integrate Steps 3, 4 and 5 through guided training. Acting without all three will dramatically weaken your tactical performance. A person who's ready

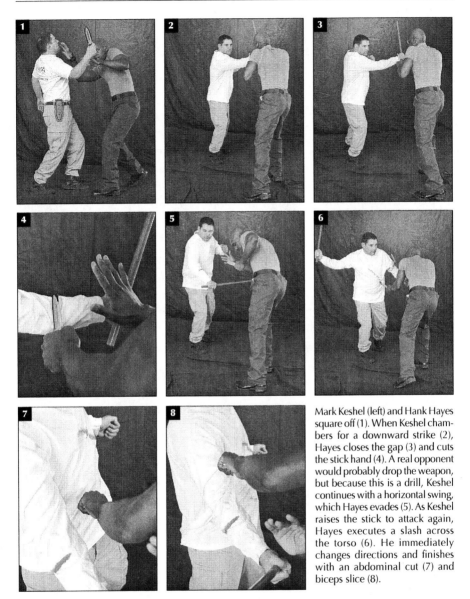

Mark Keshel (left) and Hank Hayes square off (1). When Keshel chambers for a downward strike (2), Hayes closes the gap (3) and cuts the stick hand (4). A real opponent would probably drop the weapon, but because this is a drill, Keshel continues with a horizontal swing, which Hayes evades (5). As Keshel raises the stick to attack again, Hayes executes a slash across the torso (6). He immediately changes directions and finishes with an abdominal cut (7) and biceps slice (8).

to kill with a knife has no problem with interpersonal human aggression. He's committed to taking you out, so you must commit yourself to stopping him even if you're wounded. That requires physical and, as mentioned above, mental preparation.

In *On Combat,* Grossman writes: "You must understand and accept that you might get wounded, and understand deeply and intensely that you will keep fighting until the threat is no longer present."

Step 6
Do What's Necessary to Win—Refuse to Lose

When you have an opportunity to get a piece of the attacker, take it. It may be the only chance you'll get. Consider the following defense, which is depicted in photo sequence A.

The entry starts with a high-line knife defense and an eye poke. The eye attack buys you time—from one-eighth to one-half second, at least—and tosses a wrench in your opponent's attack plan. Next, your left hand snakes over his knife arm, capturing it above the elbow, if possible. Your right arm then slips under his attacking arm, assisting in the capture. Your goal is to control the limb, inflict pain and neutralize the attack. Next is a knee thrust to the groin or any other low-line target such as the knee or the medial nerve on the thigh, after which comes a head butt, takedown and neutralizing ground control. Overkill is the name of the game, but it's all done in steps when the opportunities present themselves.

When it comes to knife defense on the ground, your odds of survival plunge. Never knowingly go to the ground with an opponent who has a knife because there's a good chance he has more than one. Criminals who come from certain blade cultures are known to carry up to five edged weapons. Grappling with such an armed enemy is tantamount to committing suicide.

No Lie Blades teaches what's known as the TNT ground game, which stands for Threat Neutralizing and Terminating. It focuses on swiftness, explosive brutality and simplicity. The goal is to escape if you're a civilian and to obtain a weapon or cover if you're a police officer. See photo sequence B for an example.

Step 7
Fight Until the Problem No Longer Exists

This step is self-explanatory.

Step 8
Expect Only the Best Effort From Yourself and Your Training Partner

Just as a person cannot sit on the sidelines and experience a football game, you cannot derive maximum benefit from this article without absorbing the content, answering the questions and undergoing the physical training, preferably with an equally committed partner. Increase the intensity of your workouts step by step. Do them at a time when you can focus on tactics and techniques without interruption. Once you've mastered

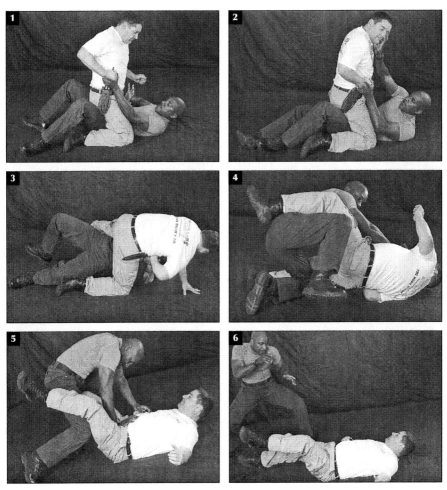

Sequence B: As soon as Mark Keshel begins to deploy his weapon, Hank Hayes seizes his knife hand (1). Hayes then executes an eye poke (2) and bridges him off (3-4). Once Hayes is on top, he palm-strikes the opponent in the groin (5) and immediately backs away in case he still wants to fight (6).

the moves, commit them to memory.

Now for the fun part: Obtain a marking blade or magic marker and head for a safe training area. Test your skills while attacking and defending at full speed. This is where the measuring and testing noted in Step 2 come in. Discover what works for you and what doesn't. Discard what doesn't work and keep the rest. All the while, maintain a conviction that you'll be successful in your defense. When something works, take note of it and vow to perfect it.

To motivate yourself in mock battle, repeat out loud your top three reasons for staying alive. After you reach the point of exhaustion, train for another half-hour using the same methods and continue to measure the results by counting "knife marks" on your body. Where are they? Would you have survived?

If all this seems a little extreme, revisit Step 1. Remind yourself that it takes time and effort to be able to conquer lethal force.

BLADE AGAINST BLADE
Realities and Simulations in Knife Fighting
by James LaFond • Photos courtesy of James LaFond • September 2006

This article is not about the blade arts. It's simply an exposition of my research, experimentation and personal findings on the subject of edged-weapon encounters. The simulation methods discussed herein can—and have—resulted in injury. Of 2,460 blade-vs.-blade simulations conducted in South Baltimore and Dundalk, Maryland, from March 1999 to October 2002, the following injuries were sustained:

- *10 facial abrasions, primarily to the bridge of the nose*
- *3 mild concussions*
- *3 bruised ribs*
- *2 severe ankle sprains*
- *2 instances of genital trauma*
- *1 severe wrist sprain*
- *4 mild thumb sprains*
- *numerous bruises to the abdominal, pectoral and biceps muscles*

—J.L.

In the winter of 1999, I was getting deep into research for my book, *The Logic of Steel: A Fighter's View of Blade and Shank Encounters*, when I became aware of a widening gulf between my findings and the expectations of the knife enthusiasts and blade-oriented martial artists who would make up the readership. While most of those people practice knife arts in the context of a blade-to-blade encounter, my research demonstrated that a statistically insignificant portion of edged-weapon encounters are blade-to-blade. In fact, of the 316 incidents I have documented, less than 3 percent were knife fights.

Knowing that readers would expect information about knife fights, I began knife sparring to collect data on what such an encounter might be like. Three problems immediately inhibited the rate at which I could proceed:

- Martial artists in central Maryland are generally unwilling to engage in any type of contact-weapon sparring, with many citing the Dog Brothers videos as proof that realistic sparring with weapons cannot be engaged in without an unacceptable risk of injury. Although it was desirable for the majority of subjects to be non-martial artists—because most participants in edged-weapon conflicts aren't martial artists—a lack of participants

295

with a knowledge of weapons techniques and empty-hand sparring hurt the experiment in regard to tactical deductions.

• Without a proven, workable sparring format, it took an entire year and three debilitating injuries to work out safety concerns within the reality-based parameters set for the experiment.

• Unable to recruit more than one sparring partner at a time until 2001, I was able to collect information only as long as my own durability and stamina, neither of which are exceptional, lasted.

Facilitating Aggression: Engaging the Ego

To simulate the hyper-aggressive action of an edged-weapon encounter, I recruited as my regular sparring partner a non-martial artist of ordinary stature and average athletic ability with an extensive history of competitive ball-play, primarily in pickup basketball games. I then developed a flow-point scoring system in which we fought until one player scored 11 clean strokes, with a torso stab or neck strike counting as two strokes.

Flow-point scoring is a compromise between break-point and continuous-contact. When a player takes a stroke, he has one beat to counter before he calls himself out, providing an opportunity to counter. Any counter that can be employed without chambering or stepping is good. A player who freezes after being stroked can be doubled in this way. In theory, players may

The author's knife study took place in an enclosed area that limited participants to three consecutive steps in any direction.

The author (right) engages a young knife fighter in a simulated duel.

stand toe-to-toe and engage in continuous contact in a flow-point bout.

Players call points on themselves to maintain accuracy because the aggressor is often found to be unaware of strokes he landed. That's because his audiovisual acuity and limited tactile sensitivity through the glove and dummy knife are markedly inferior to his opponent's sense of pain.

Evolution

While the 11-point bout system produced a lot of information, it encouraged the trading of strokes and failed to develop the players' defensive ability at the same rate as their offensive capacity. A five-point deductive bout system was implemented in August 2001, in which each player begins with five points. A butt strike, foot check, slap or stepping out deducts one point; a slash or finger jab to the goggles deducts two points; and a stab to the torso or any edge or point contact with the neck or goggles counts for three. When a player is reduced to zero, the other player is credited with the number of points retained. In this way, the testing engages the ego to encourage defense over offense in the competitive accumulation of points.

The results were as follows:

- 5-0 shutouts were extremely rare and generally achieved with lead-hand slashes.
- 4-0 victories were the rarest result, as empty-hand or butting tactics seldom succeeded without being combined with edge and point action.

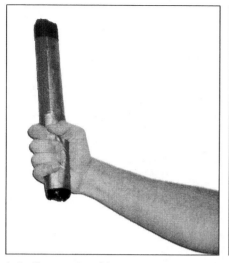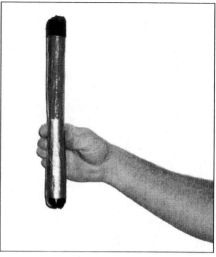

A significant portion of the sparring component of the study used a simulated butcher knife, which is the most lethal edged weapon commonly employed in actual encounters. It was constructed so that contact could be felt during a stab and so that injury to the face and hands would be minimized. In the version shown here, red marks the edge, blue the point, black the butt and gray the non-scoring portions of the grip and blade.

- 3-0 victories were the common result of duels between experienced and inexperienced players, with the veterans generally scoring three slashes or a slash-and-stab on a novice who usually managed to get in a single slash.
- 2-0 victories were rare and generally reflected a bout in which a slasher overwhelmed a stabber.
- 1-0 victories were the common result between two experienced players, with the victor typically taking two slashes to deliver three slashes or a slash-and-thrust.

Findings

- Except for an excellent heavyweight boxer who used his knife to deliver straight right stabs, all players—both martial artists and non-martial artists—fought with their knife in the lead.
- Attempts at reverse-grip knife fighting succeeded only against first-timers.
- Slashes were attempted five times as often as stabs.
- Attempted stabs were as likely to succeed as slashes but more likely to result in counter-slashes—usually one cut going in and one cut coming out, for a three- to four-point deficit.

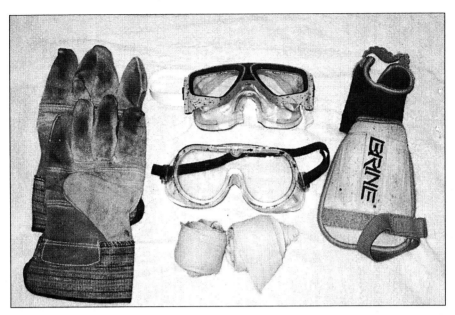

In the author's experiments, participants wore work gloves, safety goggles, boxing wraps, soccer shin pads for the wrists and a mouthpiece (not shown). It was deemed essential for the subjects to track slashes and stabs so they could later evaluate the consequences of their actions.

- Of the three participating martial artists, all of whom were knife instructors, one dominated the regular players, one held his own and one was dominated.
- The only consistently successful unarmed technique was the low kick. However, it was never decisive, having succeeded only in postponing an empty-hand-vs.-knife failure or augmented a blade-to-blade or finger-jab success.

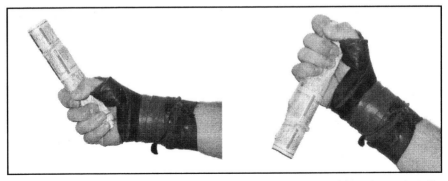

Rolled-up paper can be used to simulate a razor, folding knife or screwdriver. While working with smaller knives, boxing wraps were necessary because the subjects' hands often collided. The leather hand straps shown here helped minimize impacts to the sensitive thumb area.

- The percentages of success for empty-hand-vs.-blade simulations were:
  block, parry and dodge ....0 percent
  grappling ....2 percent
  slip, parry, trap and run................................2 percent
  finger jab..5 percent *
  kick and finger jab......................................10 percent *
  running past the knifer on approach............15 percent *

* These results are deceptive. One must remember that most of those who attempted the less-successful options such as grappling or parrying did so because they failed to get in position for something better—like running away. (In other words, most players never get into position to initiate one of the three reasonably successful defenses unless they were being attacked by an inexperienced player—who usually became an effective assassin after one session.) The credit should go to the knifer in these situations. The knifer is the initiating player, with the drill beginning with his entry into "the room."

Conclusions

Virtually all real-life blade-to-blade encounters in my study resulted in the person who had less confidence in himself—or the size and/or quality of his blade—backing down. Of the two full-blown knife fights between adult males, one was a quick one-sided slash-and-stab that resulted in the

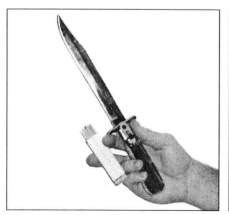 

Weapons from real-life knife-to-knife encounters: A boxcutter identical to the one pulled on the author by an older man during a heated argument in 1989, along with the knife the author drew in defense. The razor-wielder left the scene, threatening to shoot the author.

Weapons from real-life knife-to-knife encounters: The skinning knife pulled on the author by a 13-year-old panhandler in 2002 and the pocket knife the author drew as a first response. The boy stalked away, making threats.

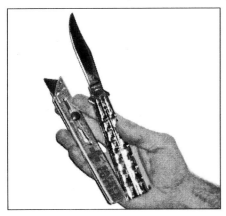

Weapons from real-life knife-to-knife encounters: The balisong that a larger man attempted to draw on the author in 1995 and the razor knife the author was wearing at the time but did not draw. Instead, the author covered the knifer's weapon hand as he attempted to deploy his blade from a belt sheath. The knifer was so focused on his blade—instead of on using his superior strength and mass to grapple—that he submitted when he was unable to take out the weapon. He later apologized to the author and handed over the knife as a peace offering.

hospitalization of the less-prepared fighter, and the other was an extended fight in which both parties were killed. It's the opinion of all the players who engaged in the flow-point sparring system that a fight between two knifers—who actually know what they're doing and have the guts to do it—is likely to produce two dead bodies.

DESIGNING A FIGHTING KNIFE

by Jim Wagner • Photos by Frank Soens/Boker • October 2006

"We want a knife that will not only be the ultimate self-defense knife for martial artists and civilians, but also one that the police and military will want," Dietmar Pohl said, extending his glass toward me over the table, waiting for me to tap mine against his.

"I have the design here," I answered, "and I know Boker is going to love it."

Pohl is the chief knife designer for a German company called Boker Baumwerk. He flew from Germany to the United Kingdom in February 2005 to attend my knife-survival course and to look at my design ideas for the first time. After an agonizingly long minute spent staring at my sketches, he nodded and said, "Yes, this is different, very different."

We discussed at length some of the concepts I'd incorporated into the knife. Then Pohl said, "I will present this to Mr. Felix, the vice president of Boker."

I first met Pohl in 1999 while training GSG9, Germany's elite counterterrorist team. One of my students, a man who'd served as my liaison, was a tough paratrooper named Hans-Peter. He said Combat Unit 2, GSG9's

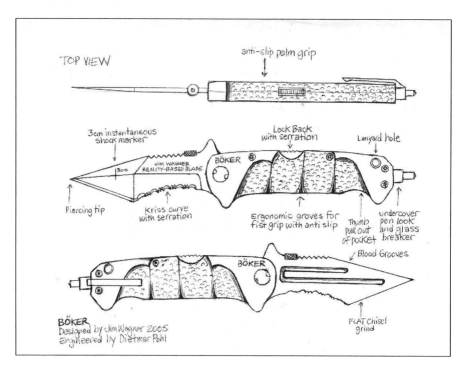

maritime interdiction unit, was working with Boker to design a combat dive knife. He asked if I was interested in accompanying him to the factory in Solingen, Germany, to view the preliminary drawings and offer my opinion before the final plans were approved. I jumped at the chance.

At the factory, Hans-Peter introduced me to Pohl. I spent several minutes examining drawings of the blade, code-named "Orca," and gave some minor suggestions.

Not until December 2004 did I hear from Pohl again. That's when he posed an interesting question: "Have you ever thought about designing a tactical knife?"

"As a matter of fact, I have," I said. Over the years, I'd often thought about the elements I'd like to see incorporated in a self-defense knife.

I let a few days pass before sitting down at my desk. Within a half-hour, I had my preliminary ideas on paper. I drew it at a 1-to-1 ratio and even cut out a "paper doll" version to see if it would fit my hand.

I submitted my ideas to Boker, returned to Los Angeles and waited for a call. A week later, the president of the company was on the phone. He said that he was impressed with my ideas and that they planned to go forward with the project.

For three months, Pohl and I sent design changes and modifications back and forth via e-mail. His mission was to ensure that my ideas remained practical with respect to the manufacturing process. My mission was to ensure that the essential features didn't get axed in an effort to save money. Fortunately, the knife had to endure only minor changes.

In July 2005, Pohl's assistant sent me three-dimensional illustrations showing the final version. On August 1, we spoke again. Pohl said: "I will send you the prototype of your handle by courier. The handle is the most difficult part of this project. Take a look at it and see if you need to make any changes."

The rest is history. I was pleased that I managed to retain the most important features of my original concept. That's because I incorporated everything I learned from my martial arts training and my service in the military, corrections, police agencies, SWAT units and counterterrorism groups, as well as thousands of hours teaching people how to use knives.

The most salient of those features are:

• **Gladius Tip** My knife is primarily a stabbing weapon. Most slashes lack stopping power—unless the blade slices an artery or opens the abdominal wall. On the other hand, puncture wounds 3 centimeters deep can induce instantaneous shock or even penetrate internal organs, shutting down the body. Therefore, I designed the tip of the blade to mirror that of the Roman *gladius* sword, which was meant to pierce. (As a conversation point, there's a line on the blade indicating the 3-centimeter mark. It's for educational purposes only.)

• **Ripping and Cutting Edge** The edge has the elegant curve of a *kris* knife. It's designed to slice muscle, to actually dig deeper as it's pulled. It also has upfront curve-serrations, which will rip into flesh and clothing whether you pull the weapon away from a solid target or slice across an incoming hand.

• **Blade Guard** The knife has a protruding blade guard to keep your hand from sliding onto the edge if you happen to strike a hard object. A hole in the blade guard permits the attachment of a lanyard for wilderness-survival use—for example, so it can be lashed to a branch to make a spear. Lastly, the blade guard can serve as a blunt-trauma striking nub when the knife is folded, transforming it into a *kubotan*.

• **Blood Grooves** There are two on one side of the blade. Blood grooves, or fullers, are typically used to lighten bayonets and swords, but many people believe that they permit blood to flow from a stab wound, thus reducing the suction effect or the clenching of muscles around the blade.

• **Ergonomic Handle** I believe the best way to maintain control of a knife in a battle is with the fist grip—the same grip you'd use on a hammer. Whether the tip is facing up or down, you'll minimize the chance of having the knife knocked out of your hand. My knife facilitates use of the fist grip by incorporating finger-grip impressions into the handle. Slippage is reduced significantly, even if blood is covering your hand. Furthermore, running the length of the top of the handle are friction grooves that make contact with your palm, whether you're holding it with a fist grip or an ice-pick grip.

• **Dual-Purpose Tip** The knife comes with two interchangeable handle ends. One looks like the end of a pen, enabling you to carry it without broadcasting that you're armed. The other is a glass breaker for use in emergencies such as car crashes.

People who see the finished knife for the first time usually say, "That's a mean-looking weapon." Of course it is. I designed it for real fighting.

EDGED-WEAPON SURVIVAL
6 Techniques to Save Your Life!

by David Hallford and Richard Nance • Photos by Rick Hustead • November 2006

The FBI Uniform Crime Reporting statistics tell us that 16,137 murders took place in the United States in 2004. Of those victims, 14.1 percent, or roughly 2,275 people, were killed with knives or other cutting instruments. In fact, edged weapons were the second most common weapon.

This should come as no surprise because no matter where a person is, chances are a knife is within reach. Think about it. If you're like most Americans, right now at least one of the following items is nearby: a pocketknife, a kitchen knife, a letter opener, a pair of scissors, a screwdriver, a box cutter or a razor blade.

Since edged weapons are not only deadly but also readily accessible, martial artists must prepare themselves to survive an assault. This article will assist you in that endeavor by debunking some of the myths associated with knife defense and providing effective techniques for stopping a real blade attack.

The Traditional Model

Many *dojo* teach edged-weapon defense. Unfortunately, most of the techniques are designed to work against unrealistic attacks: single, robotic stabs to the midsection and exaggerated overhand stabs that resemble the shower scene from *Psycho*.

Against such attacks, just about any defense will work. You can execute an X-block followed by a wrist lock and several impressive-looking counterstrikes, joint breaks and so on. You can even catch the weapon hand or redirect it by blending with the trajectory of the weapon. Often, the defensive techniques result in the disarming of the assailant.

Reality check: Try that with a man holding a razor blade. Our hats are off to anyone who can accomplish that feat against a full-speed, unscripted attack.

Sadly, real edged-weapon defense is more complex for a variety of reasons. First, you'd be hard-pressed to find a single, robotic stab outside the dojo. Real attacks are sneaky, fast and gut-wrenchingly violent. Second, most incidents involve multiple stabs and slashes from various angles.

To make matters worse, you're unlikely to see the weapon before being cut. Ask anyone who's ever been stabbed, and he'll probably tell you he had no idea he was in a knife fight until he was cut. Based on this knowledge,

Run-through: The assailant begins his swing, and Richard Nance intercepts the knife arm with his left forearm, knocking it out of the way (2). At the same time, he executes a palm-heel strike to the face and literally runs over the man (3).

you must assume that any assailant is armed until you can determine otherwise. Your punch defense must be consistent with your edged-weapon defense because you might not be able to distinguish between the two in the heat of battle.

You must also consider that you'll probably be grabbed before you're stabbed. When assailants attack in a stabbing motion, they generally hold you with their free hand to ensure that they can drive the weapon into your body. A grab isn't as likely to precede a slashing attack because penetration isn't as much of a factor.

Another major component of the traditional model is the concept of the 12 angles of attack. You're required to spend weeks, months even years practicing them so you can recognize and identify which angle a real attack might come from. Then you're supposed to master numerous techniques designed to work against a single angle of attack. Remember that having too many choices leads to hesitation, and when facing an edged weapon, hesitation is a luxury you can't afford.

If you find this critique of the traditional model a little harsh, locate a committed partner and a training knife with a marking blade, and have him try to cut you at full speed. When you're finished, count the marks.

The Progressive Model

Many instructors realized that the traditional model fails to adequately prepare students for a real knife attack and felt compelled to develop what we refer to as the "progressive model." Proponents of this approach advocate minimizing the damage by using your arms to absorb stabs and slashes until you have the opportunity to close the gap and attack the assailant. They profess that you should "expect to get cut in a knife fight." The goal, they say, is to prevent having a vital organ punctured. That sounds logical, doesn't it?

While a cut or stab to your arm isn't likely to be fatal, it'll certainly result in a potentially serious injury. After sustaining a few wounds like that, it'll be nearly impossible to use your arms to protect your vital targets, let alone mount an attack of your own. So even though getting your limbs cut or stabbed might not kill you, it can certainly lead to your demise.

Some systems that fall into the progressive-model category teach sparring with an assailant who's armed with a blade. You quickly learn that no matter how much you might outclass your opponent, you can expect to get hit eventually. Now, imagine being cut or stabbed rather than punched or kicked. Enough said.

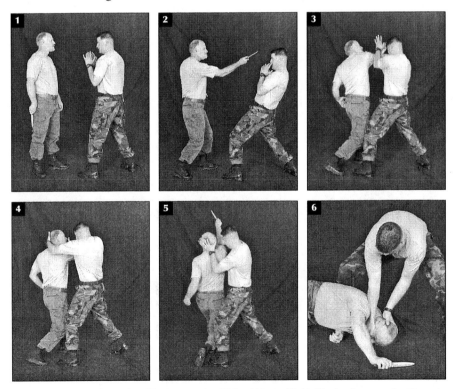

Head twist: An armed David Hallford approaches Richard Nance (1). Hallford swings, causing Nance to evade the blade (2). Once he's outside the weapon arm, Nance hits the limb with both forearms (3) and grabs the assailant's head (4). He then twists his foe (5) to the ground (6).

Another progressive-model approach is to attempt to grab the weapon arm at the wrist with both your hands or to capture and secure it with both your arms—using the two-on-one defense. Effectively executing either technique is no easy task. But let's assume that you're able to secure the weapon arm. Now what?

You're in a position of having to struggle with a thug who's grasping an edged weapon. If he's bigger or stronger than you, you'll probably be taken to the ground in a deadly wrestling match. While you have both hands tied up, he has one free. With it, he can pound you into the ground or grab the weapon and stab you. You'll then have to gain control of his other hand, which now holds the implement of your demise.

Edged-weapon defense isn't a give-and-take proposition like sparring. In fact, the term "edged-weapon defense" is really a misnomer. There is no defending against an edged weapon. All there can be is overwhelming aggression. The only thing that will stop a knife attack is your ability to be more violent than your attacker.

A Different Approach

After spending countless hours researching and attempting the most commonly taught edged-weapon defenses, we concluded that the majority work only against a cooperative partner. Neither the traditional model nor the progressive model works against a realistic attack.

Cross-face: The attacker tries to slice David Hallford, but the martial artist leans backward to avoid the strike (1-2). As the knife is swung back toward the victim, the weapon arm is blocked (3). Hallford immediately traps the limb (4) and pushes the man's head toward the ground (5).

Fold-over: Richard Nance attacks with his right arm (1-2). The defender steps to his right, stops the knife by hitting the shoulder of the arm that's grasping it and holds the man's waist with his right hand while chin-jabbing him with his left (3). The push-pull action sends the assailant to the ground (4).

Through trial and error, we came up with a viable solution to the edged-weapon dilemma. The approach is so simple that it's hard to believe no one else is using it. By avoiding the weapon, taking the assailant's balance and manipulating his head, we found that we could avoid having to perform the most difficult component of edged-weapon defense, which is catching up with and gaining control of the fast-moving weapon.

WARTAC Techniques

The Weapon Acquisition and Retention Tactics method of knife defense focuses on avoiding the blade by parrying and/or evading it, then acquiring the assailant's head. Once you control his head, you immediately compromise his balance. When someone attacks another person with a knife, he has all his focus on planting that weapon in his target, and his weapon arm is bristling with energy. If all you do is block the swing or manage to grab the limb, his focus on stabbing you hasn't changed, and the energy in his arm may intensify. You're now standing toe-to-toe with a psycho with a blade, and he's still trying to kill you.

The following are six examples drawn from the WARTAC method:

Head Twist

The assailant attacks with a horizontal slash, but you evade it by leaning backward. From outside the weapon arm, use your forearms to stop a return slash if there is one, then grab his head by placing one hand under his chin and the other at the base of his skull in a cradling fashion. Then twist his head away from you, which moves the knife away from your body. By continuing the twisting motion, you can take him to the ground or slam him into a solid object. When he's down and you're still standing, you can run away or kick him to prevent further aggression.

Cross-Face

Another technique that works from outside the weapon arm is the cross-face. After evading the inward slash, place your arms up to block the return slash, making contact above the elbow of the attacking arm. (This is more effective than blocking the forearm). After negating the slash, immediately trap the arm against your chest while pushing the assailant's head away and down to the ground with your other hand. Maintain control of his wrist as he falls on his back. From there, decide whether running or continuing the fight is the better option.

Fold-Over

The next technique is the "fold-over." We don't claim to have invented this concept; it's similar to the chin jab taught during World War II. How-

Shoulder wrap: David Hallford grabs his opponent and prepares to stab him (1). As he thrusts the weapon forward, the martial artist places his right arm between their bodies and uses his left forearm to stop the blade (2). He then grabs the man's right shoulder and inserts his left arm under the man's arm (3). Using a circular motion, the martial artist wraps the assailant's limb (4) and drives him into the ground (5).

ever, we've found that it's extremely effective against edged-weapon attacks. It can be applied from inside or outside the weapon arm. For brevity, we'll discuss its application from the inside position.

Against almost any type of attack effected with the right arm, step to your right, away from the weapon. Immediately turn toward the assailant and thrust your palms against his weapon-side shoulder. (Not only does the shoulder move more slowly than the wrist and weapon, but it's also a larger target.) Striking the shoulder disrupts the fluidity of the attack and buys you time to complete the technique.

Next, grab his waist with your right hand and pull him toward you while striking his chin with your left palm. By manipulating the head and waist, you can topple even a larger assailant. This takedown is based solely on leverage and doesn't require great size, strength or athletic ability.

Run-Through

This WARTAC technique is about as basic and gross-motor-based as you can get. It works great off a flinch response and at extreme close quarters. As the assailant initiates, thrust your closest arm to intercept the broadest area of his knife arm while palm-heeling his face and literally running right over him. This action takes him backward and off-balance, enabling you to maneuver him into an object or send him tumbling to the ground. The key to success is making it a simultaneous endeavor. If you pause after the block, he'll simply redirect the blade and cut you.

Perhaps the most important aspect of taking control of an attacker's balance is immediately distracting him, draining the energy flowing through his arm into his weapon. You must make him focus on what you're doing to him, rather than on what he's planning to do to you.

Shoulder Wrap

The shoulder wrap works at close quarters when your assailant grabs you with his left hand and tries to pump his weapon into your midsection. Place your left arm between your body and his knife arm, and grab the weapon-side shoulder with your right hand. Using a circular motion, wrap the arm so your hands are on top of his shoulder. Now you have the weapon arm locked and can turn and drive him face-first into the ground.

Turn-and-Burn

This technique was designed to minimize the damage inflicted during a surprise attack from the rear. In this worst-case scenario, your first

Turn-and-burn: Richard Nance threatens David Hallford from the rear (1). Hallford shrugs his shoulders and raises his hands for protection, then begins turning clockwise (2). Next, he pushes the weapon arm out of the way and against the man's body (3). Once he finishes the pivot (4), Hallford executes a series of palm strikes to the head (5).

indication of danger comes from being stabbed. Remember that a single stab wound is generally survivable. However, you'd better have a plan to remove your body from the trajectory of the knife and launch an immediate counterattack.

Shrug your shoulders and raise your hands to protect your head and neck. Begin turning in the direction of the threat and swing the arm that's nearest the blade downward at a 45-degree angle. That should enable you to momentarily pin the weapon arm to his body. Continue pivoting until his head presents itself as a target. Deliver a series of palm strikes to the side of the head to drive him away. Remember that against a blade, simple and brutal techniques are hard to beat.